365 Easy Italian Recipes

365 Easy Italian Recipes

Rick Marzullo O'Connell

BARNES
&NOBLE
BOOKS
NEW YORK

2004 Barnes & Noble Books

ISBN 0-7607-4046-1

Printed and bound in the United States of America

04 05 06 07 08 MC 9 8 7 6 5 4 3 2 1

Contents

with Orange-Basil Butter, Red Pepper Shrimp Calabrese, Oysters Baked with Spinach and Sambucca . . .

Italian flair with the lightest of meats. All your restaurant favorites, such as Veal Piccata, Veal Scaloppine with Two Kinds of Mushrooms, Veal Saltimbocca with Fontina Cheese, and Veal Chops Stuffed with Prosciutto and Gorgonzola.

Recipes like Pork Scaloppine with Vinegar and Garlic, Pork Braised in Milk, and Pork and Sausages Contadina, with tomatoes and peppers, offer tasty ways to use this succulent meat.

Create a pièce de résistance for company with Florentine Steak with Brandy and Mushrooms or Sicilian Braciola, or feed your family with Chuck Steak Pizzaiola or Meat Loaf with Mozzarella.

Try this less-common meat the Italian way: Rosemary Roast Lamb, Lamb Chops Milanese, Lamb with Sweet Red Peppers, Braised Lamb Shanks, Northern Italian Lamb Stew with Turnips and Mushrooms.

Experience the Italian mastery with vegetables of all kinds to produce savory side dishes, appetizers, and great vegetarian main courses, as well as frittatas, which are Italian omelets, and tortas (vegetable pies).

Here are great recipes and ideas for making your own pizzas, calzones, focaccias, bread sticks, and heroes, using store-bought ingredients to save time.

Oil and vinegar-based salads to end an Italian meal, start an American one, serve as a substantial accompaniment on a buffet or picnic table or provide a light, tasty lunch.

All your favorites, from Biscuit Tortoni and Zuppa Inglese to Italian Cheesecake and Biscotti. There are new recipes, such as Tiramisù, and classics like Zabaglione.

Introduction to Italian Cooking

It is no accident that Italian cooking is perennially popular, for this is a cuisine rich in flavor and long on love. Italian food has its roots in Mama's kitchen. There are few complicated sauces or techniques. Regional differences, which occur because of the dependence on local ingredients, add to the variety of dishes. Olive oil, tomatoes, basil, and oregano are used commonly in the south, where the strong sun heightens flavor, and the silver-green olive trees grow with abandon. The rich egg pastas with cream and butter are prevalent in the north, where there are plenty of cattle. Seafood is coveted all over Italy, which shares both the Mediterranean and Adriatic coasts.

A book on how to cook "Italian" would be remiss if it did not include some thoughts on how to eat Italian food. A meal has a very specific structure in Italy, and it is perhaps the most generally accepted part of the cuisine. Italy is a younger united country than the United States, and it still holds on to its regional differences. Great arguments take place over what is the proper way to do certain dishes, but where they are placed on the menu has a general consensus. Each part of the meal has the same value; many small, often unadorned, courses are served. The Italians feel that having starch, meat, and vegetables on the same plate is a sad and hurried way to treat your stomach. Pasta and rice, with few exceptions, are not served on a plate with meat or fish.

The progression of a meal would be an antipasto, similar to our appetizer, followed by a pasta course. A pasta course includes any pasta, rice (risotto), polenta, gnocchi, or soup containing any of the above, such as a minestrone. To serve a minestrone and a pasta would be overwhelming. A clear soup could be served in addition to a pasta. What we know as an entrée, or main course—chicken, meat, or fish—is served at this point, with little adornment—perhaps just a simple vegetable or roasted potatoes. A little salad and cheese and fruit and coffee complete the menu. Dessert has little place at an everyday meal and is served as a sweet at other times during the day or evening.

You can order this way if you wish in an Italian restaurant, or try it sometime at home. It is not as much work as it sounds, and the rhythm of the meal is delightful. You could begin with a store-bought antipasto, such as prosciutto and melon or some roasted peppers and anchovies, then serve a simple pasta, such as Spaghettini with Garlic and Pepper, allowing a pound of pasta for six to eight people, rather than the usual four. Your main course could be an easy chicken, such as Lemon and Rosemary Roast Chicken, accompanied by some Broccoli Rabe or Carrots with Marsala. For dessert, offer fresh fruit in season and some purchased cookies, such as Amaretti. See if you don't have a wonderful time.

Alternatively, I urge you to use these 365 recipes to fill in on any menu you design. For Italian food is not fussy food, and it works well in a variety of settings. Perhaps all you feel like eating is a big bowl of Spaghetti and Meat Balls for dinner, with just a green salad on the side. Indulge yourself—the comfort is indescribable. Or try an Italian vegetable with a piece of steak you've seared on the grill or an assortment of antipasti recipes for your next buffet party. I guarantee the applause.

A note on ingredients. Pasta is easy to come by in any supermarket. If you have access to an imported brand, I urge you to try it. Fresh red, ripe tomatoes are a delight, but their season is short, so substitute canned Italian peeled tomatoes when necessary. For best flavor, I prefer to drain off the canned liquid and add plain water; my recipes are designed accordingly.

A great deal of Italian food is dependent on good grating cheese. A dish that takes time and money can be diminished if it is finished with a cheese that has no more flavor than salty straw. Look for the best Parmesan or Romano you can find, and grate it freshly if possible.

Most of my recipes call for olive oil. We are lucky in America today in that whole lines of olive oils are available in supermarkets. The best is called extra-virgin. It is made from the first cold pressing of the olive, and by law it contains no more than one percent acid. It is particularly important when used as an uncooked flavoring, in salads and antipasti. For high heat sautéing and dishes where the flavor will be lost, pure or light olive oils are quite satisfactory. What's so marvelous about olive oil is not only that it tastes so good, it is a monosaturated oil, which current health studies indicate are very good for you and may help to reduce levels of serum cholesterol.

The use of herbs is very simple and specific in Italian dishes. Abundant use of basil, oregano, thyme, rosemary, sage, and mint along with Italian parsley is common. What is not common are complicated herb mixtures. If a dish has basil or sage in it, it will probably not be combined with one or two other herbs. Fresh herbs are so delicious, use them whenever possible. Substitute dried leaf herbs instead of powdered herbs, which deteriorate quickly and are often bitter. Purchase dried herbs in small quantities and store them away from light and heat.

Supermarkets and delis have answered the call for more specialty ingredients, so that fresh pasta and pasta sauces, olives, and Italian cheeses can often be found. The freezer section of your department store can offer some good-quality stuffed pastas and sauce. Doctor them up to your taste for quick cooking.

So with *365 Easy Italian Recipes, mangia*—eat and enjoy!

Chapter 1

Antipasto—Before the Pasta

An antipasto can be an elaborate table of delicious tidbits, cured meats, vinegared vegetables, cheeses, peppery seafood, and an endless display of vibrant color. There are hot antipasti of savory melting cheeses, stuffed shellfish, and wonderful purees and pâtés to pile on lovely crusty fried bread or to scoop up with bread sticks.

Literally meaning "before the pasta," these tidbits take the place of our appetizer. Antipasto can be one savory to whet your appetite at dinner, or an assortment can be enjoyed as the whole meal at lunch.

Some of the recipes are in generous portions, as they can be made and used over a period of time, so it's worth making a large batch. An individual serving of an antipasto is usually just a taste of each item, and a selection often includes strongly contrasting flavors.

It is very simple to pull together a wonderful antipasto platter without preparing everything yourself. A stop at the grocery for a few bottles of pickled vegetables, cured meats, and cheeses can be accented with one homemade recipe.

Here are five selections of antipasti, all of which include prepared deli or store-bought foods. Be sure to offer a basket of sesame bread sticks and crusty Italian bread.

ANTIPASTI

Number 1
2 or 3 different olives
Salami, such as Genoa or capocollo, thinly sliced
Peperoncini (Italian pickled hot peppers)
Marinated artichoke hearts
Kidney Beans with Salami and Scallions (page 18)

Number 2
Bread sticks wrapped in salami
Tuscan Bean Salad (page 7)
Cherry peppers
Slices of mozzarella cheese, preferably fresh
Tomatoes with olive oil and basil

Number 3
Chick-Peas with Red Onions and Pesto (page 11)
Sweet red peppers in vinegar
Thin slices of capocollo
Hard-boiled eggs
Sardines

Number 4
Fondutta (page 20)
Celery, fennel, and carrot sticks
Thin slices of prosciutto
Marinated mushrooms

Number 5
Crostini with Lima Bean Puree and Parmesan Cheese (page 15)
Mortadella
Gorgonzola cheese
Italian pickled vegetables

1   WHITE BEANS WITH TUNA
Prep: 15 minutes   Cook: none   Serves: 8 to 10

This makes a delicious antipasto plate, with hard-cooked eggs and sliced tomatoes, and it is a great Italian salad to throw together for unexpected company.

2 15-ounce cans white beans, preferably cannellini
1 garlic clove, minced
2 teaspoons minced fresh thyme leaves or ½ teaspoon dried
3 tablespoons red wine vinegar

¼ cup olive oil, preferably extra-virgin
1 teaspoon salt
¼ teaspoon pepper
¾ cup coarsely chopped red onion
2 6½-ounce cans tuna in oil, drained

1. Drain beans and rinse under cold running water. Drain well.

2. In a large bowl, combine garlic, thyme, vinegar, olive oil, salt, and pepper. Beat with fork to blend. Add beans and red onion to bowl and toss to coat.

3. Break up tuna into medium-size chunks. Toss lightly with beans. Serve at room temperature.

2   TUSCAN BEAN SALAD

Prep: 10 minutes   Stand: 1 hour   Cook: 1 hour 10 minutes
Serves: 8 to 10

Beans are ever present on the Tuscan table. They can be a delicious part of the antipasti. Use this recipe as a basic and add different tidbits and left-overs to vary the flavor.

8 ounces dried cannellini or
    Great Northern white
    beans
1 small onion
1 celery rib, halved
1 branch of fresh rosemary or
    1 teaspoon dried

2 fresh sage leaves or ¼
    teaspoon dried
1 tablespoon salt
⅛ teaspoon pepper
2 tablespoons olive oil,
    preferably extra-virgin

1. Rinse beans and pick over to remove any grit. Place in a medium sauce-pan, add enough water to cover by at least 2 inches, and bring to a boil. Boil 5 minutes. Remove from heat, cover pan, and let beans soak 1 hour. Drain beans; rinse out pan.

2. Return beans to saucepan. Add onion, celery, rosemary, sage, and 6 cups water. Bring to a boil, reduce heat to low, and simmer beans for 1 hour, or until tender.

3. Add salt and cook 5 to 6 minutes. Drain beans. Remove and discard onion, celery, and rosemary stick. Season with pepper; stir in olive oil. Serve hot or at room temperature.

3   ANTIPASTO ALLA RUSTICA

Prep: 10 minutes   Cook: none   Serves: 3 to 4

Strong flavors such as provolone cheese and salami need a strong vine-gar and oil dressing. Serve some good, thick Italian bread along with this.

1 garlic clove, minced
½ teaspoon salt
⅛ teaspoon pepper
2 teaspoons chopped fresh
    oregano or ½ teaspoon
    dried
2 tablespoons red wine
    vinegar

3 tablespoons extra-virgin
    olive oil
1 medium head romaine
    lettuce
4 ounces hot salami, thinly
    sliced
4 ounces provolone cheese,
    cut into ½-inch dice

1. In a large bowl, combine garlic, salt, pepper, oregano, vinegar, and olive oil. Beat with a fork to blend. Set aside.

2. Discard large outer leaves from romaine lettuce. Cut remaining lettuce into 2-inch pieces, making about 4 cups of greens. Quarter salami slices. Toss lettuce, salami, provolone, and dressing together until evenly coated.

4   SIMPLE CAPONATA

Prep: 20 minutes   Stand: 1 hour   Cook: 20 minutes   Serves: 10

A Sicilian dish as ever present as antipasto, great in sandwiches. Can be prepared two to three days in advance.

3 pounds eggplant
1 tablespoon coarse salt
¼ cup olive oil
2 medium onions, cut into ½-inch dice
2 celery ribs, cut into ½-inch dice
1 16-ounce can tomato puree
1 cup pitted green olives, chopped

¼ cup capers, rinsed and drained
½ cup white wine vinegar
1 tablespoon chopped fresh oregano or 1 teaspoon dried
½ teaspoon salt
¼ teaspoon pepper

1. Cut eggplant into ¾-inch dice. Sprinkle lightly with salt and place in a colander. Place a plate with a weight on top (such as two 1-pound cans) and drain for 1 hour. Pat eggplant dry with paper towels.

2. Heat oil in a nonreactive large frying pan or flameproof casserole over medium heat. Add onions and celery and cook 3 to 4 minutes, or until soft.

3. Add eggplant and cook 5 to 6 minutes, stirring, until softened. Stir in tomato puree, olives, and capers. Simmer uncovered 10 minutes to combine flavors. Remove from heat and season with oregano, salt, and pepper. Serve at room temperature.

5   SICILIAN CAPONATA WITH RAISINS AND PINE NUTS

Prep: 20 minutes   Stand: 1 hour   Cook: 30 minutes   Serves: 6 to 8

½ cup pine nuts
1½ pounds eggplant
1½ tablespoons coarse salt
2 tablespoons olive oil
1 small onion, cut into ½-inch dice
1 medium carrot, peeled and cut into ½-inch dice
1 celery rib, cut into ½-inch dice

¼ cup tomato paste
¼ cup water
¼ cup golden raisins
½ teaspoon salt
¼ teaspoon pepper
1 tablespoon white wine vinegar

1. In a medium frying pan, toast pine nuts over low heat 2 to 3 minutes, or until golden brown, shaking pan frequently. Set aside.

2. Cut eggplant into ¾-inch dice. Sprinkle lightly with salt and place in a colander. Place a plate with a weight on top (such as two 1-pound cans) and drain 1 hour. Pat eggplant dry with paper towels.

3. Heat olive oil in a large frying pan over medium heat. Add onion, carrot, and celery and cook about 3 to 5 minutes, or until softened.

4. Add eggplant and cook, stirring, 5 to 6 minutes, or until softened. Stir in tomato paste, water, and raisins. Simmer uncovered 10 minutes to combine flavors. Remove from heat and season with salt, pepper, and vinegar. When cooled to room temperature, stir in pine nuts. Serve at room temperature.

6 CAPONATA WITH RED AND GREEN PEPPERS

Prep: 20 minutes   Stand: 1 hour   Cook: 20 minutes   Serves: 8 to 10

1½ pounds eggplant	1 6½-ounce jar pitted green
1½ tablespoons coarse salt	olives, drained and
2 tablespoons olive oil	coarsely chopped
2 large green bell peppers,	¼ cup tomato paste
about 1 pound, cut into	¼ cup water
½-inch dice	1 teaspoon salt
1 large red bell pepper, about	¼ teaspoon pepper
8 ounces, cut into ½-inch	¼ teaspoon hot pepper flakes
dice	¼ cup chopped fresh parsley
1 medium onion, cut into	¼ cup red wine vinegar
½-inch dice	

1. Cut eggplant into ¾-inch dice. Sprinkle lightly with salt and place in a colander. Place a plate with a weight on top (such as two 1-pound cans) and drain for 1 hour. Pat eggplant dry with paper towels.

2. Heat oil in a nonreactive large frying pan or flameproof casserole over medium heat. Add green and red peppers and onion and cook 3 to 5 minutes, or until softened.

3. Add eggplant and cook 5 to 6 minutes, or until softened. Stir in olives, tomato paste, and water. Simmer uncovered 10 minutes to combine flavors. Remove from heat and season with salt, pepper, and hot pepper flakes. Stir in parsley and vinegar. Serve at room temperature.

7   BEANS COOKED IN THE STYLE OF LITTLE BIRDS

Prep: 5 minutes   Cook: 10 to 11 minutes   Serves: 4

Little birds called *uccelli* are often cooked with these seasonings, so the dish is called *fagioli agli uccelli*. Yes, Italians use black-eyed peas, too. You can prepare white beans or any other bean this same way.

2 tablespoons olive oil
3 garlic cloves, chopped
8 fresh sage leaves or
    ½ teaspoon dried
1 14-ounce can Italian peeled
    tomatoes, drained and
    chopped

2 10-ounce packages frozen
    black-eyed peas,
    defrosted
½ teaspoon salt
¼ teaspoon pepper

1. In a nonreactive medium saucepan, heat olive oil over medium-low heat. Add garlic and sage and cook 30 seconds, or until garlic is fragrant but not browned. Add tomatoes, raise heat to medium, and simmer 5 minutes.

2. Add black-eyed peas and cook 5 minutes longer. Season with salt and pepper. Serve hot or at room temperature.

8   MARINATED CARROTS

Prep: 15 minutes   Cook: none   Marinate: 2 hours   Serves: 8

This carrot "slaw" is best when eaten with cured meats such as salami, capocollo, or bresaola.

3 tablespoons Dijon mustard
3 tablespoons red wine
    vinegar
¼ cup olive oil, preferably
    extra-virgin
1 pound large carrots, peeled
    and cut into matchstick
    pieces

8 ounces thinly sliced hard
    salami, such as Genoa, or
    other cured meat
    (optional)
Chopped fresh parsley, for
    garnish

1. In a large bowl, combine mustard and vinegar. Whisk to blend. Gradually whisk in olive oil. Add carrots and toss to coat with dressing. Marinate at room temperature, tossing occasionally, 2 hours.

2. To serve, arrange salami (if you're using it), overlapping slices on a serving plate. Mound carrots in center and garnish with parsley.

9 CHICK-PEAS WITH RED ONIONS AND PESTO

Prep: 10 minutes   Cook: none   Serves: 6

Canned chick-peas are fine to use here. The dried variety take forever to cook, and they often cook unevenly.

1 16-ounce can chick-peas (garbanzo beans)
3 tablespoons pesto, homemade (page 77) or jarred
2 tablespoons olive oil

2 tablespoons fresh lemon juice
¾ cup chopped red onion
Chopped fresh basil or parsley

1. Drain chick-peas and rinse under cold running water. Drain well.

2. In a medium bowl, combine pesto, olive oil, and lemon juice. Whisk to blend well. Add chick-peas and red onion and toss together. Garnish with fresh basil just before serving. Serve at room temperature or slightly chilled.

10 CAULIFLOWER FRITTI

Prep: 5 minutes   Cook: 20 minutes   Serves: 4 to 6

One of my favorites, serve as a vegetable or as an appetizer with marinara sauce.

1 small head cauliflower, about 1 pound
1 cup flour
2 eggs
2 tablespoons water
2 cups dry bread crumbs

1 teaspoon salt
¼ teaspoon pepper
2 cups vegetable oil
2 cups marinara sauce, homemade (page 131) or jarred, heated

1. In a large saucepan of boiling salted water, cook cauliflower 3 to 4 minutes, until almost tender. Drain. Break into florets. Trim stems if very thick. Pat dry.

2. Place flour on a plate or sheet of wax paper. In a wide shallow bowl, beat eggs and water until well blended. On second plate, combine bread crumbs with salt and pepper.

3. Dredge cauliflower in flour, dip in egg, and roll lightly in bread crumbs.

4. In a large frying pan, heat vegetable oil over medium heat to 350° on a frying thermometer. Add cauliflower in batches without crowding and cook 3 to 4 minutes, turning once, until golden brown. Drain on paper towels. Serve with warm marinara sauce for dipping.

11 CHICK-PEA FRITTERS
Prep: 20 minutes   Cook: 15 minutes   Chill: 4 hours   Serves: 8 to 10

Chick-pea flour can be purchased in Middle Eastern groceries and health food stores. This recipe is from Sicily, the southernmost Italian island.

4½ cups cold water
1 teaspoon salt
2 cups chick-pea flour
1 tablespoon minced fresh
    parsley

¼ teaspoon pepper
1½ quarts vegetable oil, for
    deep frying

1. Put water and salt in a medium saucepan. With a wire whisk, slowly add chick-pea flour in a thin stream, whisking quickly to prevent lumps from forming. Turn on heat to medium. Add parsley and pepper. Continue to cook, whisking, until mixture boils. Reduce heat to low and simmer, stirring occasionally, 10 to 12 minutes, until thick.

2. Use 1 tablespoon of oil to grease a 14-inch sheet of plastic wrap. Turn chick-pea mixture onto oiled plastic wrap. Roll into a 2-inch-thick roll. Wrap and refrigerate at least 4 hours, or overnight.

3. When ready to cook, in a large saucepan or deep-fat fryer, heat vegetable oil over medium heat to 350° on a deep-fat thermometer. With a sharp thin knife, cut chilled mixture into ¼-inch-thick slices. Cook in batches without crowding, turning, for 2 minutes, or until lightly browned on both sides. Drain on paper towels. Serve hot.

12 CHICK-PEAS WITH MUSTARD-SAGE DRESSING
Prep: 10 minutes   Cook: none   Serves: 6 to 8

Serve with thin slices of salami or capocollo and crusty bread.

1 16-ounce can chick-peas
    (garbanzo beans)
½ cup mayonnaise
2 tablespoons Dijon mustard

2 tablespoons chopped fresh
    sage or ½ teaspoon dried
1 tablespoon chopped fresh
    parsley

1. Drain chick-peas and rinse under cold running water. Drain well.

2. In a medium bowl, combine mayonnaise, mustard, sage, and parsley. Whisk to blend well. Add chick-peas and toss to coat. Serve at room temperature or slightly chilled.

13 STUFFED CLAMS OREGANATA

Prep: 20 minutes   Cook: 10 to 12 minutes   Serves: 6 to 8

Here's a favorite in mom-and-pop Italian restaurants that's easy to make at home.

24 hard-shelled clams, such as littlenecks
1½ tablespoons olive oil
2 tablespoons minced onion
2 garlic cloves, chopped
1½ cups soft bread crumbs

1½ teaspoons fresh oregano or ½ teaspoon dried
¼ cup grated Parmesan cheese
¾ cup marinara sauce, homemade (page 131) or jarred
¼ teaspoon hot pepper flakes

1. Scrub clams under cold running water. Discard any open shells that will not close when tapped.

2. In a large saucepan or flameproof casserole, cook clams, covered, over high heat 3 to 5 minutes, shaking pan frequently until clams open. Remove from pan; discard any clams that do not open. Strain juices from pan through a fine-mesh sieve or several thicknesses of dampened cheesecloth and reserve. Remove clams from shells; discard half the shells. Chop clams.

3. In a medium frying pan, heat olive oil over medium heat. Add onions and cook 1 to 2 minutes, or until softened. Add garlic and cook, stirring, 30 seconds, or until fragrant; remove from heat. Add bread crumbs, oregano, Parmesan cheese, chopped clams, and 3 tablespoons reserved clam juice. Fill clam shells and place on a baking sheet. (Recipe can be prepared to this point up to 8 hours in advance. Cover and refrigerate.)

4. Preheat oven to 475°. Bake clams 8 to 10 minutes, or until lightly browned and crisp. Meanwhile, in a small saucepan, combine marinara sauce with hot pepper flakes and any remaining clam juice. Cook over medium heat, stirring, until hot, 2 to 3 minutes.

5. To serve, arrange clams on a platter and pass a bowl of sauce on the side.

14   CROSTINI
Prep: 5 minutes   Cook: 10 minutes   Serves: 6 to 12

For these Italian appetizer toasts, the coarser the bread, the better. Use these to accompany soup or antipasti, or turn them into hors d'oeuvres by using toppings found in the following recipes.

12 slices Italian bread, cut ½ inch thick	**¼ cup olive oil, preferably extra-virgin**

1. Preheat oven to 350°. With a pastry brush, lightly brush both sides of bread with olive oil. Place on a baking sheet.

2. Bake for 5 minutes. Turn bread slices and bake 3 to 5 minutes longer, or until lightly toasted. Serve warm or store in an airtight container for up to 2 days.

15   CROSTINI CAPONATA
Prep: 20 minutes   Stand: 1 hour   Cook: 15 minutes   Serves: 6 to 12

12 slices Italian bread, cut ½ inch thick	**½ cup water**
¼ cup plus 2 tablespoons olive oil	**1 tablespoon tomato puree**
1 small eggplant, about 8 ounces	**4 pimiento-stuffed green olives**
2½ teaspoons coarse salt	**3 tablespoons capers, rinsed and drained**
½ cup chopped onion	**¼ teaspoon pepper**
½ cup celery, cut into ¼-inch dice	**1 tablespoon white wine vinegar**
	3 plum tomatoes, sliced

1. Preheat oven to 350°. With a pastry brush, lightly brush both sides of bread with 2 tablespoons olive oil. Place on a baking sheet. Bake for 5 minutes. Turn bread slices over and bake 5 minutes longer, or until lightly toasted.

2. To make caponata, cut eggplant in ¾-inch dice. Place in a colander and sprinkle with 1 teaspoon coarse salt. Place a plate with a weight on top (such as two 1-pound cans) and drain for 1 hour. Pat eggplant dry with paper towels.

3. In a large frying pan, heat ¼ cup olive oil over medium heat. Add onions and cook 2 to 3 minutes, or until softened. Stir in celery and cook until crisp-tender, about 2 minutes longer. Stir in eggplant and water, and cook, stirring frequently, 5 to 7 minutes, or until softened.

4. Add tomato puree, olives, 1 tablespoon capers, pepper, and remaining ½ teaspoon salt. Simmer, stirring frequently, 2 minutes to blend flavors. Remove pan from heat and stir in vinegar.

5. In a food processor or blender, coarsely chop caponata. Pile onto crostini and garnish with tomatoes and remaining 2 tablespoons capers.

16   CROSTINI WITH LIMA BEAN PUREE AND PARMESAN CHEESE

Prep: 20 minutes   Cook: 10 minutes   Serves: 6

In Italy this is made with a puree of fava beans. Since fava beans are highly seasonal, hard to find, and a lot of work to peel, I use lima beans instead.

6 slices Italian bread, cut ½ inch thick	2 garlic cloves, minced
7 tablespoons olive oil, preferably extra-virgin	½ teaspoon salt
1 10-ounce package frozen lima beans, thawed	½ teaspoon pepper
	¼ cup grated Parmesan cheese

1. Preheat oven to 350°. With a pastry brush, lightly brush both sides of bread with 2 tablespoons olive oil. Place on a baking sheet. Bake for 5 minutes. Turn bread over and bake 5 minutes longer, or until lightly toasted.

2. Bring 1 cup of salted water to a boil in a medium saucepan. Add lima beans and return to a boil. Cover, reduce heat, and cook until beans are just tender, 6 to 8 minutes. Drain in a colander.

3. In a small frying pan, heat 2 tablespoons olive oil over low heat. Add garlic and cook just 30 seconds, until fragrant. Add beans, increase heat to medium, and cook 1 minute. Mash beans with a fork and continue to cook until a coarse puree is formed. Season with salt and pepper.

4. Mound bean puree on crostini and drizzle with remaining 3 tablespoons olive oil. Sprinkle 1 teaspoon Parmesan cheese over each crostini.

17   CROSTINI WITH BEL PAESE AND ANCHOVIES

Prep: 15 minutes   Cook: 8 minutes   Serves: 6

This is a Roman dish, which was originally made with local Provatura cheese, rarely available. Bel Paese or mozzarella are fine substitutes.

12 slices Italian bread, cut ½ inch thick	6 flat anchovy fillets
¼ cup olive oil	12 slices Bel Paese cheese, cut ½ inch thick, trimmed to fit bread (about 6 ounces)
4 tablespoons butter	

1. Preheat oven to 350°. With a pastry brush, lightly brush both sides of bread with olive oil. Place on a baking sheet. Bake for 5 minutes. Turn bread slices over and bake 5 minutes longer, or until lightly toasted.

2. In a small frying pan, melt butter over low heat. Add anchovies and mash into butter, about 30 seconds.

3. Arrange cheese on each crostini. Place crostini on heatproof platter, overlapping about 2 inches each. Bake 6 to 8 minutes, until cheese is melted and lightly browned. Serve warm.

18   FRIED EGGPLANT AND ZUCCHINI STICKS
Prep: 30 minutes   Cook: 15 minutes   Serves: 6 to 10

1 medium eggplant, 1 to 1½
   pounds
3 medium zucchini, about 1
   pound
1½ cups flour
3 eggs
2 tablespoons water

3 cups dry bread crumbs
1 teaspoon salt
¼ teaspoon cayenne pepper
2½ quarts vegetable oil, for
   deep frying
   Lemon wedges

1. Peel eggplant. Cut zucchini and eggplant into 4 x ½-inch sticks. Spread flour on a plate or on a sheet of wax paper. In a wide shallow bowl, beat eggs and water until well blended. On another plate, combine bread crumbs, salt, and cayenne.

2. A few at a time, dredge vegetable sticks in flour, dip in egg, and roll lightly in bread crumbs.

3. In a large saucepan or deep-fat fryer, heat vegetable oil over medium heat to 350° on a deep-fat thermometer. Add zucchini and eggplant in batches without crowding and cook, turning, until crisp and browned, 2 to 3 minutes. Drain on paper towels. Serve with plenty of lemon wedges to squeeze over vegetables.

19   PARMESAN PUFFS
Prep: 15 minutes   Cook: 5 to 8 minutes   Serves: 8 to 16

Here's an American-style hot hors d'oeuvre made with Italian ingredients.

16 slices Italian bread, cut ½
   inch thick
2 tablespoons olive oil
1½ cups mayonnaise

¾ cup grated Parmesan cheese
   (about 3 ounces)
1 teaspoon Worcestershire
   sauce

1. Preheat oven to 350°. With a pastry brush, lightly brush both sides of bread with olive oil. Place on a baking sheet. Bake 5 minutes. Turn bread slices over and bake 5 minutes longer, or until lightly toasted.

2. In a small bowl, combine mayonnaise, cheese, and Worcestershire sauce. Pile about 3 tablespoons cheese mixture on each crostini, spreading evenly.

3. Place on a baking sheet and bake for 5 to 8 minutes, or until lightly puffed and golden. Serve hot.

20 HARD-BOILED EGGS WITH BASIL AND SUN-DRIED TOMATOES

Prep: 5 minutes   Cook: 20 minutes   Serves: 6 to 12

6 large eggs
3 tablespoons mayonnaise
½ teaspoon salt
⅛ teaspoon pepper
2 tablespoons sun-dried tomatoes packed in oil, drained and chopped

1½ tablespoons chopped fresh basil or 1½ tablespoons chopped fresh parsley mixed with 1 teaspoon dried basil

1. Place eggs in cold water to cover in a medium saucepan. Bring to a boil over medium heat. Reduce heat to low, cover, and cook 5 minutes. Remove from heat and leave eggs in covered pot of hot water 15 minutes. Drain eggs and remove shells at once.

2. Cut eggs in half and remove yolks. In a small bowl, mash yolks with a fork. Blend in mayonnaise and season with salt and pepper. Fill eggs with yolk mixture. Garnish with sun-dried tomatoes and basil. Serve at room temperature or slightly chilled.

21 MARINATED EGGPLANT

Prep: 20 minutes   Stand: 1 hour   Cook: 10 minutes
Marinate: 24 hours   Serves: 10 to 12

Serve this vegetable as a salad on sliced beefsteak tomatoes or as a stuffing in small tomatoes.

2 large eggplants, 3½ to 4 pounds
2 tablespoons coarse salt
¾ cup olive oil
4 garlic cloves, minced
2 tablespoons chopped fresh mint

2 tablespoons chopped fresh basil
2 tablespoons chopped fresh parsley
½ teaspoon pepper

1. Peel eggplants. Cut into ¾-inch dice. Place in a colander and sprinkle with coarse salt. Place a plate with a weight on top (such as two 1-pound cans) and let drain for 1 hour. Pat eggplant dry with paper towels.

2. Preheat broiler. Brush a baking sheet with 1 tablespoon olive oil. Place half the eggplant on baking sheet and toss to coat with oil. Broil 3 inches from heat for 2 minutes. Turn eggplant and broil 2 to 3 minutes more, until it begins to turn golden brown. Remove eggplant to a large platter. Repeat with more olive oil and remaining eggplant.

3. Add garlic, mint, basil, parsley, and pepper to eggplant. Toss to mix. Drizzle with remaining olive oil and toss again. Cover with plastic wrap and marinate in refrigerator 24 hours, tossing several times. Serve at room temperature.

22   HARD-BOILED EGGS WITH MUSTARD AND CAPERS

Prep: 5 minutes   Cook: 20 minutes   Serves: 6 to 12

This Italian version of deviled eggs will perk up any antipasto.

6 large eggs
3 tablespoons mayonnaise
1½ teaspoons Dijon mustard

3 tablespoons capers, rinsed
   and drained
2 tablespoons finely chopped
   fresh parsley

1. Place eggs in cold water to cover in a medium saucepan. Bring to a boil over medium heat. Reduce heat to low, cover, and cook 5 minutes. Remove from heat and leave eggs in covered pot of hot water 15 minutes. Drain eggs and remove shells at once.

2. Cut eggs in half and remove yolks. In a small bowl, mash yolks with a fork. Blend in mayonnaise and mustard. Fill eggs with yolk mixture. Sprinkle capers and parsley over yolk mixture and press lightly to help adhere. Serve at room temperature or slightly chilled.

23   KIDNEY BEANS WITH SALAMI AND SCALLIONS

Prep: 15 minutes   Cook: none   Serves: 6

Sopressata is especially good in this recipe, but Genoa or any other hard Italian salami will do.

1 15-ounce can kidney beans
3 tablespoons olive oil,
   preferably extra-virgin
2 tablespoons red wine
   vinegar

Salt and pepper to taste
¾ cup diced (½-inch) salami,
   about 4 ounces
1 cup sliced scallions

1. Drain beans and rinse under cold water. Drain well.

2. In a medium bowl, combine oil, vinegar, salt, and pepper. Beat with a fork to blend. Add beans, salami, and scallions, and toss together. Serve at room temperature or slightly chilled.

24   ROASTED GARLIC

Prep: 10 minutes   Cook: 35 to 45 minutes   Serves: 6

Roasted peppers, whole baked garlic, and chunks of Parmesan cheese start a meal beautifully. Be sure to include some good Italian bread to spread the meltingly sweet garlic on and a cruet of good extra-virgin olive oil instead of butter.

6 whole heads of garlic   **6 teaspoons olive oil**

1. Preheat oven to 350°. With a sharp knife, cut off top ½ inch from garlic to expose cloves. Place each head in the middle of a 6-inch square of aluminum foil. Drizzle 1 teaspoon olive oil over top of each. Wrap garlic loosely in foil.

2. Set packets of garlic on a baking sheet and bake for 35 to 45 minutes, or until garlic is soft enough to squeeze out of cloves to spread onto bread.

25   KIDNEY BEANS WITH SHRIMP

Prep: 15 minutes   Cook: 10 minutes   Serves: 6

Serve with roasted peppers and garlic bread.

1 celery rib, halved	**1 16-ounce can kidney beans**
½ small onion	**1 tablespoon red wine vinegar**
1 sprig fresh oregano or	**3 tablespoons olive oil**
** 1 teaspoon dried**	**½ teaspoon salt**
½ lemon	**¼ teaspoon pepper**
3 whole peppercorns, crushed	**4 scallions, sliced**
⅛ teaspoon hot pepper flakes	**1 tablespoon minced fresh**
12 ounces medium shrimp,	** parsley**
** shelled and deveined**	

1. In a nonreactive medium saucepan, bring 6 cups water to a boil with celery, onion, oregano, lemon, peppercorns, and hot pepper flakes. Boil 3 minutes. Plunge shrimp into boiling water and cook 2 to 3 minutes, or until they just turn pink. Drain in a colander and rinse under cold running water. Transfer shrimp to a bowl and discard vegetables and seasonings remaining in colander. Set shrimp aside.

2. Drain beans and rinse under cold running water. Drain well. In a medium bowl, whisk together vinegar, olive oil, salt, and pepper until dressing is blended. Add beans, scallions, and parsley to dressing. Toss to coat. Add shrimp and toss lightly.

26   BAKED FONTINA CHEESE WITH MARINATED ARTICHOKES

Prep: 5 minutes   Cook: 4 to 5 minutes   Serves: 4

1 tablespoon butter, softened
1 6-ounce jar marinated
   artichokes

8 ounces Italian fontina,
   Gruyère, or Swiss cheese
Crusty Italian bread

1. Preheat oven to 475°. Generously butter a small heatproof platter or 9-inch glass pie dish.

2. Drain artichokes, discarding juices. Place artichokes in center of platter. Arrange overlapping slices of cheese in concentric circles on top.

3. Bake for 4 to 5 minutes, or until cheese begins to color around edges. Using two spoons, scoop up some of cheese with artichokes and transfer to individual warmed serving plates. Serve immediately, with crusty bread.

27   FONDUTTA

Prep: 10 minutes   Cook: 15 minutes   Serves: 4 to 6

Fondutta is Italian cheese fondue, long overdue for a comeback. If you can't find Italian fontina cheese, you can substitute Gruyère or Swiss.

12 ounces Italian fontina,
   Gruyère, or Swiss cheese
3 tablespoons butter
½ cup milk
4 egg yolks

Pinch of grated nutmeg
Pinch of white pepper
5 cups 1½-inch Italian bread
   cubes or 1 5-ounce
   package bread sticks

1. Cut cheese into 1-inch cubes. Place butter in stainless steel or earthenware fondue pot or chafing dish over very low heat. Melt butter. Add milk and cheese, stirring with wooden spoon until cheese melts, 6 to 8 minutes.

2. Whisk in egg yolks, one at a time, until well blended. Cook, stirring, 1 to 2 minutes, or until slightly thickened; do not boil. Season with nutmeg and white pepper. Serve with bread cubes, which are dipped into mixture on the end of a fork, or with bread sticks.

28 FONTINA AND VERMOUTH
Prep: 5 minutes   Cook: 5 to 8 minutes   Serves: 4

Very fast to prepare, this dip must be eaten quickly as well, before the cheese hardens. Italy produces an excellent dry vermouth; try it for authentic flavor.

3 tablespoons butter
¼ cup dry vermouth,
  preferably Italian

8 ounces Italian fontina,
  Gruyère, or Swiss cheese,
  sliced
Bread sticks

1. Preheat oven to 375°. Butter a heatproof serving platter with a lip. Pour vermouth onto platter and arrange overlapping slices of cheese in concentric circles on top.

2. Bake 5 to 8 minutes, or until cheese melts. To eat, dip bread sticks into cheese.

29 MOZZARELLA ROLLED WITH GORGONZOLA AND BASIL
Prep: 30 minutes   Cook: none   Chill: 2 hours   Serves: 6 to 12

If mascarpone is unavailable, a very good substitute is a combination of cream cheese, heavy cream, and sour cream.

12 ounces mozzarella cheese
2 cups mascarpone cheese,
  about 1 pound, or 12
  ounces cream cheese
  mixed with ¼ cup heavy
  cream and 2 tablespoons
  sour cream

6 ounces gorgonzola or other
  blue cheese
½ cup packed torn fresh basil
  leaves or 2 teaspoons
  dried basil

1. Place a piece of plastic wrap on a flat work surface. Cut mozzarella into ¼-inch slices and arrange in rows on the plastic wrap, overlapping edges by 1 inch. Place another piece of plastic wrap on top of cheese. With a rolling pin, roll cheese gently to flatten to a sheet about ¼ inch thick. Peel off top plastic wrap.

2. Spread mascarpone or cream cheese mixture over mozzarella. Crumble gorgonzola on top and sprinkle basil evenly over surface. Using plastic wrap to help lift edges, roll up, jelly-roll fashion, into a thick log. Wrap tightly in plastic wrap. Twist ends of wrap tightly to seal.

3. Refrigerate log at least 2 hours, until chilled and set, or up to 4 days. To serve, cut into slices ¾ to 1 inch thick.

30   SMOKED MOZZARELLA WITH PICKLED MUSHROOMS

Prep: 5 minutes   Cook: 8 minutes   Serves: 4

If your market doesn't carry smoked mozzarella, look for smoked Gouda or German beer cheese. Crusty Italian bread is a must to accompany this antipasto.

1 tablespoon butter, softened
1 4-ounce jar pickled mushrooms

8 ounces smoked mozzarella, thinly sliced
Crusty Italian bread

1. Preheat oven to 475°. Butter a small heatproof platter or glass pie dish.

2. Drain mushrooms, discarding juices. Place mushrooms in center of platter. Arrange overlapping slices of cheese in concentric circles on top.

3. Bake 4 to 5 minutes, or until cheese begins to lightly color around edges. Using two spoons, scoop up some of cheese with mushrooms and transfer to individual warmed serving plates. Serve immediately, with crusty bread.

31   MOZZARELLA ROLLED WITH CREAM CHEESE AND PESTO

Prep: 30 minutes   Cook: none   Chill: 2 hours   Serves: 6 to 12

½ cup pine nuts
12 ounces mozzarella cheese
¼ cup pesto, homemade (page 77) or jarred

2 cups mascarpone cheese, about 1 pound, or 8 ounces cream cheese mixed with 2 tablespoons heavy cream and 2 tablespoons sour cream

1. In a dry medium skillet, toast pine nuts over medium heat, shaking pan frequently, 2 to 3 minutes, or until golden brown and fragrant.

2. Place a piece of plastic wrap on a flat work surface. Cut mozzarella into ¼-inch slices and arrange in rows on the plastic wrap, overlapping edges by 1 inch. Place another sheet of plastic wrap on top of cheese. With a rolling pin, roll cheese gently to flatten to a sheet about ¼ inch thick. Peel off top plastic wrap.

3. Spread pesto over mozzarella. Spread mascarpone or cream cheese mixture over pesto. Sprinkle pine nuts evenly over all. Using plastic wrap to help lift edges, roll up, jelly-roll fashion, into a thick log. Twist ends of wrap tightly to seal.

4. Refrigerate log at least 2 hours, until chilled and set, or up to 4 days. To serve, cut into slices ¾ to 1 inch thick.

32 MOZZARELLA MARINATED WITH CAPERS AND ANCHOVIES

Prep: 10 minutes   Marinate: 2 days   Cook: none   Serves: 12

Marinated mozzarella cheese is a favorite in Italy, either as part of an antipasto or in a sandwich of crusty bread. This is best if you can find fresh mozzarella, which is available at Italian markets and in some supermarket delis.

12 ounces mozzarella cheese, preferably fresh
12 flat anchovy fillets, halved lengthwise
6 tablespoons capers, rinsed and drained

¼ cup fresh parsley leaves
2 cups olive oil, preferably extra-virgin
3 fresh plum tomatoes, sliced

1. Cut mozzarella into ¼-inch slices. In a glass bowl, layer slices of mozzarella with anchovies, capers, and parsley. Cover with olive oil. Marinate in refrigerator at least 2 days.

2. Using a slotted spoon, remove cheese, anchovies, and capers from oil. Serve at room temperature with slices of fresh tomato. Reuse oil if desired to marinate more cheese.

33 MOZZARELLA MARINATED WITH BASIL AND SUN-DRIED TOMATOES

Prep: 10 minutes   Marinate: 2 days   Cook: none   Serves: 12

A delicious salad to serve with fresh tomatoes or just good bread. Make this recipe when fresh basil is in season.

12 ounces mozzarella cheese, preferably fresh
1 cup packed fresh basil leaves

½ cup sun-dried tomatoes packed in oil, drained and cut into strips
2 cups olive oil, preferably extra-virgin

1. Cut mozzarella into ¼-inch slices. In a glass bowl layer slices alternately with basil and sun-dried tomatoes. Cover with olive oil. Marinate in refrigerator 2 to 3 days.

2. Using a slotted spoon, remove mozzarella, basil, and sun-dried tomatoes from oil. Serve at room temperature. Reuse oil in a dressing or to marinate more cheese.

34   STUFFED MUSHROOMS
Prep: 15 minutes   Cook: 20 minutes   Serves: 6 to 12

The ideal mushrooms for stuffing are 2 to 3 inches in diameter.

12 large fresh mushrooms
2 tablespoons butter
1 tablespoon olive oil
½ cup minced onion
1 garlic clove, minced
1 tablespoon chopped fresh parsley
1 teaspoon minced fresh marjoram or ½ teaspoon dried

1 cup bread crumbs
½ cup grated Parmesan cheese
½ cup chopped prosciutto or ham
1 teaspoon salt
¼ teaspoon pepper

1. Preheat oven to 350°. Remove stems from mushrooms and finely chop. Set caps aside.

2. In a medium frying pan, melt butter with olive oil over medium heat. Add onion and garlic and cook 2 to 3 minutes, or until onion is softened. Add mushroom stems and cook 3 minutes, or until mushroom liquid is exuded and then evaporates. Add parsley, marjoram, and bread crumbs. Cook 1 minute to combine. Stir in Parmesan cheese and prosciutto or ham. Season with salt and pepper.

3. Stuff mushrooms, mounding bread crumb mixture high in caps. Place in a buttered baking dish and bake 15 to 20 minutes, or until filling is crusty brown and mushroom caps are tender but still hold their shape.

35   MUSHROOM SALAD
Prep: 15 minutes   Cook: none   Serves: 4 to 6

This is delicious served with grilled meats. I like to put it right on top of steak. Serve it right away before the mushroom juices darken the dressing.

2 tablespoons fresh lemon juice
3 tablespoons olive oil, preferably extra-virgin
1 garlic clove, minced
2 tablespoons minced fresh parsley

1 teaspoon chopped fresh oregano or ¼ teaspoon dried
½ teaspoon salt
¼ teaspoon pepper
1 pound fresh mushrooms, very thinly sliced

1. In a medium bowl, combine lemon juice, olive oil, garlic, parsley, oregano, salt, and pepper. Beat with a fork to blend.

2. Add mushrooms and toss to coat with dressing. Serve immediately.

36   MUSHROOM AND SHRIMP ANTIPASTO
Prep: 15 minutes   Cook: 5 to 7 minutes   Serves: 6 to 8

1 celery rib, halved
½ small onion
1 sprig fresh thyme or
    1 teaspoon dried
½ lemon plus 1 tablespoon
    fresh lemon juice
3 whole peppercorns, crushed
⅛ teaspoon hot pepper flakes
12 ounces medium shrimp,
    shelled and deveined

½ cup mayonnaise
½ cup chopped tomato
1 tablespoon finely chopped
    fresh basil or ½ teaspoon
    dried
⅛ teaspoon pepper
8 ounces fresh mushrooms,
    quartered
12 romaine lettuce leaves

1. In a nonreactive medium saucepan, bring 6 cups water to a boil with celery, onion, thyme, ½ lemon, peppercorns, and hot pepper flakes. Boil 3 minutes. Plunge shrimp into boiling water and cook until they just turn pink, 2 to 3 minutes. Drain in a colander and rinse under cold running water. Transfer shrimp to a bowl; discard vegetables and lemon half.

2. In a small bowl, combine mayonnaise, tomato, basil, pepper, and 1 tablespoon lemon juice. Beat with a fork to blend. Add mushrooms and shrimp and toss to coat. Pile salad onto romaine leaves.

37   MARINATED MUSHROOMS
*Prep: 20 minutes   Cook: 5 to 6 minutes   Marinate: 8 hours
Serves: 8 to 10*

Great for parties and good snacks from the refrigerator.

1 whole lemon plus ¼ cup
    fresh lemon juice
6 cups water
1 teaspoon chopped fresh
    oregano or ¼ teaspoon
    dried
2 pounds fresh medium
    mushrooms, ends
    trimmed

2 tablespoons white wine
    vinegar
½ cup olive oil, preferably
    extra-virgin
1 teaspoon salt
½ teaspoon pepper
2 tablespoons minced parsley
1 medium onion, chopped

1. Cut lemon in half; remove seeds. Cut into very thin slices. In a large saucepan, bring water, lemon slices, and oregano to a boil. Add whole mushrooms, place a heatproof plate on top to keep mushrooms from floating to top, and cook for 5 to 6 minutes, until mushrooms turn white. Drain.

2. Meanwhile, in a large bowl, combine lemon juice, vinegar, olive oil, salt, pepper, and parsley. Beat with a fork to blend. Add hot mushrooms and onion to dressing and toss until well coated. Let cool, then cover with plastic wrap and marinate in refrigerator, tossing occasionally, at least 8 hours or overnight. Serve slightly chilled or at room temperature.

38   STUFFED MUSSELS
Prep: 15 minutes   Cook: 15 minutes   Serves: 6 to 8

2 tablespoons olive oil	1½ cups soft bread crumbs
¼ cup minced onion	2 tablespoons chopped
2 garlic cloves, minced	parsley
¼ cup dry white wine	Pinch of hot pepper flakes
2 dozen mussels, scrubbed	Lemon wedges

1. In a large frying pan, heat olive oil over medium heat. Add onion and garlic and cook 2 to 3 minutes, or until onion is softened. Add wine and mussels and raise heat to high. Cook 3 to 5 minutes, shaking pan frequently, until mussels are open. Remove from pan; discard any mussels that do not open. Strain pan juices through a fine-mesh sieve or several thicknesses of dampened cheesecloth and reserve. Remove mussels from shells; discard half the shells.

2. In a medium saucepan, boil mussel juice until reduced to 3 tablespoons. Add bread crumbs, parsley, and hot pepper flakes. Toss together. Place a mussel on each shell. Pack seasoned bread crumbs over mussels. (Recipe can be prepared to this point up to 8 hours in advance. Cover and refrigerate.)

3. Place mussels on a baking sheet and broil 4 inches from heat 3 to 4 minutes, until crumbs are lightly browned and crisp. Serve with lemon wedges.

39   SPICY MARINATED OLIVES
Prep: 5 minutes   Marinate: 24 hours   Cook: none   Serves: 4 to 6

Eat these as they are or chop them and make a sandwich. Deli olives are best, but even canned ripe olives from the supermarket will take on a new personality when prepared in this manner.

¼ cup olive oil, preferably extra-virgin	3 to 4 garlic cloves, thinly sliced
2 tablespoons red wine vinegar	1 pound black olives, preferably Mediterranean oil-cured
1 teaspoon hot pepper flakes	

In a medium bowl, whisk oil and vinegar to blend. Toss with all ingredients. Marinate in refrigerator at least 24 hours or up to 2 weeks. Serve at room temperature.

40   OLIVES MARINATED WITH CAPERS
Prep: 5 minutes   Marinate: 24 hours   Cook: none   Serves: 6 to 10

These keep well in the refrigerator, so you may want to make a double batch.

2   6-ounce cans black olives,
    drained
2   tablespoons capers, rinsed
    and drained

¼   cup olive oil, preferably
    extra-virgin
½   teaspoon freshly ground
    pepper

Toss all ingredients together. Marinate in refrigerator at least 24 hours or up to 2 weeks. Serve at room temperature.

41   CHICKEN LIVER PATE WITH MARSALA
Prep: 15 minutes   Cook: 15 minutes   Chill: 2 hours   Serves: 8

In Italy, chicken liver pâté is usually served on crostini, as it is here. It's also nice with bread sticks.

½   cup finely diced pancetta or
    bacon, about 2 ounces
1   pound chicken livers,
    trimmed
1   stick plus 2 tablespoons
    butter, softened
3   tablespoons olive oil
1   cup finely chopped onion

1   garlic clove, minced
4   bay leaves
½   cup dry Marsala or sherry
1   teaspoon salt
1   teaspoon freshly ground
    pepper
    Crostini (page 14)

1. If using bacon, simmer in 4 cups water 10 minutes to remove smoky flavor. Drain, rinse under cold running water, and drain well.

2. Rinse chicken livers and pat dry. In a large frying pan, melt 2 tablespoons butter with olive oil over medium heat. Add pancetta or bacon, onion, and garlic and cook 2 to 3 minutes, or until onion is softened. Add bay leaves and livers. Cook over medium heat, turning frequently, 6 to 8 minutes, or until livers are browned outside but still rosy inside.

3. Season livers with salt and pepper. Remove bay leaves from pan. Pour wine into pan and boil, stirring, until reduced by half, about 3 minutes.

4. In a food processor or blender, grind livers to a paste. With machine on, gradually add remaining butter in bits through feed tube. Process until blended and smooth. Season with salt and pepper.

5. Pack chicken liver pâté into a small crock or bowl. Cover with plastic wrap and refrigerate at least 2 hours or up to 2 days before serving on crostini.

42 SWEET PEPPERS WITH ROSEMARY, GARLIC, AND SALTED CHEESE
Prep: 30 minutes   Cook: 20 minutes   Serves: 8

Ricotta salata is a pressed, dry form of ricotta, with a nice tangy bite. While you can find it at some Italian markets and specialty food shops, feel free to substitute feta cheese, a Greek cousin, which is available at most supermarkets.

2 large red bell peppers, about 1 pound
2 large yellow bell peppers, about 1 pound
2 large green bell peppers, about 1 pound
4 garlic cloves, thinly sliced
5½ tablespoons olive oil, preferably extra-virgin

2 tablespoons chopped fresh rosemary or 1 teaspoon dried
½ teaspoon pepper
4 ounces ricotta salata or feta cheese, crumbled (about 1 cup)

1. Preheat oven to 475°. Set peppers on a baking sheet and brush with 1½ tablespoons olive oil to coat lightly. Set on a baking sheet. Bake, turning once or twice, 20 minutes, or until skins begin to blister.

2. Place peppers in a brown paper or plastic bag to steam for 10 minutes. Pull skins from peppers. Remove stems, seeds, and membranes. Cut peppers into thin strips.

3. Lay pepper strips flat on a serving plate. In a small bowl, combine remaining 3½ tablespoons olive oil, garlic, rosemary, and ground pepper. Pour over roasted peppers. Sprinkle cheese over top.

43 BALSAMIC ONIONS
Prep: 10 minutes   Cook: 30 to 40 minutes   Serves: 12 to 16

Use these sweetly tangy onions as part of an antipasto plate or as a side dish to accompany meat or fish.

4 large red onions, about 2 pounds

2 cups balsamic vinegar, or red wine vinegar mixed with 1 teaspoon sugar

1. Preheat oven to 350°. Cut unpeeled onions in half, from stem end to root end. Pour balsamic vinegar into an 11 x 7 x 2-inch glass baking dish. Place onions cut side down in dish. Cover with foil.

2. Bake 30 to 40 minutes, until onions are tender but still hold their shape. Remove skins and cut each onion half into 3 wedges each. Serve warm, at room temperature or slightly chilled.

44   ROASTED YELLOW PEPPERS WITH BASIL
Prep: 30 minutes   Cook: 20 minutes   Serves: 6 to 8

4 large yellow bell peppers,
   about 2 pounds
3 tablespoons olive oil,
   preferably extra-virgin

2 tablespoons shredded fresh
   basil, or 1½ tablespoons
   chopped fresh parsley
   and 1 teaspoon dried basil
   Salt and freshly ground
   pepper to taste

1. Preheat oven to 475°. Set peppers on a baking sheet and brush with 1 tablespoon olive oil to coat lightly. Bake, turning once or twice, 20 minutes, or until skins begin to blister.

2. Place peppers in a brown paper or plastic bag to steam for 10 minutes. Pull skins from peppers. Remove stems, seeds, and membranes. Tear peppers into 4 to 6 pieces each.

3. Lay roasted peppers flat on a serving plate. In a small bowl, combine remaining 2 tablespoons olive oil, basil, and salt and pepper. Pour over roasted peppers.

45   FRIED PROVOLONE
*Prep: 15 minutes   Freeze: 15 minutes   Cook: 10 minutes
Serves: 6 to 8*

The secret to the success of this recipe is chilling the cheese for only 15 minutes in the freezer, so it will not melt as the bread crumbs brown. Be sure the cheese is covered completely before frying. Serve plain or in warm tomato sauce.

1½ pounds provolone cheese,
    in 1 piece
1   cup flour
2   eggs

2   tablespoons water
2   cups dry bread crumbs
1½ quarts vegetable oil, for
    frying

1. Cut cheese into 3 x ½-inch sticks. Spread flour on a plate or sheet of wax paper. In a wide shallow bowl, beat eggs and water until well blended. On another plate, spread bread crumbs. Dredge cheese in flour, dip in egg, and roll lightly in bread crumbs, making sure it is coated completely. Place breaded cheese sticks in a single layer on a plate and freeze 15 minutes.

2. In a large saucepan or deep-fat fryer, heat vegetable oil over medium heat to 350° on a deep-fat thermometer. Add cheese in batches without crowding and cook, turning, until evenly browned, 2 to 3 minutes. Serve immediately.

46 RICE CROQUETTES WITH CHEESE
Prep: 20 minutes   Cook: 35 minutes   Serves: 6 to 8

Because the melted cheese stretches out into strings while it's being eaten, these little balls are called *suppli al telefono,* or telephone wires in Italian. Serve with your favorite tomato sauce.

3 tablespoons butter	**Pepper to taste**
½ cup minced onion	8 ounces mozzarella cheese,
2 cups Arborio rice	cut into 18 cubes
8 cups hot Chicken Stock	2 cups dry bread crumbs
(page 48) or reduced-	1½ quarts vegetable oil, for
sodium canned broth	frying
¾ cup grated Parmesan cheese	3 cups tomato sauce, heated
2 eggs, beaten	

1. In a medium saucepan, melt butter over medium-low heat. Add onion and cook 2 to 3 minutes, until softened. Add rice and stir to coat with butter. Cook, stirring, 1 to 2 minutes.

2. Add 4 cups stock and cook, stirring, until broth is almost absorbed, 4 to 5 minutes. Add 1 more cup broth and cook until almost absorbed. Continue to add broth gradually and cook, stirring, until rice is tender but still firm and liquid forms a thick sauce, 18 to 20 minutes total. Remove from heat. Stir Parmesan cheese and eggs into hot rice. Season with pepper. Spread rice out on a baking sheet to cool.

3. Divide rice into 18 portions. Flatten one portion in the palm of your hand and place one cube of mozzarella in center. Draw edges together to enclose cheese, and form into a ball. Roll in bread crumbs.

4. In a large saucepan or deep-fat fryer, heat vegetable oil over medium heat to 350° on a deep-fat thermometer. Add croquettes in batches without crowding and cook, turning, until an even golden brown, 3 to 4 minutes. Serve hot, with tomato sauce.

47   RICE CROQUETTES WITH SAUSAGE

Prep: 35 minutes   Cook: 30 minutes   Serves: 6 to 8

This is a Sicilian version called *arancini*, or little oranges. It can have various fillings of meat and mushrooms; the tomato paste gives a light orange color to the filling.

1 stick (8 tablespoons) butter	1 tablespoon olive oil
¾ cup minced onion	1 pound sweet Italian
2 cups Arborio rice	sausage, casings removed
8 cups hot Chicken Stock	¼ cup tomato paste
(page 48) or reduced-	3 ounces mozzarella cheese,
sodium canned broth	finely diced (about ¾ cup)
¾ cup grated Parmesan cheese	2 cups dry bread crumbs
2 eggs, beaten	1½ quarts vegetable oil, for
Pepper to taste	deep frying

1. In a medium saucepan, melt butter over medium-low heat. Add ½ cup minced onion and cook 2 to 3 minutes, until softened. Add rice and stir to coat with butter. Cook, stirring, 1 to 2 minutes. Add 4 cups stock and stir until broth is almost absorbed, 4 to 5 minutes. Continue to add as much stock as needed, 1 cup at a time, stirring, until rice is just barely tender. Process should take 18 to 20 minutes from time you add first stock. Remove from heat. Stir Parmesan cheese and eggs into hot rice. Season with pepper. Spread rice out on a baking sheet to cool.

2. In a small frying pan, heat olive oil over medium heat. Add remaining ¼ cup minced onion and sausage meat and cook until meat loses its pinkness, about 5 minutes. Stir in tomato paste and remove from heat. Pour off excess fat and let cool. Stir in mozzarella and divide sausage mixture into 18 portions.

3. Divide rice into 18 portions. Flatten one portion in the palm of your hand and place one portion of sausage filling in center. Draw edges together to enclose filling, and form into a ball. Roll in bread crumbs.

4. In a large saucepan or deep-fat fryer, heat vegetable oil over medium heat to 350° on a deep-fat thermometer. Add croquettes in batches without crowding and cook, turning, until an even golden brown, 3 to 4 minutes. Serve hot.

48 PISTACHIO CHICKEN LIVER PATE ROLLED IN PROSCIUTTO

Prep: 20 minutes   Cook: none   Chill: 2 hours   Serves: 12 to 14

Chicken Liver Pâté with
  Marsala (page 27)
½ cup shelled pistachio nuts,
  coarsely chopped

6 very thin slices prosciutto or
  ham
  Crostini (page 14) or slices
  Italian bread

1. Prepare chicken liver pâté through step 3. Before chilling, stir in pistachio nuts.

2. Lay a piece of plastic wrap on a work surface. In center place a row of prosciutto or ham slices, overlapping by 1 inch. Spoon liver mixture down center of prosciutto. Using plastic wrap to help lift edges, roll up, jelly-roll fashion, into a thick log. Twist ends of wrap tightly to seal.

3. Refrigerate log at least 2 hours or up to 2 days. Cut into ¾-inch slices and serve on crostini or slices of Italian bread.

49 ROASTED RED BELL PEPPERS

Prep: 30 minutes   Cook: 20 minutes   Serves: 4 to 8

Any color bell pepper can be treated this way. They are well worth the effort.

4 large red bell peppers, about
  2 pounds
3 tablespoons olive oil,
  preferably extra-virgin

2 garlic cloves, finely chopped
  Salt and pepper to taste

1. Preheat oven to 475°. Set peppers on a baking sheet and brush with 1 tablespoon olive oil to coat lightly. Bake, turning once or twice, for 20 minutes, or until skins begin to blister.

2. Place peppers in a brown paper or plastic bag to steam for 10 minutes. Pull skins from peppers. Remove stems, seeds, and membranes. Tear peppers into 4 to 6 pieces each.

3. Lay roasted peppers flat on a serving plate. In a small bowl, combine remaining 2 tablespoons olive oil, garlic, and salt and pepper. Pour over roasted peppers.

50   BAGNA CAUDA
Prep: 30 minutes   Cook: 5 minutes   Serves: 6

A fondue pot is perfect for this. A great basket of vegetables, trimmed and washed, makes a beautiful presentation.

1 fennel bulb, cut into 1-inch wide strips	4 tablespoons butter
2 large carrots, peeled and cut into 1-inch wide strips	1 cup olive oil
1 celery heart, cut into 6 pieces	6 flat anchovy fillets
1 medium head of Belgian endive, separated into leaves	4 garlic cloves, minced
1 large red bell pepper, cut lengthwise into 1-inch strips	Pepper to taste
	1 5-ounce package of bread sticks

1. Prepare vegetables as described above or choose your own assortment of raw and/or steamed for dipping.

2. In a stainless-steel or heatproof ceramic chafing dish or fondue pot, melt butter with olive oil. Add anchovies and cook, stirring, 2 to 3 minutes, or until anchovies dissolve. Reduce heat to low and add garlic and black pepper. Cook 1 minute, or until garlic is fragrant. Serve warm with vegetables and bread sticks for dipping.

51   PIEDMONTESE SPREAD WITH MASCARPONE, GORGONZOLA, AND WALNUTS
Prep: 10 minutes   Cook: none   Chill: 2 hours   Serves: 6 to 8

2 cups mascarpone cheese, about 1 pound or 12 ounces cream cheese blended with ¼ cup heavy cream and 2 tablespoons sour cream	2 tablespoons chopped fresh basil or 1 teaspoon dried
½ cup gorgonzola or other blue cheese, about 2 ounces	½ cup chopped walnuts
	Sliced apples or pears, or Crostini (page 14)

1. In a small bowl, combine mascarpone or cream cheese mixture with gorgonzola and basil. Mix to blend well. Transfer mixture to a serving bowl. Cover and refrigerate 2 hours or up to 2 days.

2. Shortly before serving, cover top with chopped walnuts. Serve with sliced pears or apples, or spread on crostini.

52   FRIED TORTELLINI

Prep: 2 minutes   Cook: 10 to 12 minutes   Serves: 8 to 10

Here's an "instant" hot hors d'oeuvre that's sure to be a hit at your next party. If made up to half an hour ahead, keep warm in a 250° degree oven.

1½ quarts vegetable oil, for
       deep frying
1 16-ounce box dried tortellini
1 cup pesto, homemade (page
       77) or jarred, or 2 cups
       marinara sauce,
       homemade (page 131) or
       jarred, for dipping

In a large saucepan or deep-fat fryer, heat vegetable oil to 350° on a deep-fat thermometer. Add uncooked tortellini in batches without crowding and cook until blisters form on the surface of the dough like an eggroll and color is golden brown, 2 to 3 minutes. Drain on paper towels. Serve hot, with pesto or marinara sauce for dipping.

Chapter 2

Soups—Like Mama Used to Make

Italian soups run the gamut from light vegetable soups prepared simply with fresh greens, a little minced garlic, and some good chicken stock, then finished off with a sprinkling of Parmesan cheese, to big, heavy bean soups, often paired with pasta, for a fortifying meal in a bowl that many find addictive. With such a range, soup can be served as a single course within a complex meal, or it can be paired with a salad or an Italian hero for a lunch like Mama used to make. Seafood soups are also popular in Italy. I've included two recipes for clam soup: one traditional and one made in a flash with pantry ingredients, like canned chopped clams.

The basis of any good soup is the stock. At the end of this chapter, you'll find a recipe for an easy chicken stock you can make at your convenience and freeze for future use. If homemade stock is not on hand when you feel like making soup, try to find a reduced-sodium canned broth, which is significantly less salty than the regular kind but still has good flavor. Or dilute regular canned broth with equal parts of water to simulate more of a homemade style.

Whether you're serving a light Fresh Tomato Soup or a hearty quintessentially Italian Neapolitan Minestrone, crusty Italian bread, preferably toasted into Crostini (page 14) or turned into irresistible Garlic Bread (page 196), is an extremely apt accompaniment.

53   PASTINA AND EGG SOUP
Prep: 5 minutes   Cook: 15 minutes   Serves: 4 to 6

This is Italian nursery food. Every child can relate to this "Mama's food." To keep the broth from becoming "starchy" and cloudy, cook pastina separately, then add it to the broth.

1 cup pastina	⅛ teaspoon grated nutmeg
4 cups Chicken Stock (page	Salt and pepper to taste
48) or reduced-sodium	¼ cup grated Parmesan cheese
canned broth	4 teaspoons butter (optional)
3 eggs	

1. Cook pastina in a large pot of boiling salted water until tender, 8 to 10 minutes. Drain.

2. In a medium saucepan bring chicken stock to a boil. Add cooked pastina.

3. In a small bowl, beat eggs. Pour all at once into soup. Remove from heat. Stir until eggs form strings. Season with nutmeg, salt, and pepper. Pour into bowls. Garnish with Parmesan cheese and butter, if desired.

54   AGUACOTTA
Prep: 15 minutes   Cook: 25 minutes   Serves: 6

Literally called "cooked water," this simple vegetable soup, enriched with eggs and served with Parmesan cheese and thick croutons of Italian bread, is a Tuscan specialty.

3 tablespoons olive oil	1½ teaspoons salt
2 cups thinly sliced onions	½ teaspoon pepper
2 red bell peppers, cored,	6 cups water
seeded, and cut into	3 eggs
½-inch strips	6 thick slices Italian bread,
2 celery ribs, chopped	toasted
1 14-ounce can Italian peeled	Grated Parmesan cheese
tomatoes, drained and	
chopped	

1. In a large pot, heat oil over medium heat. Cook onions and peppers about 10 minutes, or until soft, stirring so as not to burn. Add celery, tomatoes, salt, pepper, and water. Bring to a boil and cook uncovered 10 to 12 minutes, or until reduced to 6½ to 7 cups.

2. In a small bowl, beat eggs. Pour eggs in a steady stream into soup. Stir. Turn heat off and allow eggs to set. Pour soup over toasted Italian bread in bowls. Pass a bowl of Parmesan cheese on the side.

55   MEATBALL SOUP
Prep: 20 minutes   Cook: 20 minutes   Serves: 8

Ideally, these meatballs are the size of hazelnuts, but you can make them a little bigger. Pastina is a tiny dry pasta. Star shapes are fun for this soup.

¾ cup soft bread crumbs
3 tablespoons milk
½ pound ground chuck
1 garlic clove, minced
1 tablespoon finely chopped
   onion
¼ teaspoon dried thyme
¼ cup grated Parmesan cheese,
   plus additional for
   serving

⅛ teaspoon grated nutmeg
½ teaspoon salt
8 cups canned beef broth
¼ cup pastina, cooked
2 tablespoons chopped fresh
   parsley
   Pepper to taste

1. In a small bowl, combine bread crumbs and milk. Let stand 5 minutes. Add meat, garlic, onion, thyme, ¼ cup Parmesan cheese, nutmeg, and salt. Form into small balls. (You can use a melon baller to portion.)

2. In a large saucepan, bring beef broth to a boil over medium-high heat. Add meatballs, reduce heat to low, and cook covered 8 to 10 minutes, until cooked through. Add cooked pastina and heat through. Sprinkle with parsley and pass a pepper mill and a bowl of Parmesan cheese on the side.

56   GARLIC SOUP
Prep: 10 minutes   Cook: 5 minutes   Serves: 6

This is just as good without the egg. More garlic is up to your discretion.

2 tablespoons butter
1 tablespoon olive oil
12 garlic cloves, quartered
6 thick slices Italian bread, cut
   into 1-inch cubes
½ cup dry red wine
6 cups Chicken Stock (page
   48) or reduced-sodium
   canned chicken or beef
   broth

1 tablespoon chopped fresh
   parsley
   Salt and pepper to taste
6 small eggs
   Grated Parmesan cheese

1. In a heavy pot, melt butter with olive oil over low heat. Add garlic and cook 2 minutes; do not burn. Add bread to pan and toss. Add wine, stock, and parsley. Bring to a boil over medium heat, reduce heat to low, and cook 10 minutes. Season with salt and pepper.

2. One at a time, crack eggs and gently slip into pot without breaking yolks. Cover pot and poach eggs in soup 3 minutes, or until whites are set and yolks are medium-firm. Serve an egg in each bowl with soup around it. Pass a pepper mill and a bowl of Parmesan cheese.

57   TWO-COLOR SOUP

Prep: 10 minutes   Cook: 45 minutes   Serves: 6 to 8

3 tablespoons butter
1 medium onion, chopped
2 pounds russet potatoes, peeled and cut into 1-inch dice
8 cups Chicken Stock (page 48) or reduced-sodium canned broth

¾ cup heavy cream
1 pound spinach, stems removed, or 1 10-ounce package frozen, defrosted
1 teaspoon salt
½ teaspoon pepper
Grated Parmesan cheese

1. In a medium saucepan, melt butter over medium heat. Add onion and cook 3 minutes, or until soft but not brown. Add potatoes and chicken stock. Bring to a boil, then reduce heat to medium-low, cover, and cook 25 minutes, or until potatoes begin to fall apart.

2. Puree soup in a food processor or blender. Return to the saucepan. Add cream and heat through. Add spinach and cook 4 to 5 minutes, or until tender but still bright green. Season with salt and pepper. Pass a bowl of Parmesan cheese on the side.

58   LENTIL SOUP

Prep: 5 minutes   Cook: 1 hour   Serves: 6 to 8

3 tablespoons olive oil
1 medium onion, chopped
2 celery ribs, chopped
1 large carrot, peeled and chopped
8 ounces lentils

8 cups water
1 ham hock
1 teaspoon dried oregano
Salt and pepper to taste
Grated Romano cheese

1. In a large saucepan or flameproof casserole, heat olive oil over medium heat. Add onion, celery, and carrot and cook 5 minutes, or until softened. Add lentils, water, ham hock, and oregano. Bring to a boil, then reduce heat to low, cover, and simmer 35 to 45 minutes, or until lentils are soft but not falling apart.

2. Remove ham hock from soup. Remove any meat from bone and chop coarsely; add to soup. Season with salt and pepper. Pass a bowl of Romano cheese on the side.

59   LENTIL SOUP WITH PASTA

Prep: 5 minutes   Cook: 1 hour 10 minutes   Serves: 4 to 6

2 tablespoons olive oil
1 medium onion, chopped
1 celery rib, chopped
2 medium carrots, peeled and
   chopped
8 ounces lentils
8 cups Chicken Stock (page
   48) or reduced-sodium
   canned broth

1 teaspoon dried marjoram
½ teaspoon pepper
8 ounces spaghetti, broken
   into fourths
Salt
Grated Parmesan cheese

1. In a large saucepan or flameproof casserole, heat olive oil over medium heat. Add onion, celery, and carrots and cook, stirring occasionally, 5 minutes, or until onion is just beginning to color. Add lentils, stock, marjoram, and pepper. Bring to a boil, then reduce heat to low, cover, and simmer 35 to 45 minutes, or until lentils are soft but not falling apart.

2. Meanwhile, in a large saucepan or boiling salted water, cook spaghetti until tender but still firm, about 10 minutes. Drain and rinse under cold running water.

3. When soup is almost done, add spaghetti and simmer 5 to 10 minutes, until tender. Serve a bowl of Parmesan cheese on the side.

60   SPINACH SOUP

Prep: 10 minutes   Cook: 45 minutes   Serves: 6 to 8

2 pounds fresh spinach
8 cups Chicken Stock (page
   48) or reduced-sodium
   canned broth
1 garlic clove, chopped
1 small onion, chopped

3 tablespoons cornmeal
1 tablespoon flour
1 teaspoon salt
½ teaspoon pepper
¼ teaspoon grated nutmeg

1. Rinse spinach well. Remove stems.

2. In a large saucepan, combine 1 cup stock, garlic, and onion. Bring to a boil over high heat. Add spinach and cook, stirring, 2 minutes. Add remaining chicken stock and bring to a boil.

3. In a small bowl, combine cornmeal and flour. In a slow stream add to stock, stirring as you pour. Cover and simmer over low heat 30 minutes.

4. Puree soup, in batches if necessary, in a food processor or blender. Season with salt, pepper, and nutmeg.

61   EASY CLAM SOUP
Prep: 5 minutes   Cook: 30 minutes   Serves: 6 to 8

3 tablespoons olive oil
1 small onion, chopped
2 garlic cloves, chopped
1 14-ounce can Italian peeled
   tomatoes, drained and
   chopped
2 cups water

1 cup bottled clam juice
2 large red potatoes, peeled
   and cut into 1-inch cubes
1 teaspoon dried oregano
2 6½-ounce cans chopped
   clams
Pinch of cayenne pepper

1. In a nonreactive large saucepan, heat olive oil over medium heat. Add onion and cook 2 minutes, or until softened. Add garlic and cook 1 minute longer. Add tomatoes, water, and clam juice. Bring to a boil.

2. Add potatoes and oregano, cover, and cook 20 minutes, or until potatoes are tender. Add clams and heat through, about 1 minute. Season with cayenne.

62   TOMATO AND BREAD SOUP
Prep: 20 minutes   Cook: 30 minutes   Stand: 3 to 5 minutes
Serves: 6 to 8

Pair this thick, pulpy soup with a crisp romaine salad and gorgonzola cheese.

3 pounds ripe tomatoes
4 garlic cloves, minced
6 cups Chicken Stock (page
   48) or reduced-sodium
   canned broth
1 tablespoon chopped fresh
   basil or ¾ teaspoon dried
1 tablespoon chopped fresh
   parsley

½ teaspoon salt
¼ teaspoon pepper
6 slices Italian bread, cut
   ½ inch thick, crusts
   removed
Extra-virgin olive oil

1. Preheat oven to 350°. Plunge tomatoes into a large pot of boiling water for 30 seconds to 1 minute, until skins split. Drain immediately and cool under cold running water. Remove skins. Cut tomatoes in half and gently squeeze out seeds. Chop tomatoes.

2. In a nonreactive large saucepan, combine chopped tomatoes, garlic, stock, basil, parsley, salt, and pepper. Bring to a boil over high heat, reduce heat to low, and simmer 20 minutes.

3. Meanwhile, spread out bread slices on a baking sheet. Bake, turning once, 15 to 20 minutes, or until dried out and crisp.

4. Add bread slices to soup. Cover and remove from heat. Let stand 3 to 5 minutes, until bread is thoroughly saturated with soup. Pass a cruet of good olive oil to drizzle over soup.

63   FRESH TOMATO SOUP
Prep: 10 minutes   Cook: 45 minutes   Serves: 6 to 8

Make this summer soup in August or September, when tomatoes are plentiful. Use beefsteak, plum, or whichever variety is ripest and most flavorful.

8 cups Chicken Stock (page 48) or reduced-sodium canned broth
3 pounds ripe tomatoes, peeled and coarsely chopped

1 small onion, chopped
3 tablespoons rice
½ teaspoon salt
Pinch of sugar
2 tablespoons chopped fresh basil or parsley

1. In a nonreactive large saucepan, bring stock to a boil. Add tomatoes, onion, rice, salt, and sugar. Cover, reduce heat to medium-low, and cook 30 minutes.

2. Puree soup, in batches if necessary, in a blender or food processor. Return soup to pot and simmer 2 minutes. Stir in basil just before serving.

64   ITALIAN CLAM SOUP
Prep: 15 minutes   Cook: 15 minutes   Serves: 4 to 6

Serve with crusty garlic bread on the side or in the bowl with the soup ladled right over it.

3 dozen hard-shelled clams, such as littlenecks
2 tablespoons olive oil
4 garlic cloves, chopped
Pinch of hot pepper flakes
1 cup dry white wine

½ cup water
1 cup bottled clam juice
2 tablespoons chopped fresh parsley
Garlic Bread (page 196)

1. Scrub clams well under cold running water with a vegetable brush. Discard any open shells that will not close when tapped.

2. In a nonreactive large saucepan or flameproof casserole, heat olive oil over medium-high heat. Add garlic and hot pepper; cook 30 seconds, or until garlic is fragrant but not brown. Add wine, water, and clam juice. Bring to a boil.

3. Add clams to pan. Cover and cook 3 to 5 minutes, shaking pan frequently, until all clams open. Discard any that do not open. Sprinkle with parsley and serve at once, with garlic bread.

65   ZUCCHINI SOUP

Prep: 15 minutes   Cook: 30 minutes   Serves: 6 to 8

The rice helps thicken this soup.

1½   pounds zucchini
3   tablespoons butter
1   small onion, chopped
1   teaspoon dried thyme leaves
6   cups Chicken Stock (page 48) or reduced-sodium canned broth

¼   cup rice
¾   teaspoon salt
¼   teaspoon pepper
    Grated Parmesan cheese

1. Cut ends from zucchini. Shred on a grater.

2. In a large saucepan, melt butter over low heat. Add onion and cook 2 to 3 minutes, or until softened. Add zucchini and thyme, raise heat to medium, and add chicken stock and rice. Bring to a boil, reduce heat to low, and simmer covered 20 minutes.

3. Puree soup in a blender or food processor, in batches if necessary. Season with salt and pepper. Pass a bowl of grated Parmesan cheese on the side.

66   PASTA AND FAGIOLI

Prep: 15 minutes   Soak: 2 hours   Cook: 2 hours   Serves: 8

There are many versions of this dish. Different beans and pastas are used. Ditalini are short tubes of macaroni. If you can't find them, substitute elbow macaroni. Cranberry beans are close to the wonderful barlotti bean the Italians love, but if they are not in your market, use white beans instead.

8   ounces dried cranberry beans
2   tablespoon olive oil
1   medium onion, chopped
1   14-ounce can Italian peeled tomatoes, drained and chopped
8   cups Chicken Stock (page 48) or reduced-sodium canned broth

2   tablespoons chopped fresh parsley
8   ounces ditalini
1   teaspoon salt
½   teaspoon pepper
    Grated Parmesan cheese

1. Rinse beans and pick over to remove any grit. Cover with water and soak 2 hours. Drain.

2. In a Dutch oven, heat oil over medium heat. Add onion and cook 2 to 3 minutes, or until soft. Add tomatoes, stock, parsley, and beans. Bring to a boil. Reduce heat to low, cover, and simmer 1½ hours, or until beans are soft.

3. Meanwhile, in a large pot of boiling salted water, cook pasta until almost done, 6 to 8 minutes. Drain, rinse briefly under cold running water, and set aside.

4. When beans are tender, add cooked ditalini. Cover and simmer 15 minutes. Season with salt and pepper. Pass a bowl of grated Parmesan cheese on the side.

---

67 MAMA'S PASTA AND FAGIOLI
Prep: 10 minutes   Cook: 35 to 40 minutes   Serves: 8

Italian-Americans from southern Italy cook this dish, pronounced closer in those dialects to "pastafajol." A robust dish, it can easily be cooked from the grocery shelf.

2 tablespoons olive oil
1 medium onion, chopped
3 garlic cloves, chopped
1 30-ounce can Italian crushed
   tomatoes in puree
1 teaspoon dried oregano
   Pinch of hot pepper flakes
2 cups Chicken Stock (page
   48) or reduced-sodium
   canned broth

2 16-ounce cans kidney beans,
   drained
8 ounces spaghetti, broken in
   fourths
   Salt and pepper to taste
   Grated Parmesan cheese

1. In a large Dutch oven, heat oil over medium heat. Add onion and cook 2 to 3 minutes, or until softened. Add garlic and cook 1 minute longer. Add tomatoes with puree, oregano, hot pepper flakes, and stock. Cover and cook 5 minutes to heat through. Add beans and simmer 10 minutes.

2. Meanwhile, in a large pot of boiling salted water, cook spaghetti about 5 minutes, until half cooked; drain. Add to soup. Cook 15 to 20 minutes to combine flavors and finish cooking pasta. Season with salt and pepper. Serve in soup plates. Pass a bowl of grated Parmesan cheese on the side.

68 LA RIBOLITA
Prep: 20 minutes   Soak: 2 hours   Cook: 1¼ hours   Serves: 8 to 10

A hearty dish from Tuscany.

8 ounces dried white beans
2 tablespoons olive oil
1 cup chopped onion
1 cup chopped carrot
1 cup chopped celery
1 cup chopped leeks (white
    and tender green)
2 teaspoons dried thyme
    leaves

1 teaspoon dried rosemary
    leaves
8 cups water
1 ham hock
   Salt and pepper to taste
8 to 10 slices Italian bread, cut
   1 inch thick, lightly
   toasted
   Grated Parmesan cheese

1. Rinse beans and pick over to remove any grit. Cover with cold water and soak for 2 hours. Drain.

2. In a large pot, heat oil over medium heat. Add onion and cook 2 to 3 minutes, or until softened. Add carrots, celery, leeks, thyme, and rosemary. Cook, stirring, 1 minute. Add water, ham hock, and beans. Bring to a boil, reduce heat to low, cover, and simmer, stirring occasionally, 1 hour, or until beans begin to fall apart.

3. Remove ham hock and discard. Puree half the beans in a food processor or blender. Return to soup. Heat through and season with salt and pepper.

4. To serve, place a toast in each bowl. Ladle hot soup over toast. Pass a bowl of Parmesan cheese on the side.

69 FIVE-BEAN SOUP
*Prep: 20 minutes   Soak: 1 hour   Cook: 2 to 2¼ hours
Serves: 10 to 12*

This hearty soup from Calabria freezes well. If you're in a hurry, use rinsed and drained canned beans and add them with the cabbage in step 3.

1 cup dried white beans
1 cup dried kidney beans
1 cup dried cranberry beans
1 cup lentils
1 cup green split peas
½ pound salt pork
8 cups water
2 tablespoons olive oil
2 medium onions, chopped
3 garlic cloves, chopped

2 celery ribs, chopped
1 14-ounce can Italian peeled
   tomatoes
1 small head of cabbage,
   preferably Savoy,
   shredded
   Pinch of hot pepper flakes
1 teaspoon salt
½ teaspoon pepper

1. Rinse beans, lentils, and split peas and pick over. Place in a large pot. Add enough water to cover by at least 2 inches. Bring to a boil, remove from the heat, and let stand 1 hour; drain.

2. Meanwhile, cook salt pork in a medium saucepan of boiling water 15 minutes; drain. Cut into ¼-inch dice.

3. In a large pot, heat olive oil. Add salt pork, onions, garlic, and celery. Cook over medium heat 5 minutes, or until vegetables are softened. Add beans, lentils, peas, and water. Bring to a boil over high heat. Reduce heat to low and simmer 1½ hours, or until beans are just barely tender. Add tomatoes, cabbage, and hot pepper flakes. Simmer 20 minutes, or until cabbage is soft and beans are tender. Season with salt and pepper.

---

70 CHICK-PEA–ESCAROLE SOUP
Prep: 20 minutes   Cook: 35 to 45 minutes   Serves: 6 to 8

8 ounces salt pork
2 tablespoons olive oil
1 medium onion, chopped
2 garlic cloves, chopped
1 14-ounce can Italian peeled tomatoes, drained and chopped
1 16-ounce can chick-peas, drained and rinsed

4 cups Chicken Stock (page 48) or reduced-sodium canned broth
2 cups water
1 head of escarole, about 1 pound, coarsely chopped
¾ teaspoon salt
½ teaspoon pepper

1. Cook salt pork in a medium saucepan of boiling water 10 minutes to remove salt; drain. Cut into ¼-inch dice.

2. In a large saucepan, heat olive oil over medium heat. Add salt pork and onion and cook 2 to 3 minutes, or until onion is softened. Add garlic and cook 1 minute longer.

3. Add tomatoes, chick-peas, stock, water, escarole, salt, and pepper. Bring to a boil, reduce heat to medium-low, and cook uncovered until escarole is tender, 20 to 30 minutes.

71 NEAPOLITAN MINESTRONE

Prep: 20 minutes Cook: 40 minutes Serves: 6 to 8

A very thick soup, enough for supper in a dish.

6 **Italian sausages, 1¼ to 1½ pounds**
4 **ounces salt pork**
2 **tablespoons olive oil**
2 **garlic cloves, chopped**
1 **medium onion, chopped**
2 **celery ribs, thickly sliced**
1 **carrot, peeled and thinly sliced**
8 **cups Chicken Stock (page 48) or reduced-sodium canned broth**

1 **14-ounce can Italian peeled tomatoes, drained and chopped**
1 **small head of cabbage, cut into 2-inch squares**
1 **head of escarole, leaves cut into 3-inch lengths**
1 **cup ditalini or elbow macaroni, about 4 ounces**
   Salt and pepper
   Hot pepper flakes
   Grated Romano cheese

1. Prick sausages all over with tines of a fork. Place sausages and salt pork in a saucepan with 2 quarts of water. Bring to a boil and cook 5 minutes over medium heat; drain. Cut sausages in thirds. Cut salt pork into ¼- to ½-inch dice.

2. In a large pot, heat oil over medium heat. Add salt pork, garlic, onion, celery, and carrots. Cook 5 minutes, or until onions are soft. Add stock and tomatoes; bring to a boil. Add cabbage, escarole, and sausages. Cook 20 minutes, or until vegetables are tender.

3. Add pasta. Simmer 2 minutes. Season with salt and pepper. Pass hot pepper flakes and a bowl of Romano cheese on the side.

72 PUMPKIN MINESTRONE

Prep: 20 minutes Cook: 1 hour Serves: 10 to 12

It's hardly worth making these big soups unless you make a big batch. Freeze single or double servings in plastic bags.

2 **ounces salt pork**
2 **tablespoons olive oil**
1 **medium onion, chopped**
3 **celery ribs, chopped**
4 **medium carrots, peeled and chopped**
1 **14-ounce can Italian peeled tomatoes, drained and chopped**
8 **cups water**
2 **cups peeled, cubed (1½-inch) baking potato**
1 **teaspoon dried thyme**

½ **teaspoon dried rosemary**
3 **cups peeled, cubed (¾-inch) pumpkin or butternut squash**
1 **teaspoon salt**
½ **teaspoon pepper**
1 **cup fresh spinach leaves, washed**
2 **tablespoons chopped fresh basil or Italian flat-leaf parsley**
   Extra-virgin olive oil
   Grated Parmesan cheese

1. Cook salt pork in a medium saucepan of boiling water 15 minutes to remove salt; drain. Cut into ¼-inch dice.

2. In a large pot, heat oil. Add salt pork, onion, celery, and carrots and cook 2 minutes, or until onions are softened. Add tomatoes, water, potato, thyme, and rosemary. Bring to a boil, reduce heat to low, cover, and simmer 30 minutes. Add pumpkin and cook 15 minutes, or until pumpkin begins to fall apart.

3. Strain soup, reserving liquid and vegetables separately. In a food processor or blender, puree half the vegetables with a little of the liquid. Return puree, strained broth, and remaining vegetables to soup pot. Season with salt and pepper. Stir spinach and basil leaves into soup. Cook 2 to 3 minutes, or until spinach is tender. Pass a cruet of olive oil and a bowl of Parmesan cheese on the side.

73 MINESTRONE WITH DRY AND FRESH BEANS

Prep: 20 minutes   Soak: 1 hour   Cook: 1½ hours   Serves: 8

8 ounces dried cranberry beans or white beans
8 ounces salt pork
2 tablespoons olive oil
1 large onion, coarsely chopped
4 garlic cloves, chopped
1 14-ounce can Italian peeled tomatoes, drained and chopped
2½ quarts water

3 carrots, peeled and cut into ½-inch dice
2 celery ribs, cut into ½-inch dice
1 teaspoon dried oregano
1 teaspoon dried sage leaves
1 pound fresh green beans, cut into 2-inch pieces
1½ teaspoons salt
½ teaspoon pepper

1. Rinse beans and pick over to remove any grit. Place in a large saucepan and add cold water to cover. Bring to a boil, remove from heat, cover, and let soak 1 hour; drain.

2. Cook salt pork in a medium saucepan of boiling water 15 minutes to remove salt; drain. Cut into ¼-inch dice.

3. In a large pot, heat olive oil and salt pork over medium heat. Add onion and garlic. Cook 3 to 4 minutes, or until onion is softened. Add tomatoes, water, beans, carrots, celery, oregano, and sage. Cover partially and cook about 1 hour, or until beans are tender.

4. Add green beans and cook 10 to 15 minutes longer, or until green beans are tender. Season with salt and pepper.

74   MINESTRONE GENOA STYLE
Prep: 20 minutes   Cook: 1 hour   Serves: 8

2 tablespoons olive oil
1 medium onion, chopped
2 garlic cloves, chopped
2 carrots, peeled and thickly sliced
2 ribs celery, thickly sliced
8 cups water
1 14-ounce can Italian peeled tomatoes, drained and chopped
1 ham hock

3 cups cabbage, cut in 2-inch pieces
2 cups zucchini, cut in 1½-inch pieces
1 16-ounce can white beans, drained and rinsed
¼ cup pesto, homemade (page 77) or jarred
Extra-virgin olive oil and grated Parmesan cheese

1. In a large pot, heat olive oil over medium heat. Add onion, garlic, carrots, and celery and cook 5 minutes, or until vegetables are softened. Add water and bring to a boil. Add tomatoes and ham hock. Cover, reduce heat to low, and simmer 30 minutes. Add cabbage and zucchini and cook uncovered 15 minutes, or until tender. Remove ham hock from soup. As soon as ham is cool enough to handle, remove meat from bone and coarsely chop. Return ham to pot. Add beans and simmer 2 minutes.

2. Stir pesto into soup. Pass a cruet of olive oil and a bowl of grated Parmesan cheese on the side.

75   CHICKEN STOCK
Prep: 15 minutes   Cook: 2 hours   Yields: 4½ to 5 quarts

Italians use light chicken stock to cook with. For some dishes it is essential, particularly risotto and some soups. Too much carrot will sweeten the stock.

1 5-pound chicken
2 pounds wings, necks, and feet if available
2 medium onions, quartered
3 celery ribs with leaves, halved
1 small carrot, quartered

1 bay leaf
2 sprigs of fresh thyme or 1 teaspoon dried
4 sprigs of fresh parsley
6 peppercorns
6 quarts water

1. Rinse chicken and chicken parts in colander under cold running water. Place chicken, chicken parts, and all other ingredients in a large soup kettle with water. Bring to a boil over medium heat. Immediately reduce heat to low and simmer uncovered 1½ hours, skimming occasionally. Do not let stock boil.

2. Strain through a colander lined with cheesecloth. Let cool; then refrigerate. Lift off and discard congealed fat.

Chapter 3

Pasta—Italy's National Treasure

Pasta is so popular in this country and it's prepared in so many different ways that it could almost be claimed as an international treasure. Make no mistake about it, though, pasta is thoroughly Italian, and north to south, that country claims more varieties of shapes and sauces than you're likely to eat in a lifetime.

Dry pasta—the kind that comes in a box—was probably the first to be introduced for general consumption in America, because it was especially common to southern Italy, which is where the largest early wave of immigrants came from. This type of pasta is made from hard durum wheat and water. There are so many different shapes, it's impossible to name all of them, but they are so fanciful as well as descriptive, it's fun to remember a few.

Here are a sampling of Italian pasta shapes and their English equivalents: spaghetti (cords), penne (quills), rotelle (small wheels), farfalle (butterflies or bow ties), capellini (fine hairs), conchiglie (shells), ditalini (little thimbles), fedelini (the faithful), mostaccioli (small mustaches), vermicelli (little worms). Next time you pick up an Italian menu, the names of the dishes will come to life.

The sauces for these pasta shapes are full of strong flavors, frequently based on tomatoes and olive oil, and they are richly spiced. Generally, thinner, smoother sauces are used on thinner pasta such as capellini and linguine, while thicker, chunkier sauces are served with curled or tubular shapes such as penne and rotelle, which can hold the sauce. While the recipes in this and the next chapter pair sauces with specific shapes, you can substitute whatever pasta you have on hand; mix and match to suit your mood.

Another type of dried pasta is egg pasta, which is usually made into noodles, or fettuccine. It is richer and more delicate, and is often substituted for fresh with cream sauces.

While I am partial to imported pasta, the secret of preparing any dry pasta properly is not to overcook it. Pasta should be boiled in a large pot of salted water until it is just *al dente*, that is, tender but still offering a little resistance to the bite in the center. If it's mushy and soft, it's overdone. When the pasta is cooked to within a minute of the least amount of time specified in a recipe, taste a strand to test it. Keep checking every 30 to 60 seconds from then on, until it is just right. Then drain the pasta immediately. If there is a delay in tossing the pasta with the sauce, to prevent it from sticking together, rinse it briefly under running water to rinse off the surface starch or toss it with a tablespoon or two of olive oil.

As part of a traditional Italian meal, pasta is usually eaten in modest portions as a second course, after the antipasto and before the meat or fish course. Here in America, we love pasta so much we frequently adopt it as a main course, enjoying servings so large they might astound even a self-respecting Sicilian. However you choose to eat it, remember that pasta is gregarious food. It makes us feel good, and the process of directing spaghetti, for instance, from the plate to the mouth lends itself to a less formal, lively social occasion. Whether you twirl pasta on your plate or in a soup spoon, the ritual is part of the entertainment. So fill up your plate and twirl on.

76 FUSILLI WITH FRESH TOMATO AND CHEESE

Prep: 15 minutes   Marinate: 1 hour   Cook: 10 to 12 minutes
Serves: 8

Here is a fresh tomato pasta, best served at room temperature or lightly chilled. It's especially good with roast lamb. Ricotta salata is a hard, dry ricotta appropriate to this dish, but feta cheese, more commonly found, can be used instead.

2 pounds ripe tomatoes
1 teaspoon salt
¼ teaspoon pepper
3 tablespoons red wine vinegar
6 tablespoons extra-virgin olive oil
¼ cup shredded fresh basil or 1 teaspoon dried
2 tablespoons chopped fresh parsley
1 medium red onion, coarsely chopped
1 pound fusilli
6 ounces ricotta salata or feta cheese

1. Cut stem end from tomatoes. Cut in half and squeeze gently to remove seeds. Cut tomatoes into ½-inch dice. In a large bowl, combine salt, pepper, vinegar, olive oil, basil, and parsley. Beat with a fork to blend. Add tomatoes and red onion and toss with dressing. Let marinate at room temperature 1 hour.

2. Cook fusilli in a large pot of boiling salted water until tender but still firm, 10 to 12 minutes; drain. Cool under cold running water; drain again.

3. Combine fusilli with tomato mixture in bowl and toss to mix. Serve at room temperature, garnished with ricotta salata or feta cheese.

77   BUCATINI AMATRICIANA
Prep: 10 minutes   Cook: 20 minutes   Serves: 6 to 8

Bucatini is a spaghetti named after its "little mouth," or opening. Any size spaghetti can be used for this.

1 tablespoon olive oil
1 small onion, chopped
4 ounces pancetta or Canadian bacon, cut into ½-inch strips
Pinch of hot pepper flakes
1 28-ounce can Italian peeled tomatoes, drained and chopped

½ cup water
1 teaspoon salt
¼ teaspoon pepper
1 pound bucatini or spaghetti
¾ cup grated Parmesan cheese

1. In a large heavy saucepan, heat olive oil over medium heat. Add onion and pancetta and cook, stirring, 3 to 5 minutes, or until onion is soft. Stir in hot pepper flakes and cook 10 seconds. Add tomatoes and water and bring to a boil over medium-high heat. Cook until sauce is thick, 8 to 10 minutes. Season with salt and pepper.

2. When sauce is almost done, cook pasta in a large pot of boiling salted water, 8 to 10 minutes, or until tender but still firm; drain. Pour pasta and sauce into a warmed large bowl and toss together. Pass a bowl of Parmesan cheese on the side.

78   SPAGHETTI ALLA PUTTANESCA
Prep: 15 minutes   Cook: 15 minutes   Serves: 6

Like the harlot it's named after, this dish is quick and spicy. You can leave the pits in the olives, but be sure you warn your guests.

2 tablespoons olive oil
3 garlic cloves, thinly sliced
¼ teaspoon hot pepper flakes
6 flat anchovy fillets, finely chopped
1 6½-ounce jar oil-cured olives, pitted if desired

1 tablespoon capers, rinsed and drained
1 28-ounce can Italian peeled tomatoes, drained and chopped
½ teaspoon salt
¼ teaspoon pepper
1 pound spaghetti

1. In a large frying pan, heat olive oil over medium heat. Stir in garlic, hot pepper flakes, and anchovies. Cook about 1 minute, until fragrant. Add olives, capers, and tomatoes. Cook, stirring occasionally, 8 to 10 minutes, or until sauce thickens. Season with salt and pepper.

2. Meanwhile, cook pasta in a large pot of boiling salted water until tender but still firm, 8 to 10 minutes; drain. Pour pasta and sauce into a warmed large bowl and toss together.

79   SPAGHETTI AND MEATBALLS
Prep: 20 minutes   Cook: 1 hour   Serves: 6 to 8

We all know spaghetti and meatballs. Many Italians tell us this is our American dish. No matter—it's great.

1½ cups torn crustless Italian bread	½ teaspoon pepper
¼ cup milk	¼ cup olive oil
1½ pounds ground beef chuck	½ cup chopped onion
2 eggs	1 28-ounce can Italian crushed tomatoes in puree
⅓ cup chopped fresh parsley	½ cup dry red wine
3 tablespoons grated Parmesan cheese	½ cup water
4 garlic cloves, minced	1 pound spaghetti
1½ teaspoons salt	1 teaspoon oregano

1. In a large bowl, combine bread and milk. Let stand 5 minutes to soften bread. Add ground chuck, eggs, 3 tablespoons parsley, Parmesan cheese, half the garlic, 1 teaspoon salt, and ¼ teaspoon pepper. Blend to mix well. Form into 2-inch meatballs.

2. In a large skillet, heat 2 tablespoons olive oil. Add meatballs and cook over medium-high heat, turning, until browned, about 5 minutes. Remove with a slotted spoon and drain on paper towels.

3. In a nonreactive large Dutch oven, heat the remaining 2 tablespoons olive oil over medium heat. Add onion and cook 2 to 3 minutes, or until softened. Add remaining garlic and cook 1 minute longer. Add tomatoes, wine, water, and remaining salt and pepper. Bring to a simmer and add meatballs. Cover, reduce heat to low, and simmer 45 minutes.

4. Meanwhile, cook spaghetti in a large pot of boiling salted water 10 to 12 minutes, or until tender but still firm; drain. Pour pasta into a warmed large bowl. Add oregano and remaining parsley to sauce and pour, with meatballs, over top. Toss together.

80   SPAGHETTINI WITH SWEET PEPPERS, OLIVES, AND CAPERS

Prep: 10 minutes   Cook: 10 minutes   Serves: 4 to 5

1 pound spaghettini
¼ cup extra-virgin olive oil
1 7.25-ounce jar peeled red peppers, drained and cut into ½-inch slices
2 large garlic cloves, minced
6 ounces oil-cured black olives
¼ cup capers, rinsed and drained

Pinch of hot pepper flakes
1 teaspoon dried oregano
3 tablespoons chopped fresh parsley
½ teaspoon salt
¼ teaspoon pepper
½ cup grated Romano cheese
½ cup grated Parmesan cheese

1. Cook pasta in a large pot of boiling salted water until tender but still firm, 6 to 8 minutes.

2. Meanwhile, in a large frying pan, heat olive oil over medium-low heat. Add red peppers, garlic, olives, capers, hot pepper flakes, oregano, parsley, salt, and pepper. Cook, stirring, 2 minutes.

3. Drain pasta and pour into pan with sauce. Toss to coat. Add ¼ cup each of the Romano and Parmesan cheese. Toss again. Pass remaining cheese on the side.

81   SPAGHETTINI WITH GARLIC AND PEPPER

Prep: 10 minutes   Cook: 10 minutes   Serves: 6 to 8

A delicious something from nothing. Add more or less garlic and pepper to taste.

1 pound spaghettini
½ cup extra-virgin olive oil
4 large garlic cloves, chopped
1 teaspoon salt
¼ teaspoon hot pepper flakes

1 teaspoon pepper
3 tablespoons finely chopped parsley
Grated Romano cheese

1. Cook pasta in a large pot of boiling salted water until tender but still firm, 6 to 8 minutes.

2. Meanwhile, in a large frying pan, heat olive oil over medium-low heat. Add garlic and cook about 1 minute, or until golden. Add salt, hot pepper flakes, pepper, and parsley.

3. Drain pasta and pour into pan. Toss to coat. Pass a bowl of Romano cheese on the side.

82   LINGUINE WITH CLAMS AND RED SAUCE
Prep: 25 minutes   Cook: 10 to 12 minutes   Serves: 4 to 5

A great favorite with people who love Italian food. I have only added a pinch of hot pepper, but many prefer this dish very spicy.

4 dozen hard-shelled clams, such as littlenecks
2 tablespoons extra-virgin olive oil
2 garlic cloves, finely chopped
Pinch of hot pepper flakes
½ cup dry white wine
2 pounds ripe tomatoes, peeled, seeded, and chopped

1 tablespoon chopped fresh oregano or 1 teaspoon dried
2 tablespoons chopped fresh parsley
¾ teaspoon salt
¼ teaspoon pepper
1 pound linguine

1. Scrub clams well under cold running water with a vegetable brush. Discard any open shells that will not close when tapped.

2. In a large flameproof casserole, heat olive oil over medium-low heat. Add garlic and hot pepper flakes to pan and cook 30 seconds, or until fragrant, being careful not to burn garlic. Add wine and tomatoes, and increase heat to medium-high. Boil, stirring occasionally, until liquid from tomatoes is reduced by half, 3 to 5 minutes.

3. Add clams and oregano to pan. Cover tightly and increase heat to high. Cook, shaking pan frequently, 3 to 5 minutes, or until clams open. Discard any clams that do not open. Season with parsley, salt, and pepper.

4. Meanwhile, cook linguine in a large pot of boiling salted water until tender but still firm, 8 to 10 minutes; drain. Pour pasta and sauce into a warmed large bowl and toss together. Pass hot pepper flakes on the side.

83   LINGUINE WITH WHITE CLAM SAUCE
Prep: 10 minutes   Cook: 10 to 12 minutes   Serves: 4 to 6

Substitute 2 6½-ounce cans chopped clams and their juice if fresh clams are not available. Canned clams and dried pasta are great emergency ingredients to have on hand.

48 hard-shelled clams, such as littlenecks
2 tablespoons extra-virgin olive oil
3 garlic cloves, minced
1 cup dry white wine
¼ teaspoon hot pepper flakes

1 tablespoon chopped fresh oregano or 1 teaspoon dried
¼ teaspoon pepper
2 tablespoons finely chopped fresh parsley
2 tablespoons butter
1 pound linguine

1. Scrub clams well under cold running water. Discard any open shells that will not close when tapped.

2. In a nonreactive large saucepan over high heat, combine olive oil, garlic, wine, hot pepper flakes, oregano, and pepper. Heat over high heat. Add clams and shake pan gently to coat clams with olive oil, about 30 seconds. Cover pan and continue to cook, shaking pan frequently, 4 to 5 minutes, until clams open. Discard any clams that do not open. Stir in parsley and butter.

3. Meanwhile, cook linguine in a large pot of boiling salted water, until tender but still firm, 8 to 10 minutes; drain. Pour pasta into pan with clam sauce and toss together.

---

84 SPRING BUTTERFLIES
Prep: 20 minutes   Cook: 15 minutes   Serves: 6 to 8

This is a very clean pasta; the flavors are delicate with the first sweet vegetables of spring. Butterflies and bow ties are the same shape pasta.

1 pound butterfly or bow-tie pasta (farfalle)	2 cups Chicken Stock (page 48) or reduced-sodium canned broth
3 tablespoons butter	
2 tablespoons finely chopped onion	1 10-ounce package frozen peas
8 ounces medium asparagus, cut into ½-inch diagonal slices	¼ cup chopped fresh basil or 1 teaspoon dried
2 medium carrots, peeled and cut into ¼-inch diagonal slices	1 teaspoon salt
	¼ teaspoon pepper
2 teaspoons chopped fresh thyme or ½ teaspoon dried	Grated Parmesan cheese

1. Cook farfalle in a large pot of boiling salted water until tender but still firm, 8 to 10 minutes.

2. In a large frying pan, melt butter over medium heat. Add onion and cook 3 to 4 minutes, or until softened. Stir in asparagus, carrots, and thyme. Cook, stirring, 1 minute. Add stock, increase heat to medium-high, and cook until vegetables are crisp tender and stock is reduced to 1¼ cups, about 3 minutes. Stir in peas and basil and heat through. Season with salt and pepper.

3. Drain pasta and pour into a warmed large bowl. Pour primavera sauce on top and toss together. Pass a bowl of Parmesan cheese on the side.

85   CAPELLINI CAKE
Prep: 15 minutes   Cook: 20 minutes   Serves: 4 to 6

This way of dealing with leftover pasta is so good you probably won't wait for leftovers.

4 cups cooked and cooled pasta noodles, such as capellini, fettuccine, or linguine	3 scallions, chopped
	½ teaspoon salt
	¼ teaspoon pepper
	¾ cup grated Parmesan cheese
3 eggs, beaten	2 tablespoons olive oil

1. Preheat oven to 375°. Cut pasta into 2- to 3-inch pieces. In a large bowl, combine pasta with eggs, scallions, salt, pepper, and Parmesan cheese. Mix well, using your hands.

2. In a 9-inch ovenproof frying pan, heat olive oil, swirling to coat bottom and sides of pan. Add noodle mixture to pan and pack it in, making level on top. Cook over medium heat 2 to 3 minutes, until lightly browned on bottom. Slip a rubber spatula around edges and bottom of cake to keep crust from sticking. Place pan in oven and bake 15 minutes, or until cake is firm to touch in center.

3. Unmold cake by slipping a rubber spatula around edges and bottom to loosen. Place a large plate over top of frying pan and carefully invert pan to unmold. Cut cake into wedges to serve.

86   PENNE WITH CAULIFLOWER
Prep: 20 minutes   Cook: 20 minutes   Serves: 6

This is a very basic recipe, useful for vegetable sauces. Broccoli and bitter greens are also good this way.

1½ pounds cauliflower, trimmed and broken into florets	¼ teaspoon hot pepper flakes
	1 pound penne
	3 tablespoons grated Romano cheese
¼ cup extra-virgin olive oil	
2 large garlic cloves, minced	2 tablespoons chopped fresh parsley
6 flat anchovy fillets, finely chopped	

1. Cook cauliflower in a large saucepan of boiling salted water until tender, 6 to 8 minutes. Drain in a colander; set aside.

2. In a large frying pan, heat olive oil over medium-low heat. Add garlic, anchovies, and hot pepper flakes. Cook, mashing with back of a spoon 1 to 2 minutes, or until anchovies dissolve. Add cauliflower to the pan, toss to coat with oil, and heat through, 1 to 2 minutes.

3. Meanwhile, cook penne in a large pot of boiling salted water until tender but still firm, 8 to 10 minutes; drain. Add penne to cauliflower and cook, tossing, for 1 minute. Remove from heat and toss in Romano cheese and parsley.

87   PENNE WITH PORK AND TOMATO SAUCE
Prep: 15 minutes   Cook: 2¼ hours   Serves: 6 to 8

Pork makes one of the best tomato sauces, as the flavor of the meat adds to its sweetness. Traditionally this is layered with hard-boiled eggs and baked.

1½ pounds boneless pork shoulder, cut in 1-inch pieces	1 30-ounce can Italian crushed tomatoes in puree
2 tablespoons olive oil	2 cups water
1 small onion, chopped	¾ teaspoon salt
1 small carrot, peeled and chopped	½ teaspoon pepper
1 celery rib, chopped	1 pound penne
2 large garlic cloves, chopped	½ cup grated Romano cheese
	½ cup grated Parmesan cheese

1. Trim excess fat from pork. In a nonreactive large flameproof casserole, heat 1 tablespoon olive oil over medium heat. Add pork and cook, turning several times, 5 to 6 minutes, or until lightly browned on all sides. Remove pork from pan with a slotted spoon and set aside.

2. Heat remaining 1 tablespoon olive oil in pan. Add onion and cook over medium heat until soft, 3 to 4 minutes. Add carrot, celery, and garlic. Cook, stirring 2 to 3 minutes, or until bright in color. Add tomatoes with puree, water, and reserved pork to casserole. Bring to a boil over high heat, cover, and immediately reduce heat to low. Simmer, stirring occasionally, 1 to 1½ hours, or until pork falls apart.

3. Uncover and cook over medium heat until sauce is reduced and thickened. Season with salt and pepper.

4. When sauce is almost ready, cook penne in a large pot of boiling salted water 10 to 12 minutes, or until tender but still firm; drain. Pour pasta into a warmed large bowl, toss with 3 cups pork and tomato sauce. Cover top of pasta with remaining sauce and half each of the Romano and Parmesan cheese. Pass remaining cheese on the side.

Baked Penne and Eggs with Pork and Tomato Sauce: Preheat oven to 350°. Prepare recipe above, but add 4 hard-boiled eggs cut into ½-inch slices to ingredient list. In step 4, in a warmed large bowl, toss cooked penne with three fourths of the sauce. Layer one third of the penne with one third of the sliced eggs and one third each of the Parmesan and Romano cheeses. Repeat to make 3 layers total. Top with remaining sauce and cheese. Bake 25 minutes, or until heated through.

88   ZITI WITH SUMMER SAUCE
Prep: 10 minutes   Cook: 25 minutes   Serves: 6 to 8

For gardeners who have planted one too many zucchini plants, this is a good pasta sauce, but also great in crusty bread as a sandwich.

2 tablespoons olive oil	1 tablespoon chopped fresh
1 small onion, thinly sliced	oregano or 1 teaspoon
2 large garlic cloves, minced	dried
1 pound zucchini, cut into	½ cup water
thin strips	¼ cup chopped fresh basil or
1 medium red bell pepper, cut	1 teaspoon dried
in thin strips	1 teaspoon salt
1 pound ripe tomatoes,	¼ teaspoon pepper
peeled, seeded, and cut	1 pound ziti
into ½-inch dice	6 ounces provolone cheese,
	cut into ½-inch dice

1. In a nonreactive large frying pan, heat olive oil over medium heat. Add onion and garlic and cook 3 to 4 minutes, or until onion is softened. Add zucchini and red pepper and cook, stirring, 3 to 4 minutes, or until vegetables are slightly softened. Add tomatoes, oregano, and water. Cook until zucchini and red pepper are crisp tender, and sauce just begins to thicken, 3 to 5 minutes. Stir in basil, salt, and pepper.

2. Meanwhile, cook ziti in a large pot of boiling salted water until tender, 8 to 10 minutes; drain. Pour half of sauce onto a warmed platter. Pour hot pasta on top of sauce. Sprinkle provolone cheese over top. Pour remaining sauce over all.

89   ANGEL HAIR PASTA AND LEMON PARSLEY SAUCE
Prep: 15 minutes   Cook: 6 to 8 minutes   Serves: 4 to 5

Gremolata is a lemon rind, garlic, and parsley condiment traditionally served with veal shanks. Angel hair pasta, which is very fine, must be served immediately.

2 lemons	1 teaspoon salt
3 large garlic cloves, minced	¼ teaspoon freshly ground
¾ cup minced fresh parsley	black pepper
1 pound angel hair pasta	6 tablespoons grated
3 tablespoons extra-virgin	Parmesan cheese
olive oil	

1. Grate yellow zest from lemons, being careful not to include any bitter white pith. In a small bowl, combine lemon zest, garlic, and parsley. Set gremolata aside.

2. Cook angel hair pasta in a large pot of boiling salted water until tender but still firm, 3 to 5 minutes.

3. Meanwhile, in a large frying pan, warm olive oil over medium-low heat. Add gremolata and salt and pepper. Cook 1 minute, being careful not to burn garlic.

4. Drain pasta and pour into pan. Toss to coat. Sprinkle Parmesan on top.

---

90 ANGEL HAIR PASTA WITH SCALLOPS MARINARA

Prep: 15 minutes   Cook: 15 minutes   Serves: 5 to 6

Tiny bay scallops are best for this. If only large scallops are available, cut them into quarters.

2 **tablespoons olive oil**	2 **tablespoons chopped fresh**
3 **tablespoons finely chopped**	**basil or 1 teaspoon dried**
onion	1 **tablespoon chopped fresh**
2 **large garlic cloves, chopped**	**parsley**
12 **ounces bay scallops**	¾ **teaspoon salt**
¾ **cup dry white wine**	¼ **teaspoon pepper**
1 **14-ounce can Italian peeled**	1 **pound angel hair pasta**
tomatoes, drained and	
chopped	

1. In a nonreactive large flameproof casserole, heat olive oil over medium heat. Add onion and garlic, and cook 3 to 4 minutes, or until soft and fragrant.

2. Add scallops to pan and increase heat to medium-high. Cook, turning once, 2 to 3 minutes, or until a pale golden color. Remove with a slotted spoon and set aside. Add wine to pan and bring to a boil over high heat. Cook until reduced by half, about 2 minutes. Stir in tomatoes, basil, and parsley. Cook, stirring, 3 to 5 minutes, or until sauce thickens.

3. Reduce heat to medium. Return scallops to pan and cook 1 to 2 minutes, or until just heated through. Season with salt and pepper.

4. Meanwhile, cook angel hair pasta in a large pot of boiling salted water until tender but still firm, 4 to 6 minutes; drain. Pour pasta and sauce into a warmed large bowl and toss together.

91 MOSTACCIOLI WITH SQUID
Prep: 15 minutes   Cook: 1 hour   Serves: 4 to 6

You can buy cleaned squid to make this easier. Squid needs to be cooked either very quickly or very long. This is an old-fashioned preparation, but it is foolproof and will always give you tender squid. Use penne if you can't find "mustaches."

2 tablespoons olive oil
1 small onion, finely chopped
3 garlic cloves, finely chopped
4 ounces pancetta or Canadian bacon, cut into ½-inch dice
1½ pounds squid, cleaned and cut into ½-inch rings
½ cup dry red wine
1 14-ounce can Italian peeled tomatoes, drained and chopped

1½ cups hot water
1 tablespoon chopped fresh oregano or ½ teaspoon dried
Pinch of hot pepper flakes
¾ teaspoon salt
¼ teaspoon pepper
1 pound mostaccioli or penne
3 tablespoons chopped fresh parsley

1. In a large flameproof casserole, heat olive oil over medium heat. Add onion and garlic and cook 3 to 4 minutes, or until onion is soft. Stir in pancetta or bacon and cook 3 minutes.

2. Add squid to pan and increase heat to medium-high. Cook, stirring, 1 to 2 minutes, or until rings begin to turn pink. Add wine, tomatoes, water, oregano, and hot pepper flakes. Cover and simmer over low heat 45 minutes, stirring occasionally, until squid is tender. Season with salt and pepper.

3. When sauce is almost ready, cook mostaccioli in a large pot of boiling salted water until tender but still firm, 10 to 12 minutes; drain. Pour pasta and sauce into warmed large bowl and toss together. Garnish with parsley. Pass extra hot pepper flakes on the side.

92   SHELLS WITH SHRIMP
Prep: 20 minutes   Cook: 25 minutes   Serves: 6

2 tablespoons olive oil
1 small onion, finely chopped
1 garlic clove, chopped
¾ cup dry white wine
1 28-ounce can Italian peeled
  tomatoes, drained and
  chopped
½ cup water

1 teaspoon dried oregano
  Pinch of hot pepper flakes
1 pound medium shrimp,
  shelled and deveined
¼ cup heavy cream
½ teaspoon salt
⅛ teaspoon pepper
1 pound shell pasta

1. In a large heavy saucepan, heat olive oil over medium heat. Add onion and garlic and cook 3 to 4 minutes, or until softened but not browned. Add wine and bring to a boil. Add tomatoes, water, oregano, and hot pepper flakes. Return to a boil, reduce heat to medium-low, and simmer 20 minutes. Add shrimp and cook 2 to 3 minutes, or until they turn pink. Stir in cream and cook 2 minutes longer. Season with salt and pepper.

2. When sauce is almost ready, cook pasta in a large pot of boiling salted water until tender but still firm, 10 to 12 minutes; drain. Pour pasta and sauce into a warmed large bowl and toss together.

93   FUSILLI WITH LAMB AND TOMATO RAGU
Prep: 10 minutes   Cook: 40 minutes   Serves: 6

1 tablespoon olive oil
2 garlic cloves, chopped
1 small onion, finely chopped
1 pound ground lamb
1 cup dry red wine
1 14-ounce can Italian peeled
  tomatoes, drained and
  chopped

2 teaspoons chopped fresh
  rosemary or ½ teaspoon
  dried
2 tablespoons finely chopped
  fresh parsley
1 cup hot water
¾ teaspoon salt
¼ teaspoon pepper
1 pound fusilli or penne

1. In a large heavy saucepan, heat olive oil over medium heat. Add garlic and onion and cook, stirring, 3 to 4 minutes, or until soft. Add lamb to pan and cook 3 to 4 minutes, stirring, until lamb loses its pinkness.
Add wine, raise heat to high, and cook, stirring occasionally, 2 minutes. Add tomatoes, rosemary, parsley, and hot water. Cook, partially covered, over medium-low heat, stirring occasionally, 25 to 30 minutes, or until sauce is thick. Season with salt and pepper.

2. When sauce is almost ready, cook fusilli in a large pot of boiling salted water until tender but still firm, 10 to 12 minutes; drain. Pour pasta onto a warmed platter. Cover with sauce and toss together.

94   FUSILLI WITH TUNA
Prep: 10 minutes   Cook: 45 minutes   Serves: 6 to 8

This makes a delightful first course. As a main course to serve 4 to 6, I like to embellish it with extra tuna on top.

2   tablespoons olive oil
2   large garlic cloves, thinly sliced
1   30-ounce can Italian crushed tomatoes in puree
1   cup water
2   tablespoons chopped fresh parsley

1   6½-ounce can tuna in oil, drained
2   tablespoons capers, rinsed and drained
½   teaspoon pepper
1   pound fusilli or penne

1. In a nonreactive large saucepan, heat olive oil over medium-low heat. Add garlic and cook about 1 minute, or just until it begins to turn golden. Add tomatoes with puree, water, and parsley. Bring to a boil over medium heat. Reduce heat to medium-low and cook uncovered, stirring occasionally, 25 minutes. Add more water if sauce becomes too thick.

2. Break tuna into chunks and add to sauce. Stir in capers and pepper. Cook until heated through, 1 to 2 minutes. Remove from heat and cover to keep warm. When sauce is almost ready, cook fusilli in a large pot of boiling salted water until tender but still firm, 10 to 12 minutes; drain. Pour pasta and sauce into a warmed large bowl and toss together.

95   SPAGHETTI CARBONARA
Prep: 10 minutes   Cook: 10 minutes   Serves: 6

The Romans leave out the cream in this dish. Either way, this bacon and egg pasta is a great brunch dish. The black pepper is said to resemble coal dust, which is why it is called *carbonara*.

1   pound spaghetti
1   tablespoon olive oil
6   ounces pancetta or Canadian bacon, cut into ¼-inch dice

4   eggs
1   cup heavy cream
1   cup grated Parmesan cheese
1   teaspoon freshly ground black pepper

1. Cook pasta in a large pot of boiling salted water until tender but still firm, about 8 minutes.

2. Meanwhile, in a large frying pan, heat olive oil over medium heat. Add pancetta and cook until lightly browned, 3 to 4 minutes.

3. In a large bowl, beat eggs with cream until blended. Stir in ½ cup Parmesan cheese and pepper. Drain pasta and pour into bowl with egg-cream mixture. Toss together. Add pancetta and drippings and toss again to coat well. Serve immediately, passing remaining cheese and more freshly ground pepper on the side.

96 ZITI BAKED WITH RICOTTA CHEESE
Prep: 10 minutes   Cook: 50 minutes   Serves: 4 to 6

1 pound ziti   1¼
12 ounces ricotta cheese
2 eggs, beaten
¾ cup grated Parmesan cheese
½ teaspoon salt
¼ teaspoon pepper
2 tablespoons chopped fresh
    parsley

3 cups marinara sauce,
    homemade (page 131) or
    jarred
8 ounces mozzarella cheese,
    cut into ½-inch cubes

1. Preheat oven to 350°. Cook ziti in a large pot of boiling salted water until tender but still firm, 10 to 12 minutes. Drain and rinse under cold running water; drain well.

2. In a medium bowl, combine ricotta cheese, eggs, ½ cup Parmesan cheese, salt, pepper, and parsley. Mix to blend well.

3. Toss cooked ziti with 2 cups marinara sauce. Place half the pasta in an 11 x 7-inch baking dish. Top with ricotta mixture and half the mozzarella cubes. Top with remaining ziti, marinara sauce, mozzarella, and Parmesan cheese.

4. Bake until casserole is heated through and cheese is bubbly and lightly browned on top, 30 to 35 minutes.

97 RIGATONI WITH TOMATO SAUCE
Prep: 10 minutes   Cook: 40 minutes   Serves: 6

This is one of the simplest and most satisfying pastas.

2 tablespoons olive oil
1 medium onion, chopped
2 large garlic cloves, minced
1 30-ounce can Italian crushed
    tomatoes in puree
1 cup water

1 tablespoon chopped fresh
    oregano or 1 teaspoon
    dried
    Pinch of hot pepper flakes
½ teaspoon salt
1 pound rigatoni
1 cup grated Romano cheese

1. In a nonreactive large saucepan, heat olive oil over medium heat. Add onion and garlic and cook 2 to 3 minutes, or until onion is soft and garlic is fragrant. Add tomatoes with puree, water, oregano, and hot pepper flakes. Bring to a boil, reduce heat to medium-low, and cook partially covered 30 minutes. Season with salt.

2. Meanwhile, cook rigatoni in a large pot of boiling salted water until tender but still firm, 12 to 15 minutes; drain. Pour 2 cups of tomato sauce into a warmed large serving bowl. Add pasta and toss with sauce to coat. Pour remaining sauce over top and sprinkle with ½ cup of the Romano cheese. Pass remaining cheese on the side.

98 ZITI WITH PEPPERS

Prep: 10 minutes   Cook: 30 to 40 minutes   Serves: 4 to 6

2 tablespoons olive oil
2 garlic cloves, chopped
1 medium green bell pepper, cut into thin strips
1 medium red bell pepper, cut into thin strips
1 30-ounce can Italian crushed tomatoes in puree

3 tablespoons chopped fresh basil or 2 teaspoons dried
2 tablespoons chopped fresh parsley
1 cup water
¾ teaspoon salt
¼ teaspoon pepper
1 pound ziti
Grated Romano cheese

1. In a nonreactive large saucepan, heat olive oil over medium heat. Add garlic and cook 30 seconds, or until fragrant, being careful not to burn. Add peppers and cook, stirring occasionally, 3 to 4 minutes, or until bright in color and slightly softened. Add tomatoes with puree, basil, parsley, water, salt, and pepper. Bring to a boil over medium-high heat. Reduce heat to medium and cook partially covered 20 to 30 minutes, until thickened. Add a little water if sauce becomes too thick.

2. When sauce is almost ready, cook ziti in a large pot of boiling salted water until tender but still firm, 10 to 12 minutes; drain. Pour pasta and sauce into a warmed large bowl and toss together. Pass a bowl of Romano cheese on the side.

99 BAKED RIGATONI

Prep: 15 minutes   Cook: 1 hour 20 minutes   Serves: 10 to 15

This is a great dish for a crowd; or divide into two pans and freeze one unbaked. Increase the baking time by 30 minutes when cooking a frozen casserole.

1½ pounds rigatoni
1 tablespoon olive oil
1 large onion, chopped
2 pounds mixed hot and mild Italian sausages, casings removed
2 30-ounce cans Italian crushed tomatoes in puree
2 cups water

3 tablespoons chopped fresh basil or 2 teaspoons dried
1 tablespoon chopped fresh oregano or 1 teaspoon dried
1 tablespoon chopped fresh parsley
1 pound mozzarella cheese, shredded
1½ cups grated Parmesan cheese, about 6 ounces

1. In a large pot of boiling salted water, cook rigatoni until tender but still firm, 10 to 12 minutes; drain. Rinse under cool water; drain well.

2. In a nonreactive large saucepan, heat oil over medium heat. Add onion and cook 3 to 4 minutes, or until soft. Add sausage and cook, breaking up lumps of meat, 6 to 8 minutes, or until lightly browned. Pour off excess fat.

3. Add tomatoes with puree, water, basil, oregano, and parsley to pan. Bring to a boil over medium heat. Reduce heat to low and cook partially covered 25 minutes. Uncover, increase heat to medium, and cook, stirring occasionally, until sauce thickens, 6 to 8 minutes.

4. Preheat oven to 350°. In a large bowl, toss pasta with two thirds of the sauce. Stir in mozzarella cheese and 1 cup of Parmesan. Pour pasta into a 13 x 9-inch baking dish. Cover with remaining sauce and Parmesan cheese. Cover with foil and bake 25 minutes. Uncover and bake about 10 minutes longer, or until bubbly and lightly browned on top.

100 ORECCHIETTE WITH SWISS CHARD

Prep: 10 minutes   Cook: 15 minutes   Serves: 6

Orecchiette, cup-shaped "little ears," may be hard to find, but for those who like chewy pastas, they are well worth the search. Substitute penne or ziti if the search fails.

2 tablespoons olive oil	2 cups hot water
6 anchovy fillets, chopped	2 tablespoons butter
3 large garlic cloves, chopped	¾ teaspoon salt
Pinch of hot pepper flakes	¼ teaspoon pepper
12 ounces Swiss chard, cut into	1 pound orecchiette or penne
coarse pieces, stems	½ cup grated Romano cheese
included	½ cup grated Parmesan cheese

1. In a large frying pan, heat olive oil over low heat. Add anchovies and garlic to pan; mash with back of a spoon 1 to 2 minutes, or until anchovies dissolve. Add hot pepper flakes, Swiss chard, and water. Cover, increase heat to medium, and cook 8 to 10 minutes, or until chard is tender. Stir in butter. Season with salt and pepper. Remove from heat and cover to keep warm.

2. Cook pasta in a large pot of boiling salted water until tender but still firm, 12 to 15 minutes for orecchiette, or 10 to 12 minutes for penne; drain. Pour pasta and sauce into a warmed large bowl and toss together with ¼ cup each of the Romano and Parmesan cheese. Pass remaining cheese on the side.

101   FUSILLI WITH ARTICHOKES

Prep: 10 minutes   Cook: 25 to 30 minutes   Serves: 6

There are many varieties of artichokes in Italy, where this is usually made with tiny artichokes that are very tender and need little or no trimming. They are a good combination with this corkscrew (fusilli) pasta.

1 14-ounce can small artichokes
2 tablespoons olive oil
2 garlic cloves, finely chopped
1 28-ounce can Italian peeled tomatoes, drained and chopped

1 cup water
2 tablespoons chopped fresh basil or 1 teaspoon dried
½ teaspoon salt
¼ teaspoon pepper
Grated Romano cheese

1. Drain artichokes, rinse in cold water, and cut into quarters. In a nonreactive large saucepan, heat olive oil over medium-low heat. Add garlic and cook for 30 seconds, or until fragrant. Add tomatoes, water, and basil. Bring to a boil. Reduce heat to medium and cook uncovered about 20 minutes, or until sauce has thickened. Add artichokes and cook 1 to 2 minutes, until heated through. Season with salt and pepper.

2. When sauce is almost ready, cook fusilli in a large pot of boiling salted water until tender but still firm, 10 to 12 minutes; drain. Pour pasta and sauce into a large warmed bowl and toss together. Pass a bowl of Romano cheese on the side.

102   TORTELLINI SALAD WITH SPINACH AND PESTO

Prep: 20 minutes   Cook: 8 to 10 minutes   Serves: 8

This is a great way to buy deli food and put your mark on it.

1 pound spinach tortellini
¼ cup pesto, homemade (page 77) or jarred
5 tablespoons extra-virgin olive oil
1 tablespoon fresh lemon juice
1½ tablespoons red wine vinegar
½ teaspoon salt

¼ teaspoon pepper
1 pound fresh spinach, stemmed, washed, and dried
1 cup thinly cut red onion rings
¼ cup pine nuts
½ cup crumbled gorgonzola or other blue cheese

1. Cook tortellini in boiling salted water according to package or deli directions. Drain in a colander and cool under cold running water; drain well.

2. In a large bowl, combine pesto, 3 tablespoons olive oil, and lemon juice. Beat with a fork to blend. Add tortellini and toss to coat.

3. In a second bowl, combine remaining 2 tablespoons olive oil, red wine vinegar, salt, and pepper. Beat to blend. Add spinach to dressing and toss to coat. On a large platter, make a bed of spinach salad. Pile tortellini in center. Garnish with red onions, pine nuts, and gorgonzola.

---

103   GREEN LASAGNE WITH SPINACH AND RICOTTA

Prep: 30 minutes   Cook: 55 minutes   Stand: 10 minutes
Serves: 8 to 10

Green lasagne or spinach lasagne noodles are available in packages in grocery stores.

1 pound spinach lasagne noodles	1½ cups grated Parmesan cheese, about 6 ounces
2 pounds fresh spinach, stemmed and washed, or 2 10-ounce packages frozen chopped spinach	1 teaspoon salt
	½ teaspoon pepper
	¼ teaspoon grated nutmeg
	1 pound mozzarella cheese, cut into ½-inch dice
1½ pounds ricotta cheese	
4 egg yolks	4 cups tomato sauce

1. Cook lasagne noodles in a large pot of boiling salted water, stirring several times in the beginning to prevent noodles from sticking to each other, until tender but still firm, 12 to 15 minutes. Drain in a colander and cool under cold running water; drain again and set aside.

2. Preheat oven to 350°. In a nonreactive large saucepan, cook spinach, in water that clings to leaves, over medium-high heat, stirring frequently until leaves are limp, 2 to 3 minutes. Drain spinach in a colander and press excess water out with the back of a wooden spoon. When cool enough to handle, squeeze dry. Turn spinach out onto a cutting surface and chop fine.

3. In a large bowl, combine spinach, ricotta, egg yolks, ¾ cup Parmesan cheese, salt, pepper, and nutmeg. Mix with a wooden spoon until well blended.

4. In a greased 13 x 9-inch baking dish, alternately layer spinach pasta with spinach-ricotta mixture and mozzarella, making a total of four layers. Cover with foil and bake 25 minutes. Uncover and bake 10 minutes longer, or until bubbly. Let stand about 10 minutes before cutting into squares. Pass heated tomato sauce and remaining Parmesan cheese on the side.

104   MAMA'S LASAGNE

Prep: 40 minutes   Cook: 1½ hours   Stand: 10 minutes
Serves: 10

In Italy, lasagne is the name of a noodle, and the dishes that use it are necessarily baked. In this country, lasagne are always baked and layered. What sauces and fillings are used and in how many layers is often a personal statement. This dish can be prepared and cooked ahead of time or prepared and baked just before serving. It freezes well after baking.

3 slices Italian bread, cut 1 inch thick, trimmed of crust
½ cup milk
1 pound ground beef chuck
4 eggs
4 large garlic cloves, minced
¼ cup plus 2 tablespoons chopped fresh parsley
1 tablespoon salt
1 teaspoon pepper
3 tablespoons olive oil
1 medium onion, chopped

2 30-ounce cans Italian crushed tomatoes in puree
2 cups water
1 tablespoon chopped fresh oregano or 1 teaspoon dried
1½ pounds mild Italian sausages
2 pounds ricotta cheese
1¼ cups grated Parmesan cheese, about 5 ounces
¾ pound lasagne noodles
8 ounces mozzarella cheese, cut into ½-inch dice

1. In a small bowl, soak bread in milk 15 minutes. Squeeze excess milk from bread. In a large bowl, combine softened bread with beef, 1 egg, one fourth of the garlic, 2 tablespoons parsley, 1 teaspoon salt, and ¼ teaspoon pepper. Mix ingredients until well combined. Form into 8 to 10 meatballs.

2. In a nonreactive large flameproof casserole, heat 2 tablespoons olive oil over medium heat. Add meatballs and cook, turning several times, 6 to 8 minutes, or until evenly browned. Remove meatballs with a slotted spoon and reserve. Drain fat from casserole.

3. Heat remaining 1 tablespoon olive oil in casserole over medium heat. Add onion and remaining garlic and cook, stirring, 3 to 5 minutes, or until soft but not brown. Add tomatoes with puree, water, and oregano to pan. Bring to a simmer and return meatballs to casserole.

4. Prick sausages all over with a fork. In a medium frying pan, cook sausages with 2 tablespoons of water over medium heat, turning several times, until browned evenly, 5 to 7 minutes. Remove sausages from pan and add to casserole. Cover and simmer over low heat for 1 hour, stirring occasionally to prevent scorching on bottom of pan. Season with 1 teaspoon salt and ½ teaspoon pepper. Using kitchen tongs or a slotted spoon, remove cooked sausages and meatballs from tomato sauce to a cutting board. Cut sausages into ¼-inch slices and cut meatballs into 6 wedges each; set aside.

5. In a large bowl, beat remaining 3 eggs. Stir in ricotta cheese, ¼ cup parsley, ½ cup Parmesan cheese, 1 teaspoon salt, and ¼ teaspoon pepper. Mix with a wooden spoon until well blended.

6. Cook lasagne noodles in a large pot of boiling salted water, stirring several times in the beginning to prevent the noodles from sticking to each other, until tender but still firm, 12 to 15 minutes. Drain in a colander and rinse under cold running water; drain again.

7. To assemble lasagne, spread ¾ cup of the tomato sauce on bottom of a 13 x 9-inch baking pan. Arrange a layer of lasagne noodles on sauce. Spread another ¾ cup of sauce on noodles. Top with a layer of half each of the ricotta mixture, sausage and meatballs, and mozzarella and remaining Parmesan cheese. Repeat layers of noodles, sauce, ricotta, meat, and cheese; end with a top layer of noodles and sauce. (The recipe can be prepared to this point up to a day ahead.)

8. To cook lasagne, preheat oven to 350°. Cover with foil and bake 30 minutes; uncover and bake 15 minutes longer, or until bubbly and lightly browned on top. Let stand about 10 minutes before cutting into squares. Pass any remaining sauce on the side.

NOTE: *To freeze baked lasagne, let cool completely, wrap for freezing, and store in freezer. To bake, remove lasagne the night before baking and defrost, wrapped, in refrigerator. Bake in 350° oven 40 minutes wrapped and 15 minutes uncovered. To bake frozen, bake 1 hour covered with foil and 15 minutes uncovered, or until bubbly.*

---

105   PENNE WITH TUNA
Prep: 20 minutes   Cook: 10 to 12 minutes   Serves: 5 to 6

Penne is a short tubular pasta. Ziti or corkscrew-shaped fusilli can be substituted.

1 **pound penne**	2 **tablespoons chopped**
1 **6-ounce jar pimientos or 2**	**parsley**
large roasted and peeled	2 **scallions, chopped**
red peppers	1 **cup black olives, pitted and**
1 **teaspoon salt**	**coarsely chopped**
¼ **teaspoon pepper**	1 **6½-ounce can tuna in oil,**
3 **tablespoons red wine**	**drained and broken into**
vinegar	**chunks**
6 **tablespoons olive oil**	1 **6-ounce jar pimientos or 2**
2 **tablespoons shredded fresh**	**large roasted and peeled**
basil, or 1 teaspoon dried	**red peppers**

1. Cook penne in a large pot of boiling salted water until tender but still firm, 10 to 12 minutes. Drain in colander. Cool under cold running water.

2. In a large bowl, combine salt, pepper, vinegar, and olive oil. Beat with a fork to blend. Add basil, parsley, and scallions. Stir to mix. Add pasta to dressing along with olives, tuna, and pimientos. Toss carefully to combine, being careful to keep tuna from breaking down completely.

106   PASTA BUTTERFLIES WITH ASPARAGUS AND PROSCIUTTO

Prep: 20 minutes   Cook: 10 to 12 minutes   Serves: 8

This is a good summer lunch or buffet dish, always better with prosciutto and fresh asparagus. Bow-tie and butterfly pasta are the same shape.

1   **pound butterfly or bow-tie pasta (farfalle)**
8   **ounces fresh asparagus or 1 10-ounce package frozen asparagus tips, defrosted**
2   **large ripe tomatoes, cut into ½-inch dice**
2   **tablespoons chopped fresh parsley**
2   **tablespoons chopped fresh basil or 1 teaspoon dried**
6   **tablespoons extra-virgin olive oil**

3   **tablespoons fresh lemon juice**
1   **teaspoon salt**
½   **teaspoon pepper**
8   **ounces thinly sliced prosciutto or ham, cut into thin strips**
4   **hard-boiled eggs, cut into quarters**
    Lemon Mayonnaise (recipe follows)

1. Cook pasta in a large pot of boiling salted water until tender but still firm, 10 to 12 minutes; drain. Cool under cold running water; drain again.

2. If using fresh asparagus, trim off tough ends and cut into 1½- to 2-inch pieces. Cook in a large saucepan of boiling salted water 2 minutes, or until bright green and crisp-tender. Drain in a colander and cool under cold running water; drain again.

3. In a large bowl, combine pasta, asparagus, tomatoes, parsley, and basil. Toss gently just long enough to mix. In a small bowl combine olive oil, lemon juice, salt, and pepper. Beat with a fork to blend. Pour over pasta and toss to coat. Place in a serving bowl, cover top with prosciutto or ham, and circle with eggs. Serve with lemon mayonnaise on the side.

LEMON MAYONNAISE
Makes about 1¾ cups

In a small bowl, combine 1½ cups mayonnaise, 3 tablespoons fresh lemon juice, and ¼ teaspoon pepper. Whisk to blend well.

Chapter 4

Fresh Pasta—Try It, You'll Like It

Up to several years ago, unless you lived in an Italian neighborhood or owned your own pasta machine, fresh pasta was hard to come by. These days, not only are there entire specialty shops devoted to freshly made pasta, sauces, and cheeses, national brands market fresh pastas in both the refrigerator and frozen foods sections of supermarkets.

Fresh pastas are made with flour and eggs; some cooks add a little olive oil. Shapes are simple. Fresh pasta is usually rolled out into a sheet and cut into flat noodle shapes that vary in width from wide lasagne noodles to ribbons of fettuccine to thin strands of linguine and tagliate, such as tagliatelle and tagliarini. They are more often dressed in the northern style, with butter and cream, as well as with simple tomato sauces, and are often finished with grated Parmesan cheese.

Fresh stuffed pastas, such as ravioli or agnolotti, are much easier to find than they once were, and they make an instant meal with a simple sauce and a salad.

While I have given fresh pasta a separate chapter to help acquaint cooks with the subtle differences in recipes, keep in mind that you can substitute dried pasta for fresh in any of the following dishes. Just be sure to increase the cooking time of the pasta accordingly. In general, fresh pastas cook in anywhere from 1 to 3 minutes, whereas dried usually take 10 to 12.

107 GREEN FETTUCCINE WITH ASPARAGUS AND BACON

Prep: 15 minutes   Cook: 10 to 12 minutes   Serves: 6

This is a very fresh sauce. Don't overcook the unpeeled tomatoes at the end. Spinach or beet pasta makes this even more colorful.

1 tablespoon olive oil
4 ounces pancetta or Canadian bacon, cut into ¼-inch dice
½ cup finely chopped onion
2 cups asparagus tips, about 1 pound, trimmed and cut into ½-inch diagonal slices
1 cup Chicken Stock (page 48) or reduced-sodium canned broth

1 tablespoon minced fresh parsley
2 tablespoons chopped fresh basil or 1 teaspoon dried
1½ pounds ripe tomatoes, cut into ½-inch pieces
1 teaspoon salt
½ teaspoon ground pepper
1 pound fresh spinach fettuccine

1. In a nonreactive large frying pan, heat olive oil over medium heat. Add pancetta and onions and cook 4 to 5 minutes, or until onion is softened but not browned. Stir in asparagus. Pour in chicken stock and bring to a boil. Cook 1 to 2 minutes, or until liquid is reduced to about ¾ cup. Add parsley, basil, and tomato. Cook, stirring, over high heat 2 minutes to heat through. Season with salt and pepper and remove from heat.

2. Cook fettuccine in large pot of boiling salted water until tender but still firm, 3 to 5 minutes; drain. Pour pasta and sauce into warmed large bowl and toss together.

108 AGNOLOTTI WITH SAGE BUTTER

Prep: 10 minutes   Cook: 8 to 12 minutes   Serves: 3 to 4

For this dish, use commercially bought pasta. Technically, ravioli are stuffed with cheese and agnolotti are stuffed with meat.

30 1- to 1½-inch agnolotti or ravioli, about 1 pound
5 tablespoons butter

12 fresh sage leaves or ½ teaspoon dried
Grated Parmesan cheese
Freshly ground pepper

1. Cook agnolotti or ravioli according to package directions.

2. In a large frying pan, melt butter over medium heat. Add sage leaves and cook about 30 seconds, or until just wilted. Drain pasta and pour into a warmed large bowl. Pour sage butter over pasta and toss together. Pass grated Parmesan cheese and a pepper mill.

109   RAVIOLI WITH WALNUT SAUCE
Prep: 15 minutes   Cook: 10 to 12 minutes   Serves: 4

3 tablespoons butter
3 tablespoons finely chopped
  onion
1 garlic clove, minced
1½ cups heavy cream
1 cup grated Parmesan cheese

1 cup walnuts, about 4
  ounces, coarsely chopped
1 pound 1½-inch fresh or
  frozen ricotta cheese–
  stuffed ravioli
Freshly ground pepper

1. In a nonreactive large frying pan, melt butter over medium heat. Add onion and garlic and cook 2 to 3 minutes, or until softened but not browned. Add cream and bring to a boil. Cook 3 to 4 minutes, until reduced to 1¼ cups; be careful cream does not boil over. Add ½ cup Parmesan cheese and walnuts and stir to combine.

2. Meanwhile, cook ravioli according to package directions; drain. Pour pasta and sauce into a warmed large bowl and toss together. Pass remaining Parmesan cheese and a pepper mill.

110   FETTUCCINE IN SUN-COOKED SAUCE
*Prep: 10 minutes   Marinate: 4 to 5 hours   Cook: 5 to 6 minutes
Serves: 6 to 8*

This sauce tastes best when marinated in the sun. A sunny window or a back porch becomes the stove!

2 pounds ripe tomatoes
½ cup finely chopped red
  onion
½ cup chopped fresh basil or
  1½ teaspoons dried

2 tablespoons minced fresh
  parsley
2 tablespoons olive oil
¼ teaspoon salt
¼ teaspoon pepper
1 pound fresh fettuccine

1. Halve tomatoes and gently squeeze to extract seeds. Chop tomatoes into ½-inch pieces. In a large bowl, combine tomatoes, red onion, basil, parsley, olive oil, salt, and pepper. Stir lightly to mix. Cover bowl with a single layer of cheesecloth or a fine-mesh screen and place either outdoors in the sun or in a sunny window indoors, to marinate 4 to 5 hours.

2. Cook fettuccine in a large pot of boiling salted water 2 to 4 minutes, or until tender but still firm; drain. Pour pasta into bowl with sun-cooked sauce and toss together.

111   STRAW AND HAY WITH MUSHROOMS

Prep: 20 minutes   Cook: 15 minutes   Serves: 6 to 8

The two-colored noodles name this pasta *paglia e fieno*, or "straw and hay." If you can't find thin tagliarini, fettuccine will do.

3 tablespoons butter	1 10-ounce package frozen peas, thawed
2 tablespoons finely chopped onion	2 tablespoons chopped fresh basil or 1 teaspoon dried
12 ounces fresh mushrooms, thinly sliced	½ teaspoon salt
1½ cups Chicken Stock (page 48) or reduced-sodium canned broth	¼ teaspoon pepper
	½ pound fresh spinach tagliarini
6 ounces prosciutto or ham, cut into thin slivers	½ pound fresh egg tagliarini
	¾ cup grated Parmesan cheese

1. In a large frying pan, melt 2 tablespoons butter over medium-high heat. Add onion and cook 1 to 2 minutes, or until softened but not browned. Stir in mushrooms and cook until softened and just beginning to brown, 3 to 4 minutes.

2. Add chicken stock and bring to a boil. Cook until reduced to ¾ cup, 3 to 5 minutes. Add prosciutto or ham, peas, and basil. Cook just to heat through. Remove from heat. Season with salt and pepper and stir in remaining 1 tablespoon butter over very low heat.

3. Cook both pastas together in a large pot of boiling salted water 2 to 4 minutes, or until tender; drain. Pour pastas and sauce into warmed large bowl and toss together. Pass Parmesan cheese on the side.

112   PASTA WITH CREAM AND GORGONZOLA CHEESE

Prep: 10 minutes   Cook: 5 minutes   Serves: 6 to 8

You can use other blue cheese for this very simple sauce. Use this as a small-portion first course, as it is quite rich. A simple grilled fish would round this out beautifully.

½ cup coarsely chopped walnuts	6 ounces gorgonzola or other blue cheese
1½ cups heavy cream	1 pound fresh fettuccine

1. In a medium frying pan, toast walnuts 2 to 3 minutes over medium heat until lightly browned, shaking pan frequently. Set aside.

2. In a large saucepan, boil cream over medium heat until reduced to about 1¼ cups, about 5 minutes; be careful not to let it boil over. Stir in cheese until melted.

3. Meanwhile, cook pasta in a large pot of boiling salted water until tender, 2 to 4 minutes; drain. Pour pasta and sauce into a warmed large bowl and toss together. Sprinkle with walnuts.

113   RAVIOLI WITH TOMATO CREAM SAUCE
Prep: 10 minutes   Cook: 8 to 12 minutes   Serves: 4 to 6

Use commercially made meat-stuffed pasta such as agnolotti, tortelloni, or cappelletti. You can find them frozen, dry in packages, or freshly made in Italian delis and supermarkets. Ravioli are usually cheese. Sauces should be simple so they will not overwhelm the pasta.

2 cups marinara sauce,
      homemade (page 131) or
      jarred
½ cup heavy cream
2 tablespoons chopped fresh
      basil or 1 teaspoon dried

½ cup grated Parmesan cheese
1 pound 1- to 1½-inch fresh
      ravioli

1. In a nonreactive medium saucepan, heat marinara sauce over medium heat. Stir in cream and basil and heat together 2 to 3 minutes. Stir in 2 tablespoons of the Parmesan cheese.

2. Cook pasta in a large pot of boiling salted water until tender, about 3 minutes, or according to package directions; drain. Pour onto a warmed serving platter.

3. Pour pasta and sauce into a warmed large bowl and toss together. Pass remaining Parmesan cheese on the side.

114   RAVIOLI WITH BASIL AND NUTS
Prep: 10 minutes   Cook: 5 to 10 minutes   Serves: 6 to 8

Here's a sauce that can be changed by using walnuts, hazelnuts (filberts), or pine nuts.

1½ cups whole hazelnuts or
      ¾ cup chopped walnuts
      or pine nuts
1 pound (1- to 1½-inch) frozen
      stuffed ravioli
6 tablespoons butter

½ cup coarsely chopped fresh
      basil leaves, or 1 teaspoon
      dried basil and ⅓ cup
      chopped parsley
   Grated Parmesan cheese

1. If using hazelnuts, preheat oven to 350°. Spread nuts out on a baking sheet and roast 10 to 12 minutes, or until lightly browned and dark skins are cracked. Remove from oven and rub in a kitchen towel to remove as much brown skin as possible. Wrap in a clean towel and use a rolling pin to gently crack nuts into medium-size chunks.

2. Cook ravioli as directed on package.

3. Meanwhile, in a medium frying pan, melt butter over medium-low heat. Add nuts and cook, stirring, 1 minute. Stir in basil and remove from heat.

4. Drain ravioli and pour into a warmed large bowl. Add sauce and toss together. Pass a bowl of Parmesan cheese on the side.

115 FETTUCCINE ALL'ALFREDO
Prep: 10 minutes   Cook: 5 minutes   Serves: 6 to 8

This is the true version of Alfredo's pasta. Several variations follow.

1 **pound fresh fettuccine**	2 **cups grated Parmesan**
2 **sticks (½ pound) butter**	**cheese, about 8 ounces**

1. Cook pasta in a large pot of boiling salted water until tender, 2 to 4 minutes.

2. Meanwhile, in a large frying pan, melt butter over medium heat without allowing it to brown. Remove from heat.

3. Drain pasta and pour into pan with butter. Add 1½ cups of Parmesan cheese and toss to coat well. Pass remaining cheese on the side.

116 FETTUCCINE WITH SUN-DRIED TOMATOES, SQUID, AND HOT PEPPERS
Prep: 10 minutes   Cook: 35 minutes   Serves: 6 to 8

Sun-dried tomatoes give this sauce a delicious tart flavor. If they are not available, a bit of tomato paste will impart some of the flavor to the dish if not the complexity.

2 **tablespoons olive oil**	½ **cup sun-dried tomatoes**
¼ **cup finely chopped onion**	**packed in oil, drained**
1 **14-ounce can Italian peeled**	**and cut in thin strips**
tomatoes, drained and	½ **teaspoon salt**
chopped	¼ **teaspoon pepper**
½ **cup water**	2 **tablespoons chopped fresh**
1 **pound frozen cleaned**	**parsley**
squid, defrosted and cut	1 **pound fresh fettuccine**
in ½-inch pieces	
12 **peperoncini (Italian pickled**	
peppers), stemmed and	
seeded	

1. In a nonreactive large saucepan, heat olive oil over medium heat. Add onion and cook 2 to 3 minutes, until softened. Add tomatoes and water and bring to a boil. Add squid, reduce heat to low, cover, and cook 25 to 30 minutes, or until tender. Add peperoncini and sun-dried tomatoes. Cook 1 to 2 minutes to heat. Season with salt, pepper, and parsley.

2. When the sauce is almost ready, cook the fettuccine in a large pot of boiling salted water until tender, 2 to 4 minutes; drain. Pour pasta and half the sauce into a warmed large bowl and toss together. Pour remaining sauce over top and serve.

117   CLASSICAL PESTO WITH FETTUCCINE
Prep: 10 minutes   Cook: 4 minutes   Serves: 6 to 8

Pesto, as I like it, is sweet with basil rather than hot with garlic. A variation for garlic lovers follows.

2 **cups packed fresh basil leaves**
2 **garlic cloves, minced**
½ **cup walnuts**
1¼ **cups extra-virgin olive oil**
½ **cup grated Parmesan cheese**

½ **cup grated pecorino or Romano cheese**
¾ **teaspoon salt**
1 **pound fresh fettuccine**
2 **tablespoons butter**

1. Place basil, garlic, and walnuts in a food processor and process 15 seconds. With machine on, pour oil through feed tube in a steady stream until almost 1 cup of oil has been used. With machine still running, add Parmesan and pecorino cheese, and then the remaining oil. Taste and season pesto sauce with salt, if needed.

2. Cook fettuccine in a large pot of boiling salted water until tender but still firm, 2 to 4 minutes; drain. Pour pasta into a warmed large bowl and toss with butter, then with 1 cup of the pesto sauce. Pass remaining pesto on the side. Freeze any remaining sauce for future use.

118   FETTUCCINE PESTO WITH MASCARPONE
Prep: 10 minutes   Cook: 4 minutes   Serves: 6 to 8

Rich and sweet, this sauce coats pasta beautifully. If mascarpone is unavailable, I have included a recipe for an adequate substitute.

1 **cup pesto, homemade (page 77) or jarred**
1 **cup mascarpone cheese, about 8 ounces, or ½ cup cream cheese mixed with ¼ cup cream and ¼ cup buttermilk**

1 **pound fresh fettuccine**
Grated Parmesan cheese

1. Cook fettuccine in a large pot of boiling salted water until tender but still firm, 2 to 4 minutes.

2. Meanwhile, in a medium saucepan, warm the mascarpone or cream cheese mixture over medium-low heat. Stir in pesto and heat through.

3. Drain pasta and pour into a warmed large bowl. Add sauce and toss together. Pass a bowl of Parmesan cheese on the side.

119 FETTUCCINE ALLA ROMANA

Prep: 10 minutes   Cook: 10 minutes   Serves: 6 to 8

This dish, also called *fettuccine alla panne* (with cream) is from Rome. It is well known and very rich.

6 tablespoons butter	1 pound fresh fettuccine
2 cups heavy cream	Freshly ground pepper
¾ cup grated Parmesan cheese	

1. In a large saucepan or flameproof casserole, melt butter over medium heat. Add cream and bring to a boil. Cook until reduced to about 1½ cups, 4 to 5 minutes; be careful not to let it boil over. Stir in half the Parmesan cheese and cook 1 to 2 minutes. Remove from heat.

2. Meanwhile, cook fettuccine in a large pot of boiling salted water until tender but still firm, 2 to 4 minutes; drain. Pour pasta into pan with sauce and toss together. Pass remaining Parmesan cheese and a pepper mill on the side.

120 FETTUCCINE WITH SPINACH AND CREAM

Prep: 10 minutes   Cook: 10 to 12 minutes   Serves: 6 to 8

2 tablespoons butter	¼ teaspoon pepper
3 tablespoons finely chopped onion	1 pound fresh fettuccine
1½ cups heavy cream	3 tablespoons chopped fresh basil leaves or 1½ teaspoons dried basil
8 ounces fresh spinach, stems removed	¾ cup grated Parmesan cheese
¾ teaspoon salt	

1. In a nonreactive large saucepan, melt butter over medium heat. Add onion and cook 2 to 3 minutes, or until softened. Add cream and bring to a boil. Cook 3 minutes to thicken; be careful not to let it boil over. Add spinach and cook until wilted, 1 to 2 minutes longer. Season with salt and pepper. Remove from heat.

2. Cook pasta in a large pot of boiling salted water until tender but still firm, 2 to 4 minutes; drain. Pour pasta and sauce into a warmed large bowl, add basil, and toss together. Pass Parmesan cheese on the side.

121   FETTUCCINE IN MOUNTAIN AND SEA

Prep: 20 to 30 minutes   Cook: 25 minutes   Serves: 6 to 8

The mountains and the sea meet in this dish. Wild mushrooms and scampi are traditionally used, but we can simplify it with cultivated mushrooms and shrimp.

½ ounce dried porcini mushrooms	½ cup heavy cream
2 cups warm water	1 teaspoon dried thyme leaves
2 tablespoons butter	½ teaspoon dried sage leaves
2 tablespoons finely chopped onion	2 tablespoons minced fresh parsley
8 ounces fresh mushrooms, thinly sliced	½ teaspoon salt
½ cup dry white wine	¼ teaspoon pepper
12 ounces medium shrimp, shelled and deveined	1 pound fresh fettuccine

1. Soak porcini in warm water 20 to 30 minutes, or until softened. Remove porcini and rinse under cold running water to remove any grit. Chop fine and set aside. Strain liquid through cheesecloth to remove any grit and set aside.

2. Meanwhile, in a nonreactive large frying pan, melt butter over medium heat. Add onion and cook 2 to 3 minutes, or until softened. Add fresh mushrooms to pan and cook, stirring, until barely cooked, 2 to 3 minutes. Add wine and cook 1 to 2 minutes to reduce slightly. Add dried mushrooms and their soaking liquid and bring to a boil. Cook until liquid is reduced to 1½ cups, 4 to 5 minutes. Add shrimp and cook 2 to 3 minutes, or until they just begin to turn pink. Add cream, thyme, sage, and parsley. Bring to a simmer. Remove from heat and season with salt and pepper. Cover to keep warm.

3. Cook fettuccine in a large pot of boiling salted water until tender but still firm, 3 to 4 minutes; drain. Pour fettuccine onto a warmed serving platter. Pour sauce over top and toss together.

122 FETTUCCINE WITH CREAM, PROSCIUTTO, AND PEAS

Prep: 10 minutes   Cook: 5 minutes   Serves: 6 to 8

A gilded-lily version of Alfredo's pasta.

4 tablespoons butter
1½ cups heavy cream
1 cup frozen peas
6 ounces sliced prosciutto or other ham, cut into slivers

½ cup grated Parmesan cheese
1 pound fresh fettuccine

1. In a large frying pan, melt butter over medium heat. Add cream and bring to a boil. Cook 3 minutes to thicken; be careful not to let it boil over. Add peas and prosciutto or ham and cook 1 to 2 minutes. Remove from heat and stir in 2 tablespoons Parmesan cheese.

2. Meanwhile, cook fettuccine in a large pot of boiling salted water until tender but still firm, 2 to 4 minutes; drain. Pour pasta into pan with cream sauce and toss together. Pass remaining Parmesan cheese on the side.

123 TAGLIATELLE WITH PORK AND BEEF RAGU

Prep: 15 minutes   Cook: 1 hour 10 minutes   Serves: 6 to 8

A southern Italian specialty, pork neck bones were used for this sauce. The meat was sweet and succulent, but the bones were a nuisance and children's plates were well monitored. I like to use a boneless pork butt trimmed of fat.

2 pounds boneless pork, cut in ½-inch pieces
1 pound boneless beef chuck, trimmed of fat and cut in ½-inch pieces
1 tablespoon olive oil
1 small onion, chopped
1 small carrot, peeled and chopped
2 ribs celery, chopped

1 30-ounce can Italian crushed tomatoes in puree
1 cup water
1 tablespoon chopped fresh rosemary or 1 teaspoon dried
¾ teaspoon salt
¼ teaspoon pepper
⅛ teaspoon grated nutmeg
1 pound fresh tagliatelle
½ cup grated Romano cheese
½ cup grated Parmesan cheese

1. Trim excess fat from pork and beef. In a nonreactive large saucepan, heat oil over medium heat. Add pork and beef and cook, turning several times to brown evenly, about 4 to 5 minutes. Remove meat to a bowl and reserve. Add onion, carrot, and celery and cook 3 to 4 minutes, or until softened. Return meat to pan and add tomatoes, water, and rosemary. Bring to a boil, reduce heat to low, cover, and cook about 1 hour, or until meat is fork-tender and beginning to fall apart. Season with salt, pepper, and nutmeg.

2. When sauce is almost ready, cook tagliatelle in a large pot of boiling salted water until tender but still firm, 2 to 4 minutes; drain. Pour pasta and half the sauce into a warmed large bowl and toss together. Pour remaining sauce on top.

3. In a small bowl, combine Romano and Parmesan cheese. Pass on the side.

---

124   TAGLIATELLE IN RAGU BOLOGNESE
Prep: 20 minutes   Cook: 45 minutes   Serves: 6 to 8

Chicken livers make this one of the richest of all sauces. Try topping with lemon zest instead of cheese for a good sharp contrast.

2 tablespoons butter	¾ teaspoon salt
½ cup finely chopped onion	¼ teaspoon pepper
4 ounces pancetta or Canadian bacon, cut into ¼-inch dice	⅛ teaspoon grated nutmeg
	½ cup heavy cream
1 pound chicken livers, trimmed	1 pound fresh tagliatelle
	1 cup grated Parmesan cheese or 2 tablespoons grated lemon zest
12 ounces fresh mushrooms	
2 tablespoons tomato paste	
¾ cup dry red wine	
2 cups hot beef or veal stock or reduced-sodium canned beef broth	

1. In a large nonreactive saucepan or flameproof casserole, melt butter over medium heat. Add onion and pancetta and cook 3 to 4 minutes, or until pancetta is lightly browned and onion is soft. Add chicken livers, increase heat to medium-high, and cook, turning several times, 3 to 4 minutes, or until lightly brown but still pink in center. Remove livers with a slotted spoon and reserve.

2. Add mushrooms to pan and cook, stirring occasionally, 2 to 3 minutes to brown lightly.

3. Using a slotted spoon, remove mushrooms to a cutting board with reserved livers. Chop livers and mushrooms medium fine. Return to pan. Add tomato paste, wine, and stock. Bring to a boil, reduce heat to low, cover, and cook 30 minutes, stirring occasionally. Uncover and boil until sauce is thick. Stir in salt, pepper, nutmeg, and cream. Simmer 2 minutes.

4. When sauce is almost ready, cook pasta in a large pot of boiling salted water until tender, 2 to 4 minutes; drain. Pour pasta onto a warmed platter and pour sauce over top. Sprinkle with Parmesan cheese or grated lemon zest.

125 CANNELLONI STUFFED WITH CHICKEN, HAM, AND MUSHROOMS

Prep: 30 minutes   Cook: 45 to 55 minutes   Serves: 6

Make this with sheets of fresh pasta purchased in Italian specialty shops, or with dried tube shells, which can be purchased in grocery stores.

3 sheets of fresh pasta, cut into
    4 x 3-inch pieces, or 12
    dried cannelloni shells
2 tablespoons butter
2 tablespoons finely chopped
    onion
8 ounces mushrooms, finely
    chopped
¾ teaspoon salt

¼ teaspoon pepper
3 cups ground cooked
    chicken, about 1¼
    pounds
8 ounces ham, ground
¾ cup grated Parmesan cheese
    Bechamel Sauce (recipe
    follows)

1. Cook fresh pasta in a large pot of boiling salted water until tender but still firm, 2 to 4 minutes. Drain in colander and rinse under cold running water. Lay out pasta pieces in a single layer on a flat work surface. If using dried shells, cook until tender but still firm, 10 to 12 minutes. Drain, rinse, and drain again.

2. In a large frying pan, melt butter over medium heat. Add onion and cook 3 to 4 minutes, or until softened. Stir in mushrooms and cook until soft and all liquid has evaporated, 5 to 6 minutes. Season with salt and pepper. Transfer to a large bowl.

3. Add chicken, ham, and ½ cup Parmesan cheese to bowl. Mix to blend well. Stir in ¾ cup bechamel sauce.

4. Preheat oven to 350°. Divide equal amounts of filling along one long end of each piece of pasta. Roll up into tube shapes. Or stuff cooked cannelloni shells. Spread ½ cup bechamel sauce on bottom of a 13 x 9-inch baking dish. Place cannelloni seam side down in baking dish. Spread remaining sauce over pasta. Sprinkle with remaining ¼ cup Parmesan cheese.

5. Bake cannelloni 30 minutes, or until hot and bubbling and golden brown on top.

126 BECHAMEL SAUCE (balsamella or salsa besciamella)

Prep: 5 minutes   Cook: 5–7 minutes   Makes: 4 cups

4 tablespoons butter
¼ cup flour
4 cups hot milk

¾ teaspoon salt
¼ teaspoon grated nutmeg

In a heavy medium saucepan, melt butter over medium-low heat. Stir in flour and cook with butter for 2 to 3 minutes, being careful not to brown. Gradually whisk in hot milk. Bring to a boil, whisking, until thick and smooth. Reduce heat to low and simmer, whisking frequently, 3 to 4 minutes. Season with salt and nutmeg.

127 TAGLIARINI WITH FOUR CHEESES
Prep: 10 minutes   Cook: 8 to 10 minutes   Serves: 6 to 8

A commercially made black pepper pasta is very good for this. *Dolce latte* gorgonzola is "sweet milk gorgonzola," a milder, creamier version of this rich cheese. If unavailable, many other creamy blue cheeses can be found.

1 cup heavy cream
4 ounces Italian fontina
  cheese, grated
4 ounces dolce latte
  gorgonzola or other mild
  blue cheese, cut into
  1-inch pieces

4 ounces Bel Paese cheese, cut
  up
1 cup grated Parmesan cheese,
  about 4 ounces
½ teaspoon pepper, plus more
  for grinding
¼ teaspoon grated nutmeg
1 pound fresh tagliarini

1. In a nonreactive large saucepan, bring cream to a simmer over medium heat; be careful not to let it boil over. Add fontina, gorgonzola, and Bel Paese. Reduce heat to low and cook, stirring, until cheeses are melted and sauce is smooth, about 5 minutes. Add ½ cup Parmesan cheese and cook, stirring, 1 minute. Season with pepper and nutmeg.

2. Meanwhile, cook taglierini in a large pot of boiling salted water until tender but still firm, 2 to 4 minutes; drain. Pour pasta and sauce into a warmed large bowl and toss together. Pass remaining Parmesan cheese and a pepper mill on the side.

128 TORPEDO TAGLIARINI
Prep: 10 minutes   Cook: 30 minutes   Serves: 6 to 8

Bermudas, Walla Walla, and torpedo onions are all good for this sauce. Onion sauces are always sweet, so I prefer a sharp Romano cheese.

¼ cup olive oil
6 cups thinly sliced torpedo or
  other sweet onions
1 14-ounce can Italian peeled
  tomatoes, drained and
  chopped
  Pinch of dried rosemary
1 tablespoon chopped fresh
  basil or ½ teaspoon dried

¾ teaspoon salt
½ teaspoon pepper
2 tablespoons minced fresh
  parsley
1 pound fresh tagliarini or
  linguine
½ cup grated Romano cheese

1. In a nonreactive large pan heat olive oil over medium heat. Stir in onions and reduce heat to low. Cook 15 to 16 minutes, or until very soft but not browned. Add tomatoes, rosemary, and basil and cook 10 minutes to combine flavors. Season with salt, pepper, and parsley.

2. When sauce is almost ready, cook taglierini in a large pot of boiling salted water until tender but still firm, 2 to 4 minutes; drain. Pour pasta and sauce into a warmed large bowl. Toss with half the cheese. Pass remaining cheese on the side.

129   LINGUINE WITH KNOCK-OUT GARLIC PESTO

Prep: 10 minutes   Cook: 2 to 4 minutes   Serves: 6 to 8

This much garlic gives pesto a hot taste many enjoy. This is not for gentle souls; and be sure your neighbors love you—no matter what!

8 large garlic cloves, minced
1 cup packed fresh basil
    leaves
¼ cup pine nuts
½ cup minced fresh parsley,
    preferably Italian flat-leaf

½ cup grated Romano cheese
¼ cup grated Parmesan cheese
1 cup plus 2 tablespoons extra-
    virgin olive oil
1 pound fresh linguine or
    fettuccine

1. Place garlic, basil, parsley, and pine nuts in a food processor and process 15 seconds. With machine on, pour ¾ cup olive oil through feed tube in a steady stream until coarsely pureed. With machine still running, add cheese and then ¼ cup olive oil until combined.

2. Cook fettuccine in a large pot of boiling salted water until tender but still firm, 2 to 4 minutes; drain. Pour pasta into a warmed large bowl and toss with 2 tablespoons olive oil, then with half the pesto. Pass remaining pesto on the side.

Chapter 5

Risotto, Gnocchi, and Polenta—
The Other Italian Treats

While many of us could eat pasta every day of the week, and many Italians do, there are other dishes that serve the same function in the meal. Risotto, gnocchi, and polenta are three alternatives to pasta, either as a separate course or as an accompaniment to meat, chicken, or fish.

Risotto, common to the north of Italy where rice is grown, is a preparation of a specific type of Italian rice. Arborio rice—labled Arborio Fino or Supra Fino—is the most common type found here. It is a short-grain rice with a lot of surface starch, and it cooks up like pasta—tender on the outside with a hint of resistance remaining in the center. Simmered with broth and seasonings, the outer starch thickens the sauce, so the final texture is something like a stirred rice pudding. These rice dishes of northern Italy are delicious and soul satisfying. I encourage you to find a place for these recipes in your cooking.

While the flavorings vary, the technique of cooking any risotto has three basic parts. First the rice is cooked for a minute or two in butter or oil, until the grains are coated with fat and turn an opaque white. Then, while the rice is being stirred constantly, hot liquid—usually broth, occasionally wine—is gradually added, until enough liquid has been added and absorbed that the rice is tender but still firm in the center and the mixture has a thick, creamy, saucy consistency. Finally, a little butter, and often cheese, is added to finish the dish. The entire process takes 20 to 25 minutes, and as anyone who has ever tasted risotto in Italy or in a restaurant will tell you, it's well worth the effort.

Gnocchi, made either from flour, from flour and potatoes, or from semolina, are little cakes or dumpling-like pasta nuggets that are sauced and treated very much like pasta. They stick to your ribs, and are yet another example of Italian ingenuity with grains. The semolina cakes, in particular, are great for entertaining, because they can be made ahead and finished off in the oven just before serving.

Polenta, which you could think of as Italian cornmeal mush, was ignored in this country for years because the process of preparing it was so time consuming. I've included a recipe for Traditional Polenta, which involves stirring the mixture over heat for up to an hour, so you could see what it was all about. If you do attempt this feat, you will find the results delicious and the texture sublime. Happily, there is now on the market an instant polenta, which is ready in 10 to 15 minutes. The taste is fabulous, and that's what I've called for in most of my polenta recipes. Look for this product in Italian markets and specialty food shops.

Like pasta, polenta is bland, but lends itself almost magically to embellishments as simple as butter and Parmesan cheese or as hearty as tomato sauce and sausages.

130   MUSHROOM RISOTTO WITH WHITE WINE
Prep: 15 minutes   Cook: 30 minutes   Serves: 4 to 6

Delicious made with either wild or cultivated mushrooms. I like to serve this with additional mushrooms; just double the amount of mushrooms called for in the recipe and reserve half to serve on the side.

4 tablespoons butter	1½ cups dry white wine
1 tablespoon olive oil	2 cups Arborio rice
1 cup finely chopped onion	1 teaspoon salt
1 garlic clove, minced	½ teaspoon pepper
8 ounces fresh mushrooms, thinly sliced	6 to 8 cups hot Chicken Stock (page 48) or 2 14½-ounce cans broth mixed with 4 cups hot water
1 teaspoon dried thyme leaves	
¼ teaspoon dried rosemary	
1 tablespoon minced fresh parsley	¾ cup grated Parmesan cheese

1. In a large frying pan melt 2 tablespoons butter with olive oil over medium heat. Add ½ cup onion and garlic and cook until onion is soft, 2 to 3 minutes. Stir in mushrooms and cook until lightly browned, 3 to 4 minutes. Stir in thyme, rosemary, and parsley. Add ½ cup wine and cook until wine is absorbed, about 2 minutes. Season with ¼ teaspoon salt and ⅛ teaspoon pepper. Remove from heat and cover to keep warm.

2. Melt remaining 2 tablespoons butter in a large heavy saucepan over medium heat. Cook remaining ½ cup onion until soft, about 3 minutes. Add remaining 1 cup wine and cook over high heat until reduced to ½ cup, 4 to 5 minutes. Add rice, salt, and pepper and stir to coat evenly, allowing wine to be absorbed. Add 2 cups chicken stock, reduce heat to medium, and stir until stock is absorbed, 5 to 6 minutes. Continue to add as much stock as needed, 1 cup at a time, stirring, until rice is creamy and tender but still firm in center. Process should take 15 to 18 minutes from time you add first stock. Stir in reserved mushrooms. Remove from heat and stir in ½ cup Parmesan cheese. Pass remaining Parmesan cheese on the side.

131 RISOTTO MILANESE
Prep: 15 minutes   Cook: 25 minutes   Serves: 6

This is the signature dish of Milan. It has a lovely golden color and is a truly satisfying dish. Traditionally this is served with braised veal shank (*osso bucco*).

¼ teaspoon saffron threads	½ cup finely chopped onion
6 cups hot Chicken Stock	2½ cups Arborio rice
(page 48) or 2 14½-ounce	¾ cup dry white wine
cans broth mixed with 2	¾ teaspoon salt
cups hot water	¾ cup grated Parmesan cheese
3 tablespoons butter	

1. In a small saucepan, crush saffron into 2 cups hot stock. Let stand 15 minutes.

2. In a large heavy saucepan, melt 2 tablespoons butter over medium heat. Add onion and cook 2 to 3 minutes, or until softened. Add rice and cook, stirring, for 1 minute. Stir in wine and boil until reduced by half, about 3 minutes. Add salt and saffron-flavored stock and reduce heat to medium-low. Cook, stirring, until stock is absorbed, 5 to 6 minutes. Continue to add as much plain stock as needed, 1 cup at a time, stirring, until rice is creamy and tender but still firm in center. Process should take 15 to 18 minutes from time you add first stock. Remove pan from heat and stir in remaining 1 tablespoon butter and the Parmesan cheese.

132 GREEN RISOTTO
Prep: 15 minutes   Cook: 20 to 25 minutes   Serves: 4 to 6

A summer *risotto verde* is made with fresh herbs and spinach.

4 tablespoons butter	6 to 8 cups hot Chicken Stock
¾ cup finely chopped scallions	(page 48) or 2 14½-ounce
½ cup minced fresh parsley	cans broth mixed with 2
1½ cups finely chopped	to 4 cups hot water
spinach, about 8 ounces	3 tablespoons chopped fresh
2 cups Arborio rice	basil
½ teaspoon salt	¾ cup grated Parmesan cheese

1. In a large heavy saucepan, melt 3 tablespoons butter over medium heat. Add scallions and cook 1 to 2 minutes, or until softened. Stir in parsley and spinach and cook 1 to 2 minutes, just long enough to wilt greens.

2. Add rice and salt and stir to coat with greens. Add 2 cups chicken stock and reduce heat to medium-low. Cook, stirring, until stock is absorbed, about 5 to 6 minutes. Continue to add as much stock as needed, 1 cup at a time, stirring, until rice is creamy and tender but still firm in center. Process should take 15 to 18 minutes from time you add first stock. Remove from heat and stir in basil, remaining 1 tablespoon butter, and ¼ cup Parmesan cheese. Pass remaining Parmesan cheese on the side.

133 RISOTTO WITH HAM, PINE NUTS, AND BASIL

Prep: 15 minutes   Cook: 20 minutes   Serves: 6

Fresh basil is the only choice for this simple risotto; otherwise the flavor will not be strong enough.

¾ cup pine nuts
3 tablespoons butter
½ cup finely chopped onion
4 ounces ham, preferably prosciutto, cut into ¼-inch dice
3 cups Arborio rice
¾ teaspoon salt

⅛ teaspoon pepper
6 to 8 cups hot Chicken Stock (page 48) or 2 14½-ounce cans broth mixed with 4 cups hot water
3 tablespoons chopped fresh basil
½ cup grated Parmesan cheese

1. In a medium frying pan, roast pine nuts over low heat 2 to 3 minutes, or until golden brown, shaking pan frequently. Set aside.

2. In a large heavy saucepan, melt 2 tablespoons butter over medium heat. Cook onion 2 to 3 minutes, or until softened. Add ham, rice, salt, and pepper and stir to coat evenly. Add 2 cups stock and stir until absorbed, 5 to 6 minutes. Continue to add as much stock as needed, 1 cup at a time, stirring, until rice is creamy and tender but still firm in center. Process should take 15 to 18 minutes from time you add first stock. Remove from heat and stir in half the pine nuts, basil, remaining 1 tablespoon butter, and Parmesan cheese. Garnish with remaining pine nuts.

134 MUSHROOM RISOTTO IN BAROLO WINE

Prep: 10 minutes   Cook: 25 minutes   Serves: 6

Barolo is a very prestigious Italian red wine from the Northern Piedmont. You can use other dry red wines for this dish.

3 tablespoons butter
½ cup finely chopped onion
3 ounces pancetta, cut into ¼-inch dice
1 garlic clove, minced
2 teaspoons fresh thyme leaves or ¼ teaspoon dried
1½ cups Barolo or other dry red wine
2 cups Arborio rice

½ teaspoon salt
¼ teaspoon pepper
6 to 8 cups hot Chicken Stock (page 48) or 2 14½-ounce cans broth mixed with 4 cups hot water
8 ounces fresh mushrooms, halved
2 tablespoons minced fresh parsley
1 cup grated Parmesan cheese

1. In a heavy saucepan, melt 2 tablespoons butter over medium heat. Add onion and pancetta and cook 2 to 3 minutes, until onion is softened. Add garlic and thyme and cook 30 seconds, or until fragrant. Add red wine and boil until reduced to 1 cup, 3 to 5 minutes. Add rice, salt, and pepper and stir to coat with butter and wine.

2. Add 2 cups hot chicken broth and stir until absorbed, 5 to 6 minutes. Add mushrooms, stir to distribute evenly with rice, and cook 1 to 2 minutes. Continue to add as much stock as needed, 1 cup at a time, stirring, until rice is creamy and tender but still firm in center. Process should take 15 to 18 minutes from time you add first stock. Remove from heat and stir in remaining 1 tablespoon butter, parsley, and Parmesan cheese.

135   CORN AND SWEET PEPPER RISOTTO
Prep: 15 minutes   Cook: 25 minutes   Serves: 4 to 6

It is just in recent years that northern Italians have begun to include fresh corn in their dishes. This definitely comes under the category of *nuova cucina*, or the "new cuisine."

2 large ears of fresh corn or 1 10-ounce package frozen kernels
2 tablespoons butter
½ cup finely chopped onion
1 garlic clove, minced
3 ounces pancetta, cut into ¼-inch dice
2 cups Arborio rice
½ teaspoon salt
⅛ teaspoon pepper

6 to 8 cups hot Chicken Stock (page 48) or 2 14½-ounce cans broth mixed with 4 cups hot water
1 small red bell pepper, cored, seeded, and cut into ¼-inch dice
2 tablespoons chopped fresh basil or 1 teaspoon dried
¾ cup grated Parmesan cheese

1. If using fresh corn, remove leaves from corn and wipe with a damp towel to remove corn silk. Cut off stem end and hold corn upright on flat surface. To remove kernels, use a sharp knife to shave down ear of corn along surface of cob. If using frozen corn, defrost.

2. In a large saucepan, melt butter over medium heat. Add onion, garlic, and pancetta and cook 2 to 3 minutes, or until onion is softened but not browned. Stir in rice, salt, and pepper to coat evenly. Add 2 cups stock and stir until absorbed, 5 to 6 minutes. Stir in corn and red bell pepper. Continue to add as much stock as needed, 1 cup at a time, stirring, until rice is creamy and tender but still firm in center. The process should take 15 to 18 minutes from time you add first stock. Remove from heat and stir in basil and ½ cup Parmesan cheese. Pass remaining Parmesan cheese on the side.

136 SAUSAGE RISOTTO

Prep: 15 minutes   Cook: 30 minutes   Serves: 6

Spicy risotto is complimented beautifully with a simple salad.

12 ounces fennel sausages or
    other Italian-style sausage
4 tablespoons butter
¼ cup finely chopped onion
½ cup dry white wine
2 cups Arborio rice

6 to 8 cups hot Chicken Stock
    (page 48) or 2 14½-ounce
    cans broth mixed with
    2 cups hot water
½ cup grated Parmesan cheese
1 tablespoon minced fresh
    parsley

1. Cut sausage into ½-inch pieces and place in a small frying pan with 2 tablespoons water. Cook covered over medium-low heat, turning, 5 to 7 minutes, or until lightly browned. With a slotted spoon, remove sausages and drain on paper towels.

2. In a large heavy saucepan, melt 2 tablespoons butter over medium-low heat. Add onion and cook 2 to 3 minutes, or until softened. Add sausage meat and cook 1 to 2 minutes to reheat. Add wine and cook until reduced by half, 2 to 3 minutes. Stir in rice to coat evenly. Add 2 cups stock and cook, stirring, until absorbed, 5 to 6 minutes. Continue to add as much stock as needed, 1 cup at a time, until rice is creamy and tender but still firm in center. Process should take 15 to 18 minutes from time you add first stock. Remove from heat and stir in remaining 2 tablespoons butter, Parmesan cheese, and parsley.

137 ASPARAGUS RISOTTO

Prep: 15 minutes   Cook: 25 minutes   Serves: 6 to 8

15 medium fresh asparagus or
    1 10-ounce package frozen
    asparagus tips, defrosted
3 tablespoons butter
½ cup finely chopped onion
4 ounces pancetta or Canadian
    bacon, cut into ¼-inch
    dice
1 cup dry white wine

2 cups Arborio rice
½ teaspoon salt
¼ teaspoon pepper
6 to 8 cups hot Chicken Stock
    (page 48) or 2 14½-ounce
    cans broth mixed with
    4 cups hot water
½ cup grated Parmesan cheese

1. If using fresh asparagus trim off tough ends and cut diagonally into ¾-inch pieces, leaving tips intact. Cook in 2 quarts boiling salted water 2 to 3 minutes, until crisp-tender. Drain and rinse under cold running water. Drain and pat dry.

2. In a heavy saucepan, melt 2 tablespoons butter over medium heat. Add onion and pancetta and cook 2 to 3 minutes, or until onion is softened. Add wine and cook over high heat 2 to 3 minutes to reduce by half. Add rice, salt, and pepper and cook, stirring, 1 minute. Add 2 cups chicken stock and stir over medium to low heat until absorbed, 5 to 6 minutes. Continue to add as much stock as needed, 1 cup at a time, stirring, until rice is creamy and tender but still firm in center. Process should take 15 to 18 minutes from time you add first stock. Add asparagus and cook 1 to 2 minutes, or until heated through. Remove from heat and stir in remaining 1 tablespoon butter and the Parmesan cheese.

138 PUMPKIN, ZUCCHINI, AND HAM RISOTTO
Prep: 15 minutes   Cook: 25 minutes   Serves: 8

It is imperative to use fresh vegetables in this recipe, for any other type would turn to mush. Butternut squash is an excellent substitute for pumpkin.

3 tablespoons butter	1½ cups diced (½-inch) raw
½ cup finely chopped onion	pumpkin
1 garlic clove, minced	1½ cups diced (½-inch) zucchini
1 cup dry white wine	3 tablespoons finely chopped
2 cups Arborio rice	basil or 1½ teaspoons
½ teaspoon salt	dried
⅛ teaspoon pepper	¾ cup grated Parmesan cheese
4 ounces ham, cut into ¼-inch	
dice	
6 to 8 cups hot Chicken Stock	
(page 48) or 2 14½-ounce	
cans broth mixed with	
4 cups hot water	

1. In a large heavy saucepan, melt 2 tablespoons butter over medium-low heat. Add onion and garlic and cook 2 to 3 minutes, or until softened. Add wine and cook until reduced by half, 3 to 5 minutes.

2. Add rice, salt, pepper, and ham and stir to coat evenly. Add 2 cups stock and stir over medium heat until absorbed, 5 to 6 minutes. Stir in pumpkin and zucchini. Continue to add as much stock as needed, 1 cup at a time, stirring until rice is creamy and tender but still firm in center. Process should take 15 to 18 minutes from time you add first stock. Remove from heat and stir in remaining 1 tablespoon butter, basil, and Parmesan cheese.

139   RISOTTO WITH SHRIMP
Prep: 20 minutes   Cook: 30 minutes   Serves: 6

Seafood and fish risottos are usually a little more liquid, and they are often made with water rather than, as here, with fish stock.

1 pound large shrimp (16 to 20 per pound), shelled and deveined
2 tablespoons olive oil
½ cup finely chopped onion
1 garlic clove, minced
½ cup dry white wine
1 14-ounce can Italian peeled tomatoes, drained and chopped
Pinch of hot pepper flakes

3 tablespoons butter
2 cups Arborio rice
6 to 8 cups hot fish stock or 2 8-ounce bottles hot clam juice diluted with 4 cups hot water
½ teaspoon salt
¼ teaspoon pepper
1 tablespoon minced fresh parsley

1. Cut shrimp into 3 pieces each. In a nonreactive large frying pan, heat olive oil over medium-high heat. Add onion and garlic and cook 2 to 3 minutes, or until onion is softened. Add shrimp and cook, stirring, until they just begin to turn pink, 1 to 2 minutes. Remove shrimp to plate. Add wine and heat 1 minute. Add tomatoes and hot pepper flakes, bring to a boil, and cook 2 to 3 minutes to reduce mixture. Remove from heat.

2. In a large heavy saucepan, melt butter over medium heat. Stir in rice and toss to coat evenly. Add 2 cups stock and stir until absorbed, 5 to 6 minutes. Continue to add as much stock as needed, 1 cup at a time, stirring, until rice is creamy and tender but still firm in center. Process should take 15 to 18 minutes from time you add first stock. Add shrimp and tomatoes to rice and cook 2 to 3 minutes, stirring, to heat through. Season with salt, pepper, and parsley.

140   GNOCCHI ALLA ROMANA
Prep: 20 minutes   Cook: 35 minutes   Chill: 2 hours   Serves: 4 to 6

This is an easily prepared gnocchi from Rome. It doesn't resemble a dumpling at all and can be prepared at least a day before baking.

1 quart milk
1 cup semolina flour or farina
¾ cup grated Parmesan cheese
2 teaspoons salt

2 egg yolks
1 stick (8 tablespoons) butter, melted
Freshly ground pepper

1. In a large saucepan, heat milk over medium heat; be careful not to let it boil over. Pour semolina flour into milk in a slow steady stream, stirring with a whisk as you pour. Continue to cook, whisking, until milk is absorbed and mixture becomes too thick to pour from spoon, 10 to 12 minutes. Remove from heat and quickly whisk in ½ cup cheese, the salt, and egg yolks.

2. Moisten a 17 x 11-inch baking sheet with 2 tablespoons water. Spread semolina mixture evenly over sheet in a layer ½ to ¾ inch thick. Cover with plastic wrap and refrigerate until firm, about 2 hours.

3. Preheat oven to 450°. Using a 1- to 1½-inch biscuit cutter, cut chilled mixture into circles. Using a spatula, transfer to a buttered 13 x 9-inch baking dish, overlapping circles of gnocchi slightly. Drizzle melted butter over top. Sprinkle with remaining ¼ cup Parmesan cheese.

4. Bake gnocchi until a light golden crust begins to form on top, 15 to 20 minutes. To serve, remove gnocchi carefully with a spatula. Pass a pepper mill on the side.

141 POTATO GNOCCHI
Prep: 20 minutes   Cook: 35 minutes   Serves: 6

Gnocchi are dumplings made with either potatoes, ricotta, spinach, cornmeal, or semolina. The texture varies from very light to doughy, depending on the ingredients. Potato dumplings are substantial in texture. Butter and Parmesan are the simplest accompaniments.

4 **pounds small baking
   potatoes**
2 **egg yolks**
1 **teaspoon salt**
2 **cups flour, or more as
   needed**

**Melted butter, grated
Parmesan cheese and
pepper; or bolognese or
marinara sauce; or pesto,
homemade (page 77) or
jarred**

1. Cook potatoes in a large pot of boiling salted water over medium heat 25 to 30 minutes, or until tender; drain. Peel potatoes and return to pot. Using a potato masher, mash potatoes over very low heat, letting them dry out as you mash them and making sure that no lumps remain.

2. In a large bowl, combine mashed potatoes, egg yolks, salt, and 1½ cups flour. Turn mixture onto a clean work surface dusted with ½ cup flour. Knead several minutes, kneading in flour as necessary, until a soft dough is formed. Divide dough into 4 pieces. Dust work surface with remaining 2 tablespoons flour, if needed. With your palms, roll dough into ¾-inch-thick ropes; then cut into 1-inch pieces.

3. In a large pot of boiling salted water, cook one-quarter of the gnocchi at a time. When gnocchi rise to surface of water, remove with a slotted spoon to a warm serving bowl. Toss with melted butter, Parmesan cheese, and black pepper, or serve gnocchi with bolognese or marinara sauce, or pesto.

142 MOLDED RICE WITH CHICKEN LIVER SAUCE

Prep: 30 minutes   Cook: 40 minutes   Serves: 6 to 8

Italian rice cooked in this manner can easily be shaped in a mold. All you have to do is pack it into a mold and immediately turn it out onto a serving plate. Since the chicken liver sauce takes less than 15 minutes, you can hold the rice in the buttered mold in a 250° oven while you prepare the sauce.

3 tablespoons butter	1 10-ounce package frozen
½ cup finely chopped onion	peas, defrosted
2½ cups Arborio rice	½ cup grated Parmesan cheese
8 cups hot Chicken Stock	½ teaspoon salt
(page 48) or 2 14½-ounce	¼ teaspoon pepper
cans broth mixed with	Chicken Liver Sauce (recipe
4 cups hot water	follows)

1. Preheat oven to 275°. Butter a 6 -cup mold and set aside. In a large heavy saucepan, melt 2 tablespoons butter over medium heat. Add onion and cook 2 to 3 minutes, or until softened. Add rice, and stir to coat evenly. Add 2 cups stock and stir until absorbed, 5 to 6 minutes. Continue to add as much stock as needed, 1 cup at a time, stirring, until rice is creamy and tender but still firm in center. Process should take 15 to 18 minutes from time you add first stock. Stir in peas about 2 minutes, until heated through. Stir in remaining 1 tablespoon butter, Parmesan cheese, salt, and pepper.

2. Pack rice into prepared mold, smoothing top with a spatula. Cover tightly with foil and keep warm while preparing sauce.

3. Invert mold onto a serving plate. Gently, grasping rim of plate with your fingers and holding mold on plate with your thumbs, shake mold to release rice onto plate. Spoon chicken liver sauce on molded rice.

143 CHICKEN LIVER SAUCE

Prep: 15 minutes   Cook: 13 to 15 minutes   Serves: 6

1 pound chicken livers	2 tablespoons minced fresh
1 tablespoon butter	parsley
1 tablespoon olive oil	½ cup dry white wine
½ cup finely chopped onion	2 tablespoons tomato paste
½ cup chopped prosciutto or	diluted in ¼ cup water
ham	¼ cup heavy cream
1 teaspoon chopped fresh	½ teaspoon salt
sage or ⅛ teaspoon dried	⅛ teaspoon pepper
2 teaspoons chopped fresh	
thyme or ¼ teaspoon	
dried	

1. Rinse chicken livers in a colander under cold running water. Pat dry with a paper towel. Cut away fat or any discolored meat. Cut livers into 1-inch pieces.

2. In a large frying pan, melt butter with oil over medium-high heat. Add onion and cook 2 to 3 minutes, or until softened. Add prosciutto or ham and chicken livers, and cook, turning several times, until livers begin to brown, 4 to 5 minutes. Stir in sage, thyme, and parsley.

3. Add wine to pan and cook 3 minutes, or until wine evaporates and livers are just barely pink inside. Stir in tomato paste and water mixture and cook 2 minutes. Stir in cream and cook until it becomes bubbly and slightly thickened, about 2 minutes longer. Season with salt and pepper.

144 QUICK POLENTA
Prep: 10 minutes   Cook: 5 minutes   Serves: 6

In parts of Italy this "cornmeal mush" is a staple that often replaces pasta. The traditional variety is usually stirred and cooked slowly for almost an hour, but there is now a processed polenta that takes only 5 minutes to cook.

1½ quarts water	3 tablespoons butter
2 teaspoons salt	½ teaspoon pepper
2 cups instant polenta	½ cup grated Parmesan cheese

1. In a large saucepan, bring water and salt to a boil over high heat. Stir in polenta in a slow steady stream. Reduce heat to medium and continue stirring 5 minutes, or until polenta is thickened to consistency of hot cereal.

2. Remove polenta from heat and stir in butter, pepper, and Parmesan cheese.

145 QUICK POLENTA WITH MAPLE SYRUP AND WALNUTS
Prep: 10 minutes   Cook: 10 minutes   Serves: 6

This special breakfast dish is a combination of my "Yankee Italian" background.

2 cups milk	1 cup coarsely chopped
2 cups water	walnuts
¾ teaspoon salt	3 tablespoons butter
1 cup instant polenta	6 tablespoons maple syrup

1. Preheat oven to 350°. Bring milk, water, and salt to a boil in a large saucepan over high heat. Stir polenta into boiling liquid in a slow steady stream. Reduce heat to medium and continue stirring 5 minutes, or until thickened to consistency of hot cereal.

2. Meanwhile, spread walnuts in a single layer on a baking sheet and bake, tossing once or twice, until nuts are lightly browned all over, 5 to 8 minutes.

3. Pour polenta into shallow soup bowls and serve with a lump of butter, toasted walnuts, and maple syrup.

146   QUICK POLENTA WITH SAUSAGE RAGU
Prep: 20 minutes   Cook: 35 minutes   Serves: 6 to 8

4 tablespoons butter
1½ quarts water
2 teaspoons salt
2 cups instant polenta
1 cup grated Parmesan cheese

2 cups jarred or frozen
   sausage ragù
8 ounces mozzarella cheese,
   cut into ¼-inch-thick
   slices

1. Preheat oven to 350°. Use 1 tablespoon butter to grease an 18 x 12-inch baking pan. In a large saucepan, bring water and salt to a boil over high heat. Stir polenta into boiling water in a slow steady stream. Reduce heat to medium and continue stirring 5 minutes, or until thickened to the consistency of hot cereal. Remove from heat and stir in remaining 3 tablespoons butter and ½ cup Parmesan cheese.

2. Spread half the hot polenta into buttered baking pan. Top with half the ragù. Sprinkle with ¼ cup Parmesan cheese and half the mozzarella. Spread on remaining polenta and ragù and top with remaining mozzarella and ¼ cup Parmesan. Bake until heated through and lightly golden, 20 to 25 minutes.

147   TRADITIONAL POLENTA
Prep: 10 minutes   Cook: 50 minutes   Serves: 6 to 8

Polenta is cornmeal that is coarsely milled. Methods for cooking it have been described as taking as long as 2 to 3 hours, perhaps because of the way it was milled. For the polenta available commercially to us, 45 minutes and some stirring is long enough. If that's too long for your elbow, make Quick Polenta below.

4 cups water
1½ teaspoons salt
1 cup cornmeal polenta
½ teaspoon pepper

4 tablespoons butter, cut in
   pieces
½ cup grated Parmesan cheese

1. Bring water and 1 teaspoon salt to a boil over high heat. Reduce heat to medium. Pour polenta into water in a slow steady stream, stirring with a wooden spoon as you pour. Reduce heat to medium-low and continue to cook, stirring occasionally, 15 minutes.

2. Reduce heat to low and cook, stirring frequently, for 30 minutes. When polenta is thickness of cooked cereal and grains are no longer gritty, stir in pepper, remaining ½ teaspoon salt, butter, and Parmesan cheese.

148   BROILED POLENTA WITH HERBS

Prep: 10 minutes   Cook: 15 minutes   Chill: 6 hours
Serves: 6 to 8

This firm polenta is excellent for serving with roasted meats, stews, and saucy Italian dishes.

1½ quarts water	1 teaspoon minced fresh sage
2 teaspoons salt	or ¼ teaspoon dried
2 cups instant polenta	1 teaspoon chopped fresh
3 tablespoons butter	rosemary or ¼ teaspoon
½ cup grated Parmesan cheese	dried
	1 teaspoon pepper

1. Oil or butter a 1½- or 2-quart loaf pan and set aside. In a large saucepan, bring water and salt to a boil over high heat. Stir polenta into boiling water in a slow steady stream. Reduce heat to medium and continue stirring 5 minutes, or until thickened to consistency of hot cereal. Remove from heat and stir in butter, Parmesan cheese, sage, rosemary, and pepper. Pour polenta into prepared loaf pan and smooth top with a spatula. Cook briefly, then cover with plastic wrap. Refrigerate until firm, about 6 hours.

2. Preheat broiler. Oil or butter a baking sheet that will fit under broiler. Remove plastic wrap from loaf pan and slip a knife around edges to free polenta. Unmold onto a cutting board, tapping sharply to release, if necessary.

3. Cut polenta into ¾-inch slices and arrange in a single layer on prepared baking sheet. Broil 3 to 4 inches from heat until polenta begins to form a golden crust, about 5 minutes. Turn polenta with a spatula and broil on second side until golden, about 4 to 5 minutes longer.

149 QUICK POLENTA WITH SAGE AND FONTINA

Prep: 10 minutes   Cook: 10 minutes   Serves: 6 to 8

This is a delicious substitute for a pasta course.

1½ quarts water
2 teaspoons salt
2 cups instant polenta
5 tablespoons butter
½ teaspoon pepper

½ cup grated Parmesan cheese
8 thin slices fontina cheese,
   about 6 ounces
16 fresh sage leaves or
   ½ teaspoon dried

1. Preheat oven to 425°. In a large saucepan, bring water and salt to a boil over high heat. Stir polenta into boiling water in a slow steady stream. Reduce heat to medium and continue stirring 5 minutes, or until thickened to consistency of hot cereal.

2. Remove polenta from heat and stir in 3 tablespoons butter, pepper, and Parmesan cheese. Use the remaining 2 tablespoons of butter to grease a large heatproof serving platter. Set aside.

3. Pour polenta onto buttered platter. Scatter sage over top. Cover with fontina cheese and bake 8 to 10 minutes, until cheese has melted and polenta is heated through.

Chapter 6

Chicken and Other Birds

Chicken may be an American favorite now, but it's been a star in Italy for centuries, often served as a special treat on Sundays. Italian chicken can be simply roasted on a spit or in the oven. It can be flavored with rosemary and garlic, stuffed with sausages, cut up and stewed, or sizzled with a zesty vinegar sauce. The white meat can be treated much like veal—pounded into thin scaloppine, sautéed quickly and served with a light sauce, such as in Chicken Scaloppine with Lemon and Capers—or it can be boned and stuffed with ham and cheese.

Just as in this country there are regional squabbles about the right way to prepare fried chicken, so the different regions of Italy battle it out about what makes a proper Chicken Cacciatore, or "hunter's stew." Does it have peppers? Should there be mushrooms? Is the wine red or white? Well, in fact, all the versions are very good, and since we don't have to be purists, we can enjoy them all, which is why I've included three different recipes.

Cornish game hens make a very good substitute for the baby chickens Italians are so fond of. Recipes here pair them with dried fruit, balsamic vinegar, and Italian sausages.

Turkey was one food that was introduced to Europe from the New World, but the Italians have been avid fans of the big bird ever since. Turkey cutlets and scaloppine, which mimic veal, are particularly versatile.

To top off this chapter, there are recipes for Quail Stuffed with Apples and Raisins in Marsala Wine, Quail Flambéed with Brandy, and Duck with Cherries and Chianti, three distinctly Italian showstoppers, as well as a recipe for Bollito Misto, the Italian equivalent of a New England boiled dinner, jazzed up with a zesty Salsa Verde, or green herb vinaigrette, which makes a great Sunday dinner for a large family.

150   CHICKEN SCALOPPINE WITH LEMON AND CAPERS

Prep: 10 minutes   Cook: 10 minutes   Serves: 2 to 4

Don't try to do a quick sauté like this for more than 4 people. It is too much to do at the last minute, and it should be eaten pronto!

4 skinless, boneless chicken breast halves, about 5 ounces each	⅓ cup Chicken Stock (page 48) or reduced-sodium canned broth
½ teaspoon salt	3 tablespoons lemon juice
⅛ teaspoon pepper	2 tablespoons capers, rinsed and drained
2 tablespoons butter	
1 tablespoon olive oil	2 tablespoons finely chopped fresh parsley
⅓ cup dry white wine	

1. Pound chicken to ¼-inch thickness between sheets of wax paper or plastic wrap. Season with salt and pepper.

2. In a large frying pan, melt butter with olive oil over medium heat. Add chicken and cook 2 minutes. Turn and cook 2 minutes longer, or until white throughout. Remove to a warmed platter. Cover loosely with foil to keep warm.

3. Pour wine into pan. Add stock and boil until reduced by half, about 2 minutes. Add lemon juice, capers, and parsley. Pour over chicken and serve.

151   CHICKEN SALTIMBOCCA STYLE

Prep: 15 minutes   Cook: 10 minutes   Serves: 4

8 skinless, boneless chicken breast halves, about 5 ounces each	16 fresh sage leaves
	4 tablespoons butter
8 thin slices of ham, preferably prosciutto, cut in half	½ cup dry white wine

1. Pound chicken to ¼-inch thickness between sheets of wax paper or plastic wrap. Cut each piece in half. You should have 16 pieces of chicken; place a piece of ham on each. Top with a sage leaf. Fold in half lengthwise; fasten with a toothpick.

2. In a large frying pan, melt 2 tablespoons butter over medium-high heat. Add half of chicken and cook 3 minutes. Turn and cook 2 minutes longer, or until white throughout. Remove to a warmed platter. Cover loosely with foil to keep warm. Repeat with remaining butter and chicken.

3. Pour wine into pan and boil until reduced by half, 1 to 2 minutes. Pour over chicken.

152 CHICKEN BREASTS WITH WALNUTS AND GORGONZOLA

Prep: 15 minutes   Cook: 10 minutes   Serves: 2 to 4

Serve with sautéed spinach or buttered fettuccine.

8 skinless, boneless chicken
   breast halves, about
   5 ounces each
¼ teaspoon salt
⅛ teaspoon pepper
2 tablespoons butter
1 tablespoon olive oil
½ cup Chicken Stock (page 48)
   or reduced-sodium
   canned broth

¼ cup heavy cream
¼ cup crumbled blue cheese,
   preferably gorgonzola
½ cup coarsely chopped
   walnuts
2 tablespoons chopped fresh
   basil or 1 teaspoon dried

1. Season chicken with salt and pepper. In a large frying pan, melt butter with olive oil over medium heat. Add chicken and cook 2 minutes. Turn and cook 2 to 3 minutes longer, or until chicken is white throughout but still juicy. Remove to a platter. Cover with foil to keep warm.

2. Add stock to pan. Boil over high heat 1 minute. Add cream and blue cheese. Cook, stirring, until cheese is melted and sauce is smooth. Remove from heat; pour sauce over chicken. Garnish with walnuts and basil.

153 CHICKEN ROLLANTINI WITH PESTO

Prep: 25 minutes   Cook: 30 minutes   Serves: 8

8 skinless boneless chicken
   breast halves, about
   5 ounces each
4 thin slices ham, preferably
   prosciutto, halved
8 ounces mozzarella, cut in
   2 x ½ x ½-inch sticks

¾ cup pesto, homemade (page
   77) or jarred
½ cup flour
2 eggs beaten with
   2 tablespoons water
2 cups dry bread crumbs
2 tablespoons butter
2 tablespoons olive oil

1. Preheat oven to 350°. Cut pocket in each chicken breast. Roll a piece of ham around each piece of mozzarella. Smear inside of chicken pocket with 1½ teaspoons pesto. Place ham and cheese roll in pocket and press together.

2. Dredge chicken in flour; shake off excess. Dip in egg; dredge in bread crumbs. In a large frying pan, melt 1 tablespoon butter with 1 tablespoon olive oil over medium-high heat. Add half the chicken and cook 3 to 4 minutes on each side, until lightly browned. Remove to a baking dish. Repeat with remaining butter, oil, and chicken.

3. Transfer chicken rollantini to oven and bake 20 minutes. Pass remaining pesto on the side.

154 CHICKEN BREASTS WITH ARTICHOKES, CREAM, AND TOMATOES

Prep: 10 minutes   Cook: 45 to 50 minutes   Serves: 6

This is an elegant dish from northern Italy, perfect for company.

6 chicken breast halves, bone in, about 3½ pounds
1½ teaspoons salt
½ teaspoon pepper
3 tablespoons olive oil
1 small onion, finely chopped
1 cup dry white wine
1 cup Chicken Stock (page 48) or reduced-sodium canned broth

1 14-ounce can Italian peeled tomatoes, drained and chopped
1 10-ounce package frozen artichoke hearts, thawed
1½ cups heavy cream
1 tablespoon chopped fresh basil or ½ teaspoon dried

1. Rinse chicken and pat dry. Season with ¾ teaspoon salt and ¼ teaspoon pepper. In a large frying pan, heat olive oil over medium-high heat. Add chicken and cook 3 to 4 minutes on each side, until lightly browned. Drain excess oil from skillet. Add onion, wine, and stock to pan. Cover and simmer for 25 minutes, or until chicken is fork tender.

2. Remove chicken from pan. Boil pan juices until reduced to ½ cup, 3 to 5 minutes. Add tomatoes and artichokes to pan. Cook 1 minute. Add cream and basil; simmer until liquid is reduced to 2 cups, 6 to 8 minutes. Season with remaining ¾ teaspoon salt and ¼ teaspoon pepper. Return chicken to pan and heat together for 5 minutes.

155 CHICKEN WITH SAGE AND PEAS

Prep: 10 minutes   Cook: 35 minutes   Serves: 4

Serve with polenta or rice.

4 chicken breast halves, bone in, about 2 pounds
¾ teaspoon salt
¼ teaspoon pepper
2 tablespoons olive oil
4 ounces pancetta or Canadian bacon, finely diced

1 medium onion, chopped
1 cup dry white wine
1 tablespoon minced fresh sage or ½ teaspoon dried
1 10-ounce package frozen peas, defrosted

1. Rinse chicken and pat dry. Season lightly with salt and pepper. In a Dutch oven, heat olive oil over medium-high heat. Add pancetta and onion and cook 2 minutes, or until onion is softened. Add chicken breasts and cook 3 to 4 minutes on each side, until lightly browned.

2. Add wine and sage. Cover pan, reduce heat to low, and simmer 25 minutes, or until chicken is fork tender. Add peas and cook 5 minutes longer. Season with additional pepper and salt, if needed.

156 CHICKEN CACCIATORE
Prep: 10 minutes   Cook: 40 to 45 minutes   Serves: 4 to 6

This hunter-style chicken is from a southern Italian hunter. No effort, great reward.

6 **chicken drumsticks, about 1½ pounds**
6 **chicken thighs, about 1½ pounds**
1 **teaspoon salt**
¼ **teaspoon pepper**
2 **tablespoons olive oil**
1 **large onion, finely chopped**

3 **garlic cloves, minced**
1 **cup dry red wine**
1 **14-ounce can Italian peeled tomatoes, drained and chopped**
1 **teaspoon dried oregano**
2 **tablespoons finely chopped fresh parsley**

1. Rinse chicken and pat dry. Season with salt and pepper. In a nonreactive large frying pan or flameproof casserole, heat olive oil over medium-high heat. Add chicken, in batches if necessary, and cook, turning once, 5 minutes, or until lightly browned on all sides.

2. Add onion to pan and cook for 2 minutes, or until softened. Add garlic and cook 30 seconds. Add wine, tomatoes, and oregano. Bring to a boil, reduce heat to medium-low, cover, and simmer 30 minutes. Season with additional salt and pepper. Sprinkle with parsley just before serving.

157 CHICKEN WITH OLIVES
Prep: 15 minutes   Cook: 50 minutes   Serves: 6

Green olives stuffed with almonds or pickled onions can change this dish completely, as can ripe olives.

12 **assorted pieces of chicken, about 5 pounds**
1 **teaspoon salt**
¼ **teaspoon pepper**
2 **tablespoons olive oil**
1 **large onion, chopped**
3 **garlic cloves, chopped**
1 **cup dry red wine**

1 **14-ounce can Italian peeled tomatoes, drained and chopped**
2 **cups water**
1 **teaspoon dried rosemary**
18 **green olives stuffed with pimiento**

1. Rinse chicken and pat dry. Season with salt and pepper. In a large flameproof casserole, heat olive oil over medium-high heat. Add chicken in batches and cook, turning, 5 minutes, or until lightly browned on all sides. Pour off all but 1 tablespoon oil.

2. Add onion and cook 2 minutes, or until softened. Return all chicken to pan, along with garlic, wine, tomatoes, water, and rosemary. Bring to a boil, reduce heat to low, cover, and simmer 20 minutes. Add olives to pan, cover, and simmer 10 minutes. Remove chicken; cover with foil to keep warm.

3. Boil sauce in pan over medium-high heat until reduced to about 3 cups. Season with additional salt and pepper. Pour sauce over chicken and serve.

158   CHICKEN AND HOT ITALIAN SAUSAGES
Prep: 15 minutes   Cook: 1 hour 5 minutes   Serves: 4 to 6

Serve with crusty bread or garlic croutons.

1 bunch Swiss chard, about 12 ounces	12 small red potatoes, peeled
6 large chicken thighs, about 1½ pounds	6 medium carrots, peeled and halved
3 tablespoons olive oil	2 cups water
6 links hot Italian sausage, about 1½ pounds	1 14-ounce can Italian peeled tomatoes, drained and chopped
1 large onion, chopped	Salt and pepper to taste

1. In a large pot of boiling salted water, cook Swiss chard 8 minutes, or until tender; drain. Coarsely chop stems and leaves. Set aside.

2. Rinse chicken and pat dry. In a large flameproof casserole, heat 2 tablespoons olive oil over medium-high heat. Add thighs and cook, turning, 5 minutes, or until lightly browned on all sides. Remove thighs from pan.

3. Prick sausages with a fork. Add to pan and cook over medium heat, turning, for 5 minutes, or until lightly browned; remove from pan. Discard grease and wipe out pan.

4. Heat remaining 1 tablespoon olive oil in casserole over medium heat. Add onion and cook until soft, 3 to 5 minutes. Add chard, chicken, sausages, potatoes, and carrots. Pour in water and tomatoes. Bring to boil, reduce heat to low, cover, and simmer over medium-low heat 45 minutes. Season with salt and pepper. Serve in soup plates.

159   CHICKEN MARSALA
Prep: 10 minutes   Cook: 40 to 45 minutes   Serves: 2 to 4

Use dry sherry if you can't find dry Marsala, but don't use sweet Marsala except in desserts.

4 chicken drumsticks, about 1 pound	2 tablespoons olive oil
4 chicken thighs, about 1 pound	1 small onion, chopped
1 teaspoon salt	¼ cup dry Marsala
¼ teaspoon pepper	1 cup Chicken Stock (see page 48) or reduced-sodium canned broth
2 tablespoons butter	

1. Rinse chicken and pat dry. Season with salt and pepper. In a large frying pan, melt butter with oil over medium heat. Add chicken, in batches if necessary, and cook 5 minutes, turning, until lightly browned on all sides. Remove chicken and set aside. Drain off almost all fat.

2. Add onion to pan and cook over medium heat 2 minutes, or until softened. Return chicken to pan, along with Marsala and stock. Bring to a boil, reduce heat to low, cover, and simmer 25 to 30 minutes, or until chicken is fork tender. Season with additional salt and pepper.

160 ROASTED CHICKEN
Prep: 10 minutes   Cook: 45 to 55 minutes   Serves: 2

Roast chicken is one of the most typical dishes to follow a Sunday pasta. In my grandmother's home, Sunday roast chicken was simple, served with roast potatoes followed by a salad. Broiling chickens, which range from 2½ to 4 pounds, are perfect for roasting. I like to cook two that size instead of a big 5- to 7-pounder.

1 **whole chicken, 2½ to**	½ **celery rib**
3½ pounds	1 **sprig of fresh thyme or**
1 **teaspoon salt**	½ **teaspoon dried**
¼ **teaspoon pepper**	2 **teaspoons olive oil**
½ **small onion**	

1. Preheat oven to 425°. Rinse chicken and pat dry inside and out. Rub cavity with salt and pepper. Put onion, celery, and thyme in cavity. Cross bone ends of legs and tie together. Rub skin with olive oil.

2. Place chicken in a small roasting pan. Roast 45 to 55 minutes, or until juices run clear when meatiest part of thigh is pierced.

161 ROAST CHICKEN STUFFED WITH FENNEL SAUSAGE
Prep: 15 minutes   Cook: 1½ to 1¾ hours   Serves: 6

If you can't find fennel sausage, use sweet Italian sausage mixed with 1 teaspoon fennel seeds.

4 **slices Italian bread, trimmed**	½ **teaspoon dried oregano**
of crust	½ **cup finely diced mozzarella**
¼ **cup milk**	**cheese**
8 **ounces fennel sausage, or**	1 **whole roasting chicken,**
other Italian-style	**4½ to 5 pounds**
sausage, casings removed	1 **tablespoon olive oil**
¼ **cup chopped onion**	

1. In a small bowl, soak bread in milk 5 minutes. Squeeze bread to remove excess liquid.

2. Crumble sausage meat into a small frying pan. Cook, stirring, over medium heat with 2 tablespoons water 2 minutes, or until no longer pink. Add onion, oregano, and bread; blend well. Remove from heat and set aside.

3. Preheat oven to 425°. Rinse chicken and pat dry inside and out. Add mozzarella cheese to sausage mixture. Spoon stuffing into cavity of chicken. Cross bone ends of legs and tie together with string. Rub skin with olive oil.

4. Place chicken in a roasting pan just big enough to fit. Roast 15 minutes. Turn heat down to 375° and roast, basting several times with any pan juices, 1¼ to 1½ hours longer, or until juices run clear. Allow chicken to rest 10 minutes before carving.

162   CHICKEN CACCIATORE WITH SWEET PEPPERS

Prep: 10 minutes   Cook: 40 to 45 minutes   Serves: 4 to 6

This is just as good the day after.

6   chicken legs, about
        1½ pounds
6   chicken thighs, about
        1½ pounds
1   teaspoon salt
¼   teaspoon pepper
3   tablespoons olive oil
1   large onion, finely chopped
3   garlic cloves, chopped
1   14-ounce can Italian peeled
        tomatoes, drained and
        chopped

1   cup water
1   large green bell pepper, cut
        into 1-inch squares
1   large red bell pepper, cut
        into 1-inch squares
2   teaspoons chopped fresh
        oregano or ½ teaspoon
        dried
2   tablespoons minced fresh
        parsley

1. Rinse chicken and pat dry. Season with salt and pepper. In a Dutch oven, heat 1½ tablespoons olive oil over medium-high heat. Add chicken, in batches if necessary, and cook, turning, 5 minutes, or until lightly browned on all sides. Remove chicken and set aside. Pour off fat.

2. Add remaining 1½ tablespoons olive oil to Dutch oven. Add onion and cook over medium heat 3 minutes, or until softened. Add garlic and cook 1 minute longer. Return chicken to pan. Add tomatoes, water, bell peppers, oregano, and parsley. Bring to a boil, reduce heat to low, cover, and simmer 25 to 30 minutes, or until chicken is fork tender. Season sauce with additional salt and pepper, if needed.

163   CHICKEN WITH VINEGAR SAUCE

Prep: 10 minutes   Cook: 40 minutes   Serves: 2 to 4

This has become my favorite chicken. Balsamic vinegar is well worth the search it may take to find it. Serve with simple roasted potatoes.

1   chicken, 2½ to 3 pounds,
        split in half
1   teaspoon salt
¼   teaspoon pepper
2   tablespoons olive oil
½   cup Chicken Stock (page 48)
        or reduced-sodium
        canned broth

½   cup dry white wine
½   cup balsamic vinegar or
        ½ cup red wine vinegar
        with a pinch of sugar
2   tablespoons cold butter

1. Rinse chicken and pat dry. Season with salt and pepper. In a nonreactive large frying pan, heat olive oil over medium heat. Add chicken and cook, turning once, 8 to 10 minutes, or until browned on all sides.

2. Add stock to pan. Bring to a boil, then reduce heat to low, 20 to 25 minutes, or until chicken is white throughout but still juicy. Remove chicken from pan.

3. Add wine and vinegar to pan. Bring to a boil over high heat, scraping up brown bits from bottom of pan. Boil until sauce is reduced to about ½ cup, 2 to 3 minutes. Remove from heat and swirl in butter until melted and smooth. Season with additional salt and pepper. Pour over chicken and serve.

164   CHICKEN CACCIATORE WITH MUSHROOMS

Prep: 15 minutes   Cook: 30 to 35 minutes   Serves: 4

Use several kinds of mushrooms if you can.

8 assorted pieces of chicken, 3 to 4 pounds
1 teaspoon salt
¼ teaspoon pepper
¼ cup flour
2 tablespoons olive oil
1 cup dry white wine
1 cup Chicken Stock (page 48) or reduced-sodium canned broth

2 tablespoons butter
1 small onion, finely chopped
8 ounces pancetta or Canadian bacon, diced
1 pound fresh mushrooms, sliced
1 teaspoon dried thyme

1. Rinse chicken and pat dry. Season with salt and pepper. Dust with flour. In a large frying pan over medium-high heat, heat olive oil. Add chicken, in batches if necessary, and cook, turning, 5 minutes, or until lightly browned on all sides. Drain off oil. Return all chicken to pan. Add white wine and ½ cup stock. Cover and simmer 25 minutes, or until chicken is fork tender.

2. Meanwhile, in another large frying pan, melt butter over medium heat. Add onion and pancetta or Canadian bacon and cook, stirring, about 3 minutes, or until onion is softened. Add mushrooms and cook 3 minutes. Add remaining ½ cup stock and thyme; cook uncovered 5 minutes.

3. When chicken has cooked 25 minutes, add mushrooms and any juices to pan. Simmer 2 minutes to blend flavors. Season with additional salt and pepper.

165 LEMON AND ROSEMARY ROAST CHICKEN

Prep: 15 minutes   Cook: 45 to 55 minutes   Serves: 2

Feel free to substitute thyme, tarragon, or any favorite herb for the rosemary in this recipe. For those who love crisp skin, this is a great one.

1 whole chicken, 2½ to 3½ pounds	1 tablespoon olive oil
½ lemon	1 teaspoon salt
1 tablespoon chopped fresh rosemary or ½ teaspoon dried	¼ teaspoon pepper
½ small onion	

1. Preheat oven to 425°. Rinse chicken and pat dry inside and out. Cut lemon into 8 thin slices, discarding end; remove seeds. Scatter a few rosemary leaves over each lemon slice.

2. With cavity of chicken toward you, slip your fingers between skin and meat of bird, gently separating up through thighs and breast without tearing the skin. Slip lemon slices under skin. Put onion in cavity. Cross bone ends of legs and tie together. Rub skin with olive oil, salt, and pepper.

3. Place chicken in a small roasting pan. Roast 45 to 55 minutes, or until juices run clear when meatiest part of thigh is pierced.

166 CORNISH GAME HENS WITH FIGS AND PEARS

Prep: 20 minutes   Cook: 50 minutes   Serves: 4

This is good summer food, served cold with a rice salad.

4 dried figs	¾ teaspoon salt
½ cup port wine	¼ teaspoon pepper
1 tablespoon fresh rosemary or ½ teaspoon dried	2 tablespoons olive oil
4 Cornish game hens, about 1 pound each	4 dried pears or apricots

1. Preheat oven to 375°. Place figs in a small heatproof bowl. Pour enough boiling water over figs to cover. Let stand 2 minutes; drain. Return figs to bowl. Add port and rosemary; let steep 10 minutes.

2. Rinse hens and pat dry inside and out. Rub inside and out with salt, pepper, and olive oil. Place 1 pear and 1 fig into cavity of each hen, along with about 1 tablespoon port. Cross bone ends of legs and tie together.

3. Place birds in a small roasting pan. Roast 15 minutes. Turn heat down to 350° and roast 35 minutes longer, or until juices run clear when meatiest part of thigh is pierced. Serve with fruit from cavity of hens.

167 CORNISH GAME HENS WITH BALSAMIC ONIONS

Prep: 10 minutes   Cook: 1½ hours   Serves: 4

2 medium red onions,
   unpeeled
½ cup balsamic or red wine
   vinegar

4 Cornish game hens, about
   1 pound each
¾ teaspoon salt
¼ teaspoon pepper
2 tablespoons olive oil

1. Preheat oven to 350°. Cut onions in half from stem to root end. Pour vinegar into nonreactive casserole just big enough to hold onions cut side down. Put onions in casserole. Cover with foil and bake 40 minutes, or until onions are tender but still hold their shape.

2. Meanwhile, rinse game hens and pat dry inside and out. Season inside and out with salt, pepper, and olive oil. Let stand at room temperature 30 minutes.

3. Remove onions from oven. Increase oven temperature to 475°. As soon as onions are cool enough to handle, remove skin. Cut each piece in half so onions are quartered lengthwise.

4. Stuff each bird with a piece of onion. Cross bone ends of legs and tie together. Place birds in a roasting pan. Roast 15 minutes. Turn heat down to 350° and roast 30 minutes longer, until juices run clear when meatiest part of thigh is pierced. Serve remaining onion pieces as a room-temperature garnish.

168 CORNISH GAME HENS WITH SAUSAGES

Prep: 10 minutes   Cook: 1 hour 5 minutes   Serves: 4

4 links Italian sausage, about
   1 pound
4 Cornish game hens, about
   1 pound each

2 tablespoons olive oil

1. Preheat oven to 475°. Cut sausage links into 1-inch pieces. In a large frying pan, cook sausages over medium heat 3 minutes, or until partially cooked. Drain and let cool.

2. Rinse hens and pat dry inside and out. Stuff cavities with sausages. Cross bone ends of legs and tie together. Rub skin with olive oil.

3. Place birds in a small roasting pan. Roast 15 minutes. Turn heat down to 350° and roast 45 minutes longer, or until juices run clear when meatiest part of thigh is pierced.

169 GRILLED TURKEY CUTLETS WITH ITALIAN GREEN HERB SAUCE

Prep: 10 minutes   Cook: 5 to 7 minutes   Serves: 6

Do this easy recipe on your barbecue with lean, low-calorie sliced turkey breast. Turkeys were brought to Europe in the sixteenth century. The Italians love turkey, especially in the northern regions, where it is often cooked in the style of veal and chicken.

6 turkey breast cutlets, 4 to
    5 ounces each
2 tablespoons olive oil
   Salt and pepper to taste
	Lemon wedges
	Italian Green Herb Sauce
	   (recipe follows)

Prepare a medium-hot fire in a charcoal or gas grill, or preheat a broiler. Brush slices of turkey with olive oil; season with salt and pepper. Grill or broil 4 minutes on one side and 3 minutes on other, or until turkey is white throughout and tender. Serve with wedges of lemon to squeeze over meat and pass herb sauce on the side.

ITALIAN GREEN HERB SAUCE
Makes about 2 cups

¼ cup capers, rinsed, drained,
    and chopped
¼ cup pickled cocktail onions,
    finely chopped
1 cup chopped fresh parsley
2 tablespoons chopped fresh
    basil or 1 teaspoon dried
	¼ cup red wine vinegar
	1 cup extra-virgin olive oil
	½ teaspoon salt
	¼ teaspoon freshly ground
	    pepper

Combine all ingredients in a small bowl. Can be made way ahead of time.

170 TURKEY SCALOPPINE WITH BACON

Prep: 10 minutes   Cook: 15 minutes   Serves: 6

Pancetta is the same cut as American bacon, but the meat is not smoked. It is rolled, often with aromatic spices.

6 turkey breast cutlets, 4 to
    5 ounces each
   Salt and pepper to taste
6 slices pancetta or bacon
	3 tablespoons olive oil
	6 ounces mozzarella cheese,
	    sliced
	2 cups tomato sauce

1. Preheat oven to 375°. Pound turkey cutlets to ¼-inch thickness between sheets of wax paper or plastic wrap. Season with salt and pepper.

2. In a large frying pan, cook bacon or pancetta over medium heat 3 to 4 minutes, or until almost crisp; drain on paper towels. Pour off fat. Add olive oil to pan. Add turkey cutlets and cook over medium heat, turning once, 2 to 3 minutes per side, until lightly browned.

3. Arrange cutlets in a single layer on a large baking sheet. Top with cheese, then bacon. Bake 10 minutes, or until cheese melts. Serve with warmed tomato sauce.

171 DUCK WITH CHERRIES AND CHIANTI

Prep: 30 minutes   Cook: 1 hour 50 minutes   Serves: 2 to 4

The Italians are very fond of cherries, especially in the north. Cherries have such a short growing season, when they are available use them as much as possible. You can use canned cherries.

1 duck, 4½ to 5 pounds, neck and giblets reserved	4 cups water
1 teaspoon salt	1 celery rib, cut in half
¼ teaspoon pepper	1 cup Chianti wine
1 tablespoon olive oil	1 pound fresh sweet cherries, pitted, or 1 16-ounce can Bing cherries, drained
2 small onions, cut in half	
3 garlic cloves	

1. Preheat oven to 450°. Rinse duck and pat dry inside and out. Remove any excess fat from cavity of duck; discard. Rub inside of duck with salt, pepper, and olive oil. Prick skin in about 10 places with a needle. Place one halved onion and garlic cloves in cavity.

2. Meanwhile, put duck neck and giblets in a medium saucepan. Add water along with one halved onion and the celery. Bring to a boil, reduce heat to low, and simmer uncovered 1 hour. Boil if necessary to reduce liquid to 1 cup; strain. Set duck stock aside.

3. Place duck in a roasting pan and roast for 15 minutes. Reduce oven temperature to 350° and roast 1½ hours longer, or until juices run clear when thickest part of thigh is pierced.

4. Remove duck to a carving board. Drain off grease from pan. Place roasting pan over moderate heat. Add wine and bring to a boil, scraping up browned bits from bottom of pan. Add 1 cup duck stock to pan; cook 1 minute. Add cherries and heat through. Season with additional salt and pepper. Carve duck and serve with cherry sauce.

172   BOLLITO MISTO

Prep: 30 minutes   Cook: 4¼ hours   Serves: 10 to 12

Literally, this means "mixed boil," and it is not too far from a New England boiled dinner or the French *pot au feu*. The meats are sliced and served on a platter along with the vegetables and a little broth. Side dishes of *salsa verde* (literally "green sauce," an herbed vinaigrette), mustard, and pickles are offered as condiments along with the jewellike tiny fruits preserved in mustard syrup called *mostarda di Cremora*, which can be found in many specialty food shops. *Bollito misto* comes from Piedmont in the very northern part of Italy, and hardy vegetables such as turnips and cabbage are often included. A dinner of *bollito misto* is a grand event. The dish takes a long time, but can be made ahead. It can be made as simple or elaborate as you like.

3 pounds beef brisket	4 pounds cotechino or other
4 lamb tongues (optional)	Italian-style sausage
1 large onion, quartered	1 whole chicken, 5 to
2 large carrots, each cut in	6 pounds, rinsed with
half, plus 6 medium	cold water and patted dry
carrots, peeled but left	12 medium turnips, peeled and
whole	halved
2 ribs celery, each cut in half	1 medium cabbage, cored and
2 bay leaves	quartered
5 sprigs of fresh thyme or	12 medium boiling potatoes,
1½ teaspoons dried	peeled and halved
1 teaspoon salt	Salsa Verde (recipe follows)
¼ teaspoon pepper	

1. In a large pot, cover beef and tongues with 4 inches water. Add onion, 2 halved carrots, celery, bay leaves, thyme, salt, and pepper. Cover and cook over high heat until liquid comes to a boil, skimming off foam. Immediately reduce heat to low and continue cooking 2½ hours.

2. Add sausage and chicken to pan; add more hot water if needed to cover. Cover pan and simmer until all meats are tender, about 1 hour.

3. Add turnips, potatoes, whole carrots, and cabbage and cook for an additional 30 to 35 minutes, or until vegetables and meats test tender when pricked with a fork.

4. Remove lamb tongues to a carving board and peel by slipping a small sharp knife between skin and meat and removing outer skin. Carve into ¼-inch slices and place on a warmed large rimmed platter; cover with foil to keep warm. Remove brisket from liquid and carve across grain into ¼-inch slices. Place on platter with tongue and again cover with foil. Cut sausages diagonally into 1-inch pieces and arrange on platter. Remove chicken to carving board and cut into serving pieces. Add to platter. Arrange vegetables on same platter with meats and spoon a bit of broth over all. Serve additional broth at the table. Pass Salsa Verde on the side.

SALSA VERDE
Makes about 2 cups

1 small baking potato, about 6 ounces
1½ cups coarsely chopped fresh parsley
4 to 6 flat anchovy fillets, drained

6 small pickled onions or cornichons
2 garlic cloves, minced
2 tablespoons minced onion
¾ cup extra-virgin olive oil
2 tablespoons white wine vinegar

1. In a medium saucepan of boiling salted water, cook potato until tender, about 25 minutes. Drain and rinse under cold running water to cool. Peel off skin and coarsely chop potato.

2. In a food processor or blender, process parsley, anchovy, pickled onions, potato, garlic, and onion until it becomes a soft paste. With machine running, slowly pour olive oil through feed tube until mixture resembles mayonnaise. Stir in vinegar. Serve at room temperature.

173   QUAIL FLAMBEED WITH BRANDY
Prep: 10 minutes   Cook: 15 minutes   Serves: 6

Italians love game birds, and they eat many varieties. Quail, which have rich, succulent dark meat, are more available now and are very easy to cook.

3 to 4 tablespoons olive oil
2 garlic cloves
6 slices of French bread, cut 1 inch thick
6 quail, split in half

¾ teaspoon salt
¼ teaspoon pepper
2 tablespoons butter
½ cup brandy, warmed

1. In a large frying pan, heat 3 tablespoons olive oil. Add garlic and cook 3 to 4 minutes, or until golden brown. Remove and discard garlic. Using more oil if needed, add bread and cook, turning, until golden brown, 2 to 3 minutes. Remove garlic toasts from pan. Set pan aside.

2. Rinse quail and pat dry. Rub skin with salt and pepper. Add remaining olive oil and butter to any remaining garlic oil in frying pan. Add quail, skin side down, and cook over medium-high heat until browned, about 4 minutes. Turn over and cook 3 minutes, or until done.

3. Reduce heat to medium. Add brandy and carefully ignite with a match. As soon as it flames, spoon over quail, shaking pan until flames subside. Place quail on garlic toasts and pour brandy drippings over. Fingers are best for eating this one.

174   QUAIL STUFFED WITH APPLES AND RAISINS IN MARSALA WINE

Prep: 10 minutes   Marinate: 20 minutes   Cook: 25 minutes
Serves: 3

These little birds are delicious cold and would make an elegant picnic.

3 tablespoons golden raisins
3 tablespoons dry Marsala or
  sherry
2 green apples, such as
  Granny Smith

6 quail
2 tablespoons olive oil
¾ teaspoon salt
¼ teaspoon pepper

1. Steep raisins in Marsala for 20 minutes. Meanwhile, peel and core apples. Cut into 6 wedges each.

2. Preheat oven to 425°. Rinse quail and pat dry inside and out. Rub skin with olive oil, salt, and pepper. Stuff cavities with apples and raisins. Cross bone ends of legs and tie together. In a roasting pan just large enough to hold quail, roast birds in oven 25 minutes, or until juices run clear when thickest part of thigh is pierced. Serve hot or cold.

Chapter 7

Seafood Italian Style

If you look at a map of Italy, you'll see that it forms a large boot that kicks out into the Mediterranean Sea. In fact, more than three quarters of the country is surrounded by water, so it's not surprising that Italian cuisine boasts a wealth of ways to cook fish and shellfish.

This chapter explains how to cook everything from Sole Oreganata to Lobster Fra Diavolo with that particular flair Italian cooking lends. While I've specified the fish that is ideal for each recipe, know that many can be used interchangeably. If your fish market does not carry fresh tuna, swordfish will probably work just as well, since both are rich, deep-sea fish. Likewise, some of the more delicate white-fleshed fish, such as sole, perch, and trout, substitute well for each other.

Shellfish preparations, from Shrimp Scampi to Clams and Mussels in Fennel Sauce, come from Italy, while Cioppino, the classic seafood stew, was actually developed by the Italian fishing community around the San Francisco Bay area. However, it has become so much a part of Italian menus, and it is so good, I have included my favorite recipes for it here.

175 SWORDFISH WITH ORANGE-BASIL BUTTER

Prep: 10 minutes   Marinate: 1 hour   Cook: 8 to 10 minutes
Serves: 4

2 tablespoons extra-virgin
   olive oil
¾ cup plus 2 tablespoons
   orange juice
¼ teaspoon pepper
¼ cup chopped fresh basil or
   1 tablespoon dried

4 swordfish steaks, cut ¾ inch
   thick, 6 to 8 ounces each
¼ teaspoon salt
1 stick (8 tablespoons) butter,
   softened
   Grated zest of 1 orange

1. Combine oil, ¾ cup orange juice, pepper, and one fourth of basil. Brush each side of fish with mixture. Place on plate, cover with plastic wrap, and refrigerate 1 hour.

2. Preheat broiler. Season fish with salt. Broil 3 to 4 inches from heat, turning once, 8 to 10 minutes, or until lightly browned outside and just opaque inside.

3. In small bowl, beat butter with an electric mixer until soft. Add remaining basil, orange zest, and 2 tablespoons orange juice. Beat just to combine. Serve hot fish with cold butter.

176 NEAPOLITAN SWORDFISH IN MARINARA SAUCE

Prep: 10 minutes   Cook: 30 to 35 minutes   Serves: 4

2 tablespoons extra-virgin
   olive oil
2 tablespoons chopped onion
1 garlic clove, minced
1 cup soft bread crumbs
¼ cup grated Romano cheese
1 tablespoon chopped fresh
   oregano or 1 teaspoon
   dried

½ teaspoon salt
¼ teaspoon pepper
4 pieces swordfish, cut ½ inch
   thick, 4 to 5 ounces each
2 cups marinara sauce,
   homemade (page 131) or
   jarred

1. Preheat oven to 350°. In small frying pan, heat olive oil over medium heat. Add onion and garlic and cook 2 to 3 minutes, or until onion is softened. Remove from heat and stir in bread crumbs, Romano cheese, oregano, salt, and pepper.

2. Place fish pieces on a flat work surface. Spread surface of each with one fourth of bread mixture and roll up jelly-roll fashion. Fasten with toothpicks. Place fish in a single layer in an oiled glass baking dish. Pour marinara sauce around rolls and cover with foil. Bake until fish is cooked through, 25 to 30 minutes.

177 BAKED SWORDFISH WITH HOT TOMATO, ANCHOVY, AND CAPER SAUCE

Prep: 15 minutes   Cook: 25 to 30 minutes   Serves: 4

- 2 tablespoons extra-virgin olive oil
- 4 flat anchovy fillets
- ¼ teaspoon hot pepper flakes
- 2 garlic cloves, minced
- 1 14-ounce can Italian peeled tomatoes, drained and chopped

- 1 cup water
- 2 tablespoons capers, rinsed and drained
- 2 tablespoons minced fresh parsley
- 4 swordfish steaks, cut ½ inch thick, about 7 ounces each

1. Preheat oven to 375°. In a large frying pan over medium heat, heat olive oil. Add anchovies, hot pepper flakes, and garlic and mash together with back of a wooden spoon until anchovies dissolve in oil, 2 to 3 minutes. Stir in tomatoes and water and bring to a boil. Cook uncovered until sauce is reduced to a thick puree, 6 to 8 minutes. Remove from heat and stir in capers and parsley.

2. Spread one third of sauce over bottom of a 13 x 11-inch baking pan. Place swordfish on sauce and spoon remaining sauce over top. Cover with foil and bake 15 to 18 minutes, or until fish is opaque throughout but juicy when tested with a fork.

178 SICILIAN STUFFED SWORDFISH

Prep: 10 minutes   Cook: 30 to 35 minutes   Serves: 4

- 2 tablespoons extra-virgin olive oil
- 2 tablespoons chopped onion
- 1 cup soft bread crumbs
- ¼ cup finely chopped prosciutto
- 1 tablespoon currants or raisins

- 1 tablespoon chopped fresh mint or 1 teaspoon dried
- ½ teaspoon salt
- ¼ teaspoon pepper
- 4 pieces swordfish, cut ¼ inch thick, 4 to 5 ounces each
- Lemon wedges

1. Preheat oven to 350°. In small frying pan, heat oil over medium heat. Add onion and cook 2 to 3 minutes, or until softened. Remove from heat and stir in bread crumbs, prosciutto, currants, mint, salt, and pepper.

2. Place fish pieces on a flat work surface. Spread surface of each with one fourth of bread mixture and roll up jelly-roll fashion. Fasten with toothpicks. Place fish in a single layer in an oiled glass baking dish. Cover with foil and bake until fish is cooked through, 25 to 30 minutes. Serve with lemon wedges.

179 GRILLED FRESH TUNA WITH COLD TOMATO-CAPER SAUCE

Prep: 20 minutes   Cook: 10 minutes   Serves: 4

The tuna catch is a grand event in Sicily, and this popular fish is cooked in any number of ways. This is one of my favorite sauces.

3 large ripe tomatoes, about 1½ pounds
3 tablespoons capers, rinsed and drained
1 garlic clove, minced
1 tablespoon chopped fresh oregano or 1 teaspoon dried

2 tablespoons minced parsley
3 tablespoons extra-virgin olive oil
¾ teaspoon salt
½ teaspoon pepper
4 tuna steaks, cut ¾ inch thick, 6 to 8 ounces each

1. Prepare a hot fire in a charcoal or gas grill, or preheat a broiler.

2. Cut ½ inch top from the top of each tomato and gently squeeze to extract seeds and juice. Chop tomatoes coarsely and place in a medium bowl. Stir in capers, garlic, oregano, parsley, and 2 tablespoons of the olive oil. Season with ½ teaspoon salt and ¼ teaspoon pepper. Set tomato-caper sauce aside.

3. Brush fish with remaining 1 tablespoon olive oil and season with remaining ¼ teaspoon each salt and pepper. Place fish on an oiled grill set 4 to 6 inches from coals. Grill tuna, turning once, until opaque throughout but still moist inside, about 8 to 10 minutes. Top each tuna steak with tomato-caper sauce.

180 GRILLED FRESH TUNA WITH HERBS

Prep: 10 minutes   Cook: 8 to 10 minutes   Serves: 4

½ cup extra-virgin olive oil
1 tablespoon chopped fresh thyme or ½ teaspoon dried
2 teaspoons chopped fresh sage or ¼ teaspoon dried
1 tablespoon minced fresh parsley

1 tablespoon chopped fresh rosemary or ½ teaspoon dried
½ teaspoon salt
¼ teaspoon pepper
4 tuna steaks, cut ¾ inch thick, 6 to 8 ounces each
Lemon wedges

1. Prepare a hot fire in a charcoal or gas grill, or preheat a broiler.

2. In a small bowl, combine olive oil, thyme, sage, parsley, rosemary, salt, and pepper. Brush tuna on both sides with herb oil.

3. Place fish on an oiled grill rack set 4 to 6 inches from coals. Grill, turning once, 8 to 10 minutes, or until opaque throughout but still moist inside. Serve fish with any remaining herb oil and lemon wedges.

181 TUNA BAKED WITH ONIONS AND OLIVES
Prep: 10 minutes   Cook: 30 to 35 minutes   Serves: 4

The flavors of this dish are well worth the effort of removing the olive pits, which you can do days ahead of time.

3 tablespoons extra-virgin olive oil	1 teaspoon dried oregano
2 large onions, thinly sliced	½ teaspoon salt
2 garlic cloves, minced	¼ teaspoon pepper
1 pound oil-cured black olives, loose or jarred, pitted	6 tuna steaks, cut ¾ inch thick, 6 to 8 ounces each
2 tablespoons red wine vinegar	2 teaspoons minced fresh parsley

1. Preheat oven to 350°. In a nonreactive medium frying pan, heat 2 table-spoons olive oil over medium heat. Add onion and garlic and cook, stirring occasionally, 10 to 12 minutes, or until onions are soft but not browned. Add olives, vinegar, oregano, salt, and pepper. Cook, stirring, 2 minutes.

2. Brush a 13 x 9-inch baking dish with remaining 1 tablespoon olive oil and place tuna in dish. Spoon sauce over tuna. Cover with foil and bake 15 to 20 minutes, or until fish is opaque throughout but still moist. Sprinkle with parsley.

182 SOLE OREGANATA
Prep: 10 minutes   Cook: 15 to 20 minutes   Serves: 6

6 sole fillets, 5 to 6 ounces each	½ cup water
½ cup flour	1 14-ounce can Italian peeled tomatoes, drained and chopped
½ teaspoon salt	
¼ teaspoon pepper	
2 tablespoons butter	1 tablespoon chopped fresh oregano or 1 teaspoon dried
¼ cup olive oil	
½ cup dry white wine	
½ cup bottled clam juice	

1. Pat sole fillets dry with paper towels. On a large flat plate or sheet of wax paper, combine flour, salt, and pepper. Dredge fish in seasoned flour; shake off any excess.

2. In a large frying pan, melt butter with olive oil over medium heat. Cook fish, turning once, 2 to 3 minutes per side, or until browned outside and just opaque throughout. Remove to a heated platter and cover with foil to keep warm.

3. Add wine, clam juice, water, tomatoes, and oregano to pan. Boil uncovered over high heat until sauce thickens but still pours from a spoon, 5 to 10 minutes. Pour sauce over fish and serve.

183   PIKE WITH SALSA DI NOCE GRATINATA

Prep: 5 minutes   Soak: 20 to 30 minutes   Cook: 20 to 25 minutes   Serves: 6

The lakes of northern Italy are full of freshwater fish. This sauce is typically northern with its use of walnuts and porcini.

1   ounce dried porcini
    mushrooms
1   cup warm water
1   pike, 2 to 2½ pounds, cut
    into serving pieces
½   teaspoon salt
½   teaspoon pepper
¼   cup flour
5   to 8 tablespoons extra-virgin
    olive oil
½   cup chopped onion

¼   cup chopped celery
½   cup dry white wine
½   cup clam juice
½   cup water
¾   cup finely chopped walnuts
½   cup shredded Italian fontina
    or Gruyère cheese
2   tablespoons grated
    Parmesan cheese

1. Soak porcini in warm water 20 to 30 minutes, or until softened. Remove porcini and rinse under running water to remove any grit. Chop fine; place in a medium bowl. Strain liquid through cheesecloth into bowl with mushrooms. Set aside.

2. Meanwhile, season fish with salt and ¼ teaspoon pepper. Place flour on a piece of wax paper or flat plate. Dredge fish in flour, shaking to remove any excess.

3. In a nonreactive medium frying pan, heat 2 tablespoons olive oil over medium heat. Add onion and cook 2 to 3 minutes, or until softened. Stir in celery and continue to cook, stirring, 2 to 3 minutes, or until crisp tender. Add mushrooms and their liquid, wine, clam juice, and water and bring to boil over high heat. Cook until liquid is reduced to 1 cup, 3 to 5 minutes. Stir in walnuts and cook 1 minute. Season with remaining pepper. Set aside.

4. In a nonreactive large frying pan, heat 3 tablespoons olive oil over medium-high heat. Cook a few pieces of fish at a time, being careful sides don't touch, 3 to 4 minutes on each side, or until golden brown on outside and opaque but still juicy on inside. Add more olive oil if needed. Using a wide spatula, remove fish to a flameproof 13 x 9-inch baking dish or gratin dish. Cover loosely with foil to keep warm.

5. Heat broiler. Pour reserved walnut sauce over fish. Sprinkle fontina and Parmesan cheese over top. Broil about 3 inches from heat 2 to 3 minutes, or until cheese melts and begins to brown.

184   SALMON WITH LEMON-CAPER BUTTER

Prep: 10 minutes   Cook: 15 to 18 minutes   Serves: 6

1 stick (8 tablespoons) butter
3 tablespoons minced fresh
   parsley
2 garlic cloves, minced
2 tablespoons capers, rinsed
   and drained
2 tablespoons grated lemon
   zest

1 teaspoon salt
¼ teaspoon pepper
6 salmon steaks, cut ¾ to
   1 inch thick, 6 to 8 ounces
   each
1 tablespoon extra-virgin olive
   oil

1. Preheat oven to 350°. In a medium bowl, beat butter with an electric mixer until soft. Add parsley, garlic, capers, lemon zest, ¼ teaspoon salt, and ⅛ teaspoon pepper. Beat just to combine. Set lemon-caper butter aside.

2. Brush salmon with olive oil and season with remaining ¾ teaspoon salt and ⅛ teaspoon pepper. Bake until just opaque throughout, 15 to 18 minutes depending upon thickness of steak. Serve hot fish with cold lemon-caper butter.

185   WHOLE TROUT WITH PROSCIUTTO AND BREAD CRUMBS

Prep: 10 minutes   Cook: 12 to 15 minutes   Serves: 6

6 whole trout, about 1 pound
   each
6 tablespoons soft bread
   crumbs
3 garlic cloves, minced
2 tablespoons minced fresh
   parsley

3 tablespoons chopped
   prosciutto or other ham
3 tablespoons plus 1 teaspoon
   olive oil
¼ teaspoon pepper
   Lemon wedges

1. Preheat oven to 475°. Slash trout diagonally twice on each side, ¼ to ½ inch.

2. In a small bowl, combine bread crumbs, garlic, parsley, prosciutto, 1 teaspoon olive oil, and pepper. Lightly fill slashes in trout with bread mixture.

3. Rub ½ tablespoon olive oil over each fish. Place fish in an oiled baking dish and bake 12 to 15 minutes, or until fish is just opaque near bone. Serve with lemon wedges.

186 MACKEREL PIZZAIOLA

Prep: 10 minutes   Cook: 35 minutes   Serves: 4

A very oily fish rich in flavors and especially good with the "pizza man's sauce."

2 whole mackerel, 1½ to
   2 pounds each
1 14-ounce can Italian peeled
   tomatoes, drained and
   chopped
3 garlic cloves, chopped
2 teaspoons chopped oregano
   or ½ teaspoon dried

2 tablespoons chopped fresh
   basil or ½ teaspoon dried
1 tablespoon chopped fresh
   parsley
   Pepper to taste

1. Preheat oven to 350°. Slash mackerel diagonally, 3 times on each side, ¾ to 1 inch deep. Place fish in an oiled 13 x 9-inch baking dish. Cover fish with tomatoes, garlic, oregano, basil, parsley, and pepper.

2. Bake 35 minutes, or until fish flakes when tested with a fork. Serve with pan sauce.

187 BURRIDA

Prep: 15 minutes   Cook: 30 minutes   Serves: 6 to 8

This fish stew from Genoa has many variations. Many of the fish traditionally used are not available in this country.

4½ to 5 pounds firm-fleshed
   assorted thick fish fillets,
   such as snapper, halibut,
   cod, and bluefish
3 tablespoons extra-virgin
   olive oil
1 medium onion, chopped
2 medium carrots, peeled and
   chopped
2 celery ribs, chopped
2 garlic cloves, chopped

2 flat anchovy fillets, finely
   chopped
1 8-ounce bottle clam juice
1 cup water
1 14-ounce can Italian peeled
   tomatoes, drained and
   chopped
½ teaspoon pepper
   Salt to taste
2 tablespoons chopped fresh
   parsley

1. Cut fish into 2- by 3-inch serving pieces and pat dry with paper towels. In a nonreactive flameproof casserole large enough to hold all ingredients, heat olive oil over medium heat. Add onion and cook 2 to 3 minutes, or until softened. Add carrots, celery, and garlic and cook until onions are just beginning to turn golden, 3 to 4 minutes.

2. Stir in anchovies, clam juice, water, and tomatoes. Bring to a boil over high heat, then reduce heat to medium and cook uncovered 10 minutes to combine flavors.

3. Add fish to pan and cover. Reduce heat to medium-low and simmer 15 minutes, or until fish is just opaque throughout. Season with pepper and salt if needed, remembering anchovies are salty. Sprinkle parsley over top. Serve in warmed shallow soup bowls.

188 FRITTO MISTO DI MARE
Prep: 30 minutes   Cook: 20 to 25 minutes   Serves: 6

This is not an easy dish to do because deep frying is a pest. It's well worth the trouble if you can get a good variety of fish.

12 smelts, cleaned	8 ounces squid, cleaned and cut into rings
12 large shrimp, about 12 ounces, shelled and deveined	3 cups flour
12 sea scallops, about 12 ounces	2 teaspoons salt
1 pound cod or snapper fillet, cut into 12 2 x 1-inch pieces	1 teaspoon pepper
	1½ quarts peanut oil, for frying Lemon wedges Garlic Anchovy Sauce (recipe follows)

1. Rinse all fish under cold running water and pat dry with paper towels. On a large piece of wax paper or flat plate, combine flour, salt, and pepper. Dredge fish in seasoned flour.

2. In a deep-fat fryer or large saucepan, heat oil to 350° on a deep-fat thermometer. Fry fish in batches without crowding, turning once, 2 to 3 minutes, or until golden brown. Remove and drain on paper towels. Garnish with lemon wedges and pass Garlic Anchovy Sauce on the side.

GARLIC ANCHOVY SAUCE
Makes about 1½ cups

1½ cups extra-virgin olive oil	6 flat anchovy fillets, chopped
4 garlic cloves, minced	Pinch of hot pepper flakes

In a small frying pan, warm olive oil over medium-low heat. Add garlic, anchovies, and hot pepper flakes. Cook for 1 to 2 minutes, until garlic is softened and fragrant but not brown. Remove from heat.

189 CLAMS AND MUSSELS IN FENNEL SAUCE
Prep: 15 minutes   Cook: 15 minutes   Serves: 4

Fennel and shellfish are good partners. If fennel is not available, you can use celery for texture and 2 teaspoons crushed fennel seeds for flavor.

18 hard-shelled clams, such as littlenecks	½ cup dry white wine
18 mussels	1 14-ounce can Italian peeled tomatoes, drained and chopped
3 tablespoons olive oil	
1 small onion, chopped	½ teaspoon salt
2 fennel bulbs, thinly sliced	¼ teaspoon pepper

1. Scrub clams and mussels well under cold running water with a vegetable brush. Discard any open shells that will not close when tapped.

2. In a nonreactive large frying pan, heat olive oil over medium heat. Add onion and cook 2 to 3 minutes, or until softened. Stir in fennel and cook 2 minutes. Add wine and tomatoes. Cook 5 minutes to reduce liquid and blend flavors.

3. Add shellfish. Cover and cook over high heat, shaking pan frequently, 4 to 5 minutes, or until clams open. Discard any clams or mussels that do not open. Season with salt and pepper. Serve shellfish with fennel and sauce in heated soup bowls.

190 CLAMS IN BRODO
Prep: 10 minutes   Cook: 8 to 10 minutes   Serves: 4

A combination of mussels and clams is delicious. Serve with thick pieces of garlic bread.

2 pounds hard-shelled clams, such as littlenecks	Pinch of hot pepper flakes
½ cup extra-virgin olive oil	1 cup dry white wine
4 garlic cloves, chopped	3 tablespoons minced fresh parsley
1 tablespoon chopped fresh oregano or 1 teaspoon dried	

1. Scrub clams well under cold running water. Discard any open shells that will not close when tapped.

2. In a nonreactive large frying pan or flameproof casserole, heat oil over medium-high heat. Add clams, garlic, oregano, hot pepper flakes, and white wine. Cover and cook, shaking pan frequently, 4 to 5 minutes, or until clams open. Discard any clams that do not open. Add parsley to pan and toss gently. Serve clams and broth in warmed soup bowls.

191 OYSTERS BAKED WITH SPINACH AND SAMBUCCA

Prep: 30 minutes   Cook: 13 to 18 minutes   Serves: 8

1 pound fresh spinach, stems removed and washed, or 1 10-ounce package frozen, defrosted
2 tablespoons butter
2 tablespoons chopped onion
1 tablespoon chopped fresh basil or parsley
2 tablespoons Sambucca
¼ cup heavy cream

¼ teaspoon grated nutmeg
½ teaspoon salt
1 cup soft bread crumbs
2 tablespoons grated Parmesan cheese
16 oysters, scrubbed and shucked (see note), half the shells reserved
Rock salt

1. Preheat oven to 475°. Cook fresh spinach, with water that clings to leaves, in a medium saucepan over medium heat 2 to 3 minutes, or until limp. Drain in colander. When cool enough to handle, squeeze to remove as much liquid as possible. Or drain defrosted spinach in a colander and squeeze dry. Chop fine.

2. In a small frying pan, melt butter over medium heat. Add onion and cook 2 to 3 minutes, or until softened. Add spinach and basil and cook, stirring, 2 minutes. Add Sambucca, cream, nutmeg, and salt. Cook 2 minutes, or until thick and bubbly.

3. Spoon spinach mixture over oysters. Sprinkle bread crumbs and Parmesan cheese on top; press gently to help adhere. Place oysters on a bed of rock salt in a baking pan. Bake 7 to 8 minutes, or until oysters are plump and juicy and crumbs begin to brown.

NOTE: *If you don't have a good friend who will open oysters for you, here are some instructions: Hold oyster with cup side down on a firm work surface. Use a cooking mitt to hold oyster in place and protect your hand. Insert tip of an oyster knife into hinge of oyster and twist knife to release hinge. This takes a good amount of steady strength, depending on the type of oyster. Slide oyster knife along inside edge of shell to detach muscle and release top shell. Discard shell. Slip knife under oyster to cut muscle attaching meat to bottom shell. Keep shell level to avoid spilling the tasty oyster liquor. Or ask your fishmonger to shuck oysters for you just before you pick them up and pack them on ice.*

192 BROILED MARINATED SHRIMP WITH GARLIC AND ROSEMARY

Prep: 10 minutes   Marinate: 2 hours   Cook: 5 minutes
Serves: 2 to 4

16 extra-large shrimp, about
   1 pound, shelled and
   deveined
¾ cup extra-virgin olive oil
3 garlic cloves, chopped

2 tablespoons chopped
   fresh rosemary or 2
   teaspoons dried
1 teaspoon salt
½ teaspoon pepper
3 lemons, cut into wedges

1. Place shrimp on four long metal skewers, threading through tails and body.

2. Combine oil, garlic, rosemary, salt, and pepper in a shallow dish. Place skewered shrimp in dish and turn to coat well. Marinate shrimp, turning several times, 2 hours in refrigerator.

3. Preheat broiler. Set skewers on a baking sheet set 3 inches from heat and broil shrimp, turning once, until lightly browned and just opaque inside, about 5 minutes. Brush with any remaining herb oil just before serving. Pass lemon wedges on the side.

193 BLACK PEPPER SHRIMP OREGANATA

Prep: 10 minutes   Cook: 3 to 4 minutes   Serves: 2 to 4

The best way to cook this is to leave the shells on the shrimp. Serve with lots of crusty bread and plenty of napkins.

1 pound large shrimp in their
   shells (16 to 20 pieces per
   pound)
2 tablespoons butter
3 tablespoons extra-virgin
   olive oil
4 garlic cloves, chopped

1 tablespoon chopped fresh
   oregano or 1 teaspoon
   dried
1 tablespoon pepper
1 cup dry white wine
   Crusty bread

1. Remove little "legs" from shrimp if you see any; leave shells and tails on. Rinse under cold running water. Pat dry with paper towels.

2. In a nonreactive large frying pan, melt butter with olive oil over medium-high heat. Add garlic, oregano, and pepper, then immediately stir in shrimp. Cook, tossing, 30 seconds. Add white wine and cook 2 to 3 minutes, or until shrimp turn pink. Serve immediately, accompanied by bread, each diner peeling off his or her shrimp shells.

194 RED PEPPER SHRIMP CALABRESE
Prep: 10 minutes   Cook: 5 to 7 minutes   Serves: 4

Calabrians especially seem to love hot pepper flakes.

¼ cup olive oil	1 cup dry white wine
3 garlic cloves, chopped	½ cup sliced scallions
½ teaspoon hot pepper flakes	½ teaspoon salt
1 pound large shrimp (16 to	Lemon wedges
20 pieces per pound),	
shelled and deveined	

1. In a nonreactive large frying pan, heat olive oil over medium heat. Add garlic and hot pepper flakes and cook about 30 seconds, or until fragrant. Stir shrimp into pan and cook 1 to 2 minutes to coat with oil.

2. Add wine and cook, stirring, 3 to 4 minutes, or until shrimp turns pink and wine reduces to about ¾ cup. Stir in scallions just to heat. Remove from heat, season with salt, and pass lemon wedges on the side.

195 SHRIMP SCAMPI
Prep: 15 minutes   Marinate: 2 hours   Cook: 12 minutes   Serves: 4

The word *scampi* is often used on menus for large shrimp in this country. The true scampi are from Venetian waters. Large shrimp are a good substitute, so you might want to call this "shrimp cooked like scampi."

½ cup extra-virgin olive oil	2 garlic cloves, chopped
½ teaspoon salt	1½ pounds jumbo shrimp,
¼ teaspoon pepper	shelled and deveined
2 teaspoons chopped fresh	2 lemons, cut into wedges
oregano or ½ teaspoon	
dried	

1. On a large flat plate, combine olive oil, salt, pepper, oregano, and garlic. Add shrimp to oil mixture and turn them to coat well. Marinate shrimp, turning several times, 2 hours in refrigerator.

2. Skewer marinated shrimp, threading them through the middle of the body and fitting them so they just barely touch. Place skewers in broiler pan and brush with marinade. Broil 3 inches from the heat 7 minutes on one side. Turn shrimp over and brush with marinade. Continue to cook 5 minutes, or until succulent and opaque inside and well seared on outside. Pass lemon wedges on the side.

196   SHRIMP IN PESTO CREAM
Prep: 25 minutes   Cook: 10 minutes   Serves: 4 to 6

3 tablespoons butter	½ cup dry white wine
½ cup chopped onion	¾ cup cream
1½ pounds large shrimp, shelled and deveined	¼ cup pesto, homemade (page 77) or jarred

1. In a large frying pan, melt butter over medium-low heat. Add onions and cook 2 to 3 minutes, or until softened. Add shrimp and toss to coat with butter. Raise heat to medium-high.

2. Add wine and cook, stirring, until shrimp begin to turn pink, about 2 minutes. Stir in cream and pesto. Cook 4 to 5 minutes, or until cream and pesto are thick and bubbly, and shrimp are pink and opaque throughout.

197   CIOPPINO TUTTO MARE
Prep: 10 minutes   Soak: 20 to 30 minutes   Cook: 25 to 30 minutes Serves: 6

Save fish stews for friends who don't mind a little juice on their fingers. This dish can be costly, so it is ideal for a "share the expense" cooking party.

1 ounce dried porcini mushrooms	3 pounds assorted thick fish fillets such as cod, halibut, and snapper, cut into 2 x 3-inch pieces
1 cup warm water	
3 tablespoons extra-virgin olive oil	
1 large onion, chopped	¾ pound shrimp, shelled and deveined
4 garlic cloves, chopped	½ pound scallops, trimmed
1 28-ounce can Italian crushed tomatoes in puree	6 frozen lobster tails, 5 to 6 ounces each, defrosted
1 tablespoon chopped fresh oregano or 1 teaspoon dried	3 tablespoons minced fresh parsley
	Garlic Bread (page 196)

1. Soak porcini in warm water 20 to 30 minutes, or until softened. Remove porcini and rinse under running water to remove any grit. Coarsely chop; place in a small bowl. Strain liquid through cheesecloth into bowl with mushrooms. Set aside.

2. In a 9- to 10-quart flameproof casserole or stockpot, heat olive oil. Add onion and cook over medium heat 2 to 3 minutes, or until softened. Add garlic and cook 1 minute longer. Add tomatoes, mushrooms and their liquid, and oregano. Simmer uncovered 10 minutes to blend flavors.

3. Add fish, shrimp, scallops, and lobster to casserole. Cover and cook over medium-low heat 15 to 18 minutes, or until shrimp are pink and lobster is bright red. Sprinkle parsley over top.

4. If possible, bring whole casserole to table. Serve a portion of each shellfish and fish to each person, along with some of the sauce. Serve with generous portions of Garlic Bread.

198 SHELLFISH CIOPPINO
Prep: 15 minutes   Cook: 35 minutes   Serves: 4

Actually from San Francisco, this is an Italian-American version of *ciuppin* from Genoa, usually made with local Dungeness crab. You really need to get into this gregarious stew with your fingers, so have available some shell crackers, side plates for discarded shells, and plenty of napkins.

¼ cup extra-virgin olive oil
1 large onion, chopped
3 large garlic cloves, chopped
¼ teaspoon crushed hot pepper flakes
2 celery ribs, chopped
2 medium carrots, peeled and chopped
1 cup dry red wine
1 28-ounce can Italian crushed tomatoes in puree
1½ cups water
1 tablespoon chopped fresh oregano or 1 teaspoon dried
1 teaspoon chopped fresh rosemary or ⅛ teaspoon dried

12 cracked crab claws, preferably Dungeness, fresh or defrosted frozen
12 to 14 clams, soft-shell or cherrystones, scrubbed clean
12 to 14 mussels, scrubbed clean
3 tablespoons chopped fresh parsley
2 tablespoons chopped fresh basil or 1 teaspoon dried
Crusty Italian bread
Freshly ground pepper

1. In a nonreactive large, flameproof casserole, heat olive oil over medium heat. Cook onion 3 to 4 minutes, or until softened. Add garlic and hot pepper flakes and cook 30 seconds, or until fragrant. Stir in celery and carrots and cook until softened and just turning golden, 3 to 4 minutes. Add wine, tomatoes, water, oregano, and rosemary. Cook, uncovered, over medium heat until liquid is reduced by one fourth, 8 to 10 minutes.

2. Add crab and cover. Cook over medium-high heat 3 minutes. Add clams and mussels and cook until opened and crab claws are bright red, 3 to 4 minutes longer. Discard any clams or mussels that did not open. Sprinkle with parsley and basil. Serve in shallow soup bowls with thick crusty bread, passing a pepper mill on the side.

199   SCALLOPS WITH LEMON, GARLIC, AND PARSLEY

Prep: 15 minutes   Cook: 5 to 6 minutes   Serves: 4 to 6

Gremolata—this fragrant combination of lemon rind, garlic, and parsley—usually garnishes veal shanks. It's delicious with fish, too.

2 lemons	½ pounds sea scallops,
½ cup fresh chopped parsley	trimmed
2 garlic cloves minced	½ cup dry vermouth
2 tablespoons butter	¼ teaspoon salt
2 tablespoons olive oil	⅛ teaspoon pepper

1. Grate yellow zest from lemons, being careful not to include any bitter white pith. In a small bowl, combine lemon zest, parsley, and garlic. Set *gremolata* aside.

2. In a nonreactive large frying pan over medium-high heat, melt butter with olive oil. Add scallops to pan and cook 2 minutes on each side, or until opaque but still tender and juicy. Add vermouth and heat, 1 to 2 minutes. Remove from heat. Season with salt and pepper. Add half the *gremolata* to pan and toss together. Pass remaining *gremolata* on the side.

200   LOBSTER FRA DIAVOLO

Prep: 15 minutes   Cook: 35 minutes   Serves: 4

Lobster as we know it in this country is not native to Italy, but this dish has been enjoyed by Italian-Americans for years.

2 Maine lobsters, 1½ to 2 pounds each, split in half, or 8 frozen lobster tails, 4 to 6 ounces each, defrosted	¼ teaspoon pepper
	3 tablespoons chopped fresh parsley
	4 cups marinara sauce, homemade (page 131) or jarred
½ cup extra-virgin olive oil	
2 garlic cloves, minced	1 pound spaghettini
1 medium onion, chopped	
¼ teaspoon hot pepper flakes, plus more for accompaniment	

1. If using whole lobster, twist claws from lobster to remove. With a cleaver, cut lobster into large pieces (or ask your fishmonger to do this). Remove and discard sac near head and intestinal vein in tail. Remove the gray-green liver and any roe.

2. In a nonreactive large frying pan, heat olive oil over medium heat. Stir in garlic and onion and cook 2 to 3 minutes, or until softened. Add hot pepper flakes, pepper, and parsley. Cook, stirring, until just fragrant, about 30 seconds. Place lobster, cut side down, in pan and cook covered over medium-low heat 15 minutes, or until lightly browned.

3. Add marinara sauce to pan and cook, spooning sauce over lobster, 1 minute. Add lobster claws, cover, and continue cooking, stirring occasionally, until lobster is tender and juicy, about 15 minutes.

4. When lobster is almost ready, in a large pot of boiling salted water, cook spaghettini until tender, 5 to 6 minutes; drain. Pour pasta onto a large serving platter. Spoon diavolo sauce from pan over pasta and arrange lobster around it. Serve with shellfish crackers, forks, and plenty of napkins. Pass extra hot pepper flakes.

201 MARINARA SAUCE
Prep: 10 minutes   Cook: 35 minutes   Makes: 5 to 6 cups

1 tablespoon butter
2 tablespoons olive oil
2 garlic cloves, chopped
3 flat anchovy fillets, chopped
2 tablespoons tomato paste
2 30-ounce cans Italian whole
    tomatoes in puree
1 cup water

2 tablespoons chopped fresh
    parsley
2 tablespoons chopped fresh
    oregano or 2 teaspoons
    dried
½ teaspoon salt
¼ teaspoon pepper

1. In a nonreactive large saucepan, melt butter with olive oil over medium heat. Stir in garlic and cook 1 minute, being very careful not to burn. Stir in anchovy until dissolved, 1 to 2 minutes.

2. Add tomato paste and stir to heat. Stir in tomatoes with puree, water, parsley, oregano, salt, and pepper. Bring to a boil, reduce heat to low, and simmer uncovered 30 minutes.

Chapter 8

Veal

      Stews and savory little sautés of veal are a very important part of Italian cooking. Veal is often the meat of choice for Italians who enjoy the meat from naturally raised animals.

      Veal takes a little care, and preparation often involves pounding it into thin fillets or scaloppine and quick-cooking them over high heat. There is not a middle stage for cooking veal. It should be cooked quickly or long, the middle stage producing a tough result, as there is little fat to keep it tender. Braising in a little stock and wine will make delicious little stews. As for roasting, a rare veal roast will be rubbery and difficult to cut, as it hasn't developed the muscle and fat to make it flavorful. Season well and cook to almost well done.

      Many of the pounded veal dishes can be done with chicken or turkey fillets; cooking times will vary accordingly.

---

202 VEAL MARSALA
Prep: 20 minutes   Cook: 12 to 13 minutes   Serves: 4 to 6

Marsala is a fortified wine originally from Sicily. There is a sweet and a dry Marsala; be sure to use the *dry* Marsala. You can substitute dry sherry if you have to.

1½ **pounds veal cutlets**	½ **cup dry Marsala or dry**
½ **teaspoon salt**	**sherry**
¼ **teaspoon pepper**	1 **cup Chicken Stock (page**
¼ **cup flour**	**48) or reduced-sodium**
2 **tablespoons butter**	**canned broth**
2 **tablespoons olive oil**	

1. Season veal with salt and pepper; dust lightly with flour. In a nonreactive large frying pan, melt 1 tablespoon butter with 1 tablespoon olive oil over medium heat. Add as many pieces of veal as will fit in pan without crowding and cook 4 minutes, or until lightly browned on both sides. Remove to a warmed platter; cover with foil and keep warm. Repeat with remaining veal, adding remaining butter and oil as needed.

2. Add Marsala and bring to a boil, scraping up browned bits from bottom of pan. Add stock and boil to reduce liquid to ½ cup, 3 to 4 minutes. Return veal to pan and heat through, about 1 minute. Season with additional salt and pepper.

203 VEAL PICCATA

Prep: 20 minutes   Cook: 10 to 15 minutes   Serves: 4

If you are lucky enough to have a good butcher, let him do most of the work for you, and ask him to pound the cutlets for scaloppine. Don't try to do these quick sauté dishes for more than 4 people.

1½ pounds veal cutlets	3 tablespoons fresh lemon
1 teaspoon salt	juice
¼ teaspoon pepper	2 tablespoons capers, rinsed
¼ cup flour	and drained
2 tablespoons butter	1 tablespoon finely chopped
2 tablespoons olive oil	fresh parsley
½ cup dry white wine	
1 cup Chicken Stock (page 48)	
or reduced-sodium	
canned broth	

1. Pound veal cutlets between two sheets of wax paper or plastic wrap to ¼-inch thickness. Cut each cutlet in half. Season veal pieces with ¾ teaspoon salt and ¼ teaspoon pepper. Dust lightly with flour; shake off excess.

2. In a nonreactive large frying pan, melt 1 tablespoon butter with 1 tablespoon olive oil over medium heat. Add as many veal pieces as will fit in pan without crowding and cook 2 minutes on each side, or until lightly browned. Remove veal to a warmed platter; cover with foil to keep warm. Repeat with remaining veal, adding remaining butter and oil as needed.

3. Add wine to pan and bring to a boil, scraping up browned bits from bottom of pan. Add stock and boil to reduce liquid to ¾ cup, 4 to 5 minutes.

4. Add lemon juice and capers to pan and cook 1 minute. Return veal to pan and heat through, about 1 minute. Season with remaining ¼ teaspoon salt and garnish with parsley. Serve immediately.

204 VEAL SALTIMBOCCA ALLA ROMANA

Prep: 20 minutes   Cook: 10 minutes   Serves: 4 to 6

These delicious tidbits are said by the Romans to "jump into your mouth."

8 veal cutlets, about 3 ounces	8 thin slices of prosciutto or
each	ham, cut in half
Salt and pepper to taste	5 tablespoons butter
16 fresh sage leaves or	1 to 2 tablespoons olive oil
1½ to 2 teaspoons dried sage	1 cup dry white wine

1. Preheat oven to 350°. Pound veal cutlets between two sheets of wax paper or plastic wrap to ¼-inch thickness. Cut each cutlet in half. Season with salt and pepper. Place 1 fresh sage leaf on each piece of veal or sprinkle with ⅛ teaspoon dried sage. Cover with a piece of prosciutto or ham.

2. In a nonreactive large frying pan, melt 2 tablespoons butter with 1 table-spoon oil over medium-high heat. Add as many pieces of veal as will fit in pan without crowding and cook 1 to 1½ minutes, or until lightly browned on bottom. Remove veal to a heatproof platter. Repeat with remaining veal, adding 1 more tablespoon oil if pan becomes dry.

3. When all veal is removed to platter, place platter in oven and bake 2 to 3 minutes to reheat and finish cooking.

4. Meanwhile, add wine to frying pan and bring to a boil over high heat, scraping up any brown bits from bottom of pan. Cook until reduced to ½ cup. Whisk in remaining 3 tablespoons butter until just melted. Season sauce with salt and pepper to taste. Pour sauce over veal and serve at once.

---

205   VEAL SCALOPPINE WITH TWO KINDS OF MUSHROOMS

Prep: 10 minutes   Soak: 20 to 30 minutes   Cook: 10 to 12 minutes
Serves: 4

Porcini are very flavorful mushrooms. Be sure to rinse them off, as they can be sandy.

1 ounce dried porcini mushrooms	8 ounces fresh mushrooms, thinly sliced
2 cups warm water	1½ cups Chicken Stock (page 48) or reduced-sodium canned broth
1½ pounds veal cutlets, cut ¼ inch thick and then halved	1 tablespoon minced fresh sage or 1 teaspoon dried
1 teaspoon salt	1 tablespoon minced fresh parsley
¼ teaspoon pepper	2 tablespoons butter
3 tablespoons flour	½ cup dry red wine
3 tablespoons olive oil	
1 small onion, chopped	
1 garlic clove, minced	

1. Soak porcini in 2 cups warm water for 20 to 30 minutes, or until softened. Remove porcini and rinse under running water to remove any grit. Coarsely chop and place in a small bowl. Strain liquid through cheesecloth into bowl with mushrooms.

2. Season veal with salt and pepper. Dust lightly with flour.

3. In a large frying pan, heat 2 tablespoons olive oil over medium heat. Add onion and garlic and cook 2 to 3 minutes, or until onion is softened. Stir in fresh mushrooms until well mixed, then add 1 cup stock, porcini and their liquid, sage, and parsley. Simmer uncovered 5 minutes.

4. Meanwhile, in a nonreactive large frying pan, melt butter with remaining 1 tablespoon olive oil over medium-high heat. Add veal slices and cook, turning once, 1 to 2 minutes, or until lightly browned on both sides. Stir in wine and remaining ½ cup stock and simmer uncovered 3 minutes to reduce slightly. Add mushroom mixture and simmer 2 minutes longer.

206 VEAL PARMIGIANA
Prep: 20 minutes   Cook: 30 minutes   Serves: 4 to 8

8 veal cutlets, about 3 ounces each	1½ teaspoons chopped fresh oregano or ½ teaspoon dried
1 teaspoon salt	¼ to ⅓ cup olive oil
¼ teaspoon pepper	2 cups tomato sauce
⅓ cup flour	8 thin slices of mozzarella cheese
2 eggs	½ cup grated Parmesan cheese
2 tablespoons water	
1 cup dry bread crumbs	

1. Preheat oven to 350°. Pound veal cutlets between two sheets of wax paper or plastic wrap until flattened to ¼-inch thickness. Season with ½ teaspoon salt and ¼ teaspoon pepper.

2. Spread flour on a plate or sheet of wax paper. In a wide shallow bowl, beat eggs and water until well blended. On another plate or sheet of wax paper, toss bread crumbs with oregano and remaining ½ teaspoon salt and ¼ teaspoon pepper. Dredge veal in flour. Dip in egg mixture and coat with seasoned bread crumbs. Pat crumbs gently to help them adhere.

3. In a large skillet, heat 2 tablespoons olive oil over medium-high heat. Add as many cutlets as will fit in pan without crowding and cook, turning once, 4 minutes, or until browned on both sides. Remove to a 13 x 11-inch baking dish. Repeat with remaining cutlets, adding more oil as needed.

4. Spoon 2 or 3 tablespoons tomato sauce over each cutlet. Top each with a slice of mozzarella and 1 tablespoon Parmesan cheese. Bake for 20 minutes, or until veal is tender.

207 VEAL STEW WITH ARTICHOKES AND POTATOES
Prep: 10 minutes   Cook: 1¼ hours   Serves: 4 to 8

2 pounds boneless veal shoulder, cut into 2-inch pieces	1 tablespoon fresh thyme leaves or 1 teaspoon dried
1 teaspon salt	8 small red potatoes, peeled
½ teaspoon pepper	1 10-ounce package frozen artichoke hearts, defrosted
¼ cup flour	2 tablespoons minced fresh parsley
2 tablespoons olive oil	
1 small onion, chopped	
½ cup dry white wine	
1½ cups Chicken Stock (page 48) or reduced-sodium canned broth	

1. Trim excess fat from veal. Season with ½ teaspoon salt and ¼ teaspoon pepper. Dust with flour; shake off excess. In a nonreactive Dutch oven, heat oil over medium-high heat. Add veal and cook, turning, 5 to 7 minutes, or until lightly browned on all sides.

2. Add onion and cook about 1 minute. Add wine, stock, thyme, and remaining ½ teaspoon salt and ¼ teaspoon pepper. Bring to a simmer and reduce heat to medium-low. Add potatoes, cover, and simmer for 30 minutes. Add potatoes, re-cover, and simmer 30 to 35 minutes longer, or until veal and potatoes are tender.

3. Add artichokes and simmer 5 minutes. Garnish with parsley just before serving.

208 VEAL STEW WITH TOMATOES, PEAS, AND OREGANO

Prep: 10 minutes   Cook: 1¼ hours   Serves: 4 to 6

Those of you who are lucky enough to find yellow tomatoes in the summer will be able to make this an even more elegant dish.

2 pounds boneless veal
   shoulder, cut into
   2-inch pieces
1 teaspoon salt
½ teaspoon pepper
¼ cup flour
2 to 3 tablespoons olive oil
1 medium onion, chopped
2 garlic cloves, chopped
½ cup dry white wine
1 cup Chicken Stock (page 48)
   or reduced-sodium
   canned broth

1 14-ounce can Italian peeled
   tomatoes, drained
   and chopped
1 tablespoon fresh oregano
   leaves or 1 teaspoon
   dried
1 10-ounce package frozen
   peas

1. Trim excess fat from veal. Season with ½ teaspoon salt and ¼ teaspoon pepper. Dust with flour; shake off excess. In a nonreactive Dutch oven, heat 2 tablespoons olive oil over medium-high heat. Add veal and cook, turning, 5 to 7 minutes, or until lightly browned on all sides. Remove with a slotted spoon and set aside.

2. If pan is dry, add another 1 tablespoon olive oil. Add onion and cook over medium heat 2 to 3 minutes, or until softened. Add garlic and cook until fragrant, about 1 minute longer.

3. Return veal to pan. Add wine, stock, tomatoes, oregano, and remaining ½ teaspoon salt and ¼ teaspoon pepper. Bring to a boil, reduce heat to medium-low, cover, and simmer about 1 hour, or until veal is tender. Add peas and simmer 5 minutes longer.

209   VEAL STEW PEPERONATA
Prep: 10 minutes   Cook: 1 hour   Serves: 4 to 6

When my mother prepared this dish, she always made enough for left-overs, as it makes a great hero sandwich.

2 pounds boneless veal shoulder, cut into 2-inch pieces
1 teaspoon salt
½ teaspoon pepper
¼ cup flour
2 to 3 tablespoons olive oil
1 medium onion, chopped
2 garlic cloves, minced

1 pound red and/or green bell peppers, cut into 1½-inch squares
1 14-ounce can Italian peeled tomatoes, drained and chopped
1 cup water
2 tablespoons minced fresh parsley
1 tablespoon minced fresh basil or ½ teaspoon dried

1. Trim excess fat from veal. Season veal with ½ teaspoon salt and ¼ tea-spoon pepper. Dust with flour; shake off excess. In a nonreactive Dutch oven, heat 2 tablespoons olive oil over medium-high heat. Add veal and cook, turning, 5 to 7 minutes, or until browned on all sides. Remove with a slotted spoon and set aside.

2. If pan is dry, add another 1 tablespoon olive oil. Add onion and cook over medium heat 2 to 3 minutes, or until softened. Add garlic and bell peppers and cook 1 minute longer.

3. Return veal to pan. Add tomatoes, water, and remaining ½ teaspoon salt and ¼ teaspoon pepper. Partially cover and cook about 1 hour, or until veal is tender. Stir in parsley and basil just before serving.

210   VEAL SALTIMBOCCA WITH FONTINA CHEESE
Prep: 25 minutes   Cook: 10 minutes   Serves: 4 to 6

The traditional saltimbocca has no cheese, but this addition has become very popular.

8 veal cutlets, about 3 ounces each
8 thin slices prosciutto or ham
8 thin slices of fontina cheese
24 sage leaves

5 tablespoons butter
1 to 2 tablespoons olive oil
1 cup dry white wine
Salt and pepper

1. Preheat oven to 350°. Pound veal cutlets between two sheets of wax paper or plastic wrap to ¼-inch thickness. Cut each cutlet into 3 pieces. Cut each ham and cheese slice into three pieces. Place 1 sage leaf on each piece of veal, cover with ham and then with cheese.

2. In a nonreactive large frying pan, melt 2 tablespoons butter with 1 table-spoon olive oil over medium-high heat. Add as many pieces of veal, cheese side up, as will fit in pan without crowding and cook 1 to 1½ minutes, or until lightly browned on bottom. Remove veal to a heatproof platter. Repeat with remaining veal, adding 1 more tablespoon oil if pan becomes dry.

3. When all veal is removed to platter, place platter in oven and bake 2 to 3 minutes, or until cheese begins to melt.

4. Meanwhile, add wine to frying pan and bring to a boil over high heat, scraping up any browned bits from bottom of pan. Cook until reduced by half. Whisk in remaining 3 tablespoons butter until just melted. Season with salt and pepper. Pour sauce over veal and serve immediately.

211 ROLLED VEAL BIRDS
Prep: 20 minutes   Cook: 50 minutes   Serves: 4 to 8

These neatly rolled packages can be served whole as an entree or appe-tizer; but when sliced pinwheel-fashion, they make wonderful party food.

8 veal cutlets, about 3 ounces each	8 thin slices prosciutto or ham
6 tablespoons soft bread crumbs	8 thin slices fontina cheese
2 garlic cloves, minced	1 cup Chicken Stock (page 48) or reduced-sodium canned broth
1 tablespoon olive oil	1 cup tomato sauce
1 tablespoon finely chopped fresh parsley	½ cup dry red wine

1. Preheat oven to 350°. Pound veal cutlets between two sheets of wax paper or plastic wrap until flattened to ¼-inch thickness.

2. In a small bowl, combine bread crumbs, garlic, olive oil, and parsley; blend well. Place veal on a flat work surface. Cover each piece of veal with a slice of prosciutto or ham; sprinkle with about 1 tablespoon bread crumb mixture and top with a slice of cheese. Roll up veal jelly-roll fashion. Fasten with toothpicks or tie with string. Place in a baking dish just large enough to hold "birds."

3. In a nonreactive small saucepan, combine chicken stock, tomato sauce, and red wine. Pour around veal birds. Cover with foil. Bake 40 to 50 min-utes, turning once or twice, until tender. Remove picks or string. Serve from baking dish.

212 VITELLO TONNATO

Prep: 15 minutes   Cook: 1¼ hours   Serves: 6 to 8

This is a cold dish, which can be easily prepared a day in advance.

1 boneless veal shoulder roast, about 2½ pounds, trimmed of fat, rolled, and tied
2 garlic cloves, cut into slivers
2 cups dry white wine
2 cups Chicken Stock (page 48) or reduced-sodium canned broth
1 celery rib, quartered
1 small onion, chopped
1 6½-ounce can tuna in olive oil, drained but oil reserved

2 hard-cooked eggs, coarsely chopped
8 flat anchovy fillets, coarsely chopped
2 tablespoons capers, plus additional for garnish, rinsed and drained
½ cup olive oil
½ teaspoon salt
¼ teaspoon pepper
   Thin slices of lemon

1. With a sharp paring knife, make 10 tiny slits in veal roast and stud with slivers of garlic. Place meat in a nonreactive small, flameproof casserole. Add wine, stock, celery, and onion. Cover and bring to a simmer over medium-low heat. Simmer 1 hour, or until tender. Remove meat from pan and strain juices. Return juices to pan and boil until reduced to 1 cup.

2. Place tuna with oil, eggs, anchovies, and capers in a food processor or blender. With machine on, pour oil through feed tube. Blend until smooth. Slowly add 1 cup reduced juices while blending. Season with salt and pepper.

3. When veal is cool, slice thin. Arrange on a platter and cover with tuna sauce. Garnish with capers and thin lemon slices.

213 VEAL BOLOGNESE

Prep: 20 minutes   Cook: 25 minutes   Serves: 4 to 8

8 veal cutlets, about 3 ounces each
½ teaspoon salt
¼ teaspoon pepper
½ cup flour
2 eggs
2 tablespoons water

1 cup dry bread crumbs
⅓ cup olive oil
2 cups tomato sauce
8 thin slices prosciutto or ham
8 thin slices mozzarella cheese
¼ cup grated Parmesan cheese

1. Preheat oven to 375°. Pound veal cutlets between two sheets of wax paper or plastic wrap until flattened to ¼-inch thickness. Season with salt and pepper.

2. Spread flour on a plate or sheet of wax paper. In a wide shallow bowl, beat eggs and water until well blended. Spread bread crumbs on another plate or sheet of wax paper. Dredge veal in flour; shake off excess. Dip in egg mixture and coat with bread crumbs. Pat crumbs gently to help them adhere.

3. In a large frying pan, heat 2 tablespoons olive oil over medium-high heat. Add as many cutlets as will fit in pan without crowding and cook, turning once, about 6 minutes, or until browned on both sides. Remove to a baking dish. Repeat with remaining cutlets, adding more oil as needed.

4. Spoon 2 or 3 tablespoons tomato sauce over each cutlet. Top each with a slice of prosciutto or ham, mozzarella, and a sprinkling of Parmesan cheese. Bake 10 to 12 minutes, or until cheese is melted and bubbly. Serve immediately.

---

214 VEAL ROAST (ARROSTO)
Prep: 10 minutes   Cook: 1 hour 20 minutes   Serves: 4

If you have fresh rosemary, tuck the branches and leaves under the string that ties the roast together.

1 teaspoon dried sage leaves	1 boneless veal shoulder
1 tablespoon dried rosemary	roast, 2½ to 3 pounds,
2 garlic cloves, minced	trimmed of fat, rolled,
3 tablespoons olive oil	and tied
1 teaspoon salt	2 cups Chicken Stock (page
¼ teaspoon pepper	48) or reduced-sodium
	canned broth
	1 cup dry white wine

1. Preheat oven to 350°. In a small bowl, combine sage, rosemary, garlic, olive oil, salt, and pepper. Rub surface of veal with seasoned oil. Place roast in a nonreactive large, flameproof casserole with a lid. Pour 1 cup stock and the wine around veal. Roast partially covered 1 hour, turning 2 or 3 times, until barely tender. Uncover and roast until lightly browned, about 15 minutes longer.

2. Remove meat from pan and tent with foil to keep warm. Set pan over medium heat and bring juices to a boil, scraping up brown bits from bottom of pan with a wooden spoon. Add remaining ½ cup stock to pan. Season juices with additional salt and pepper to taste. Slice veal roast and serve with pan juices.

215 VEAL CHOPS STUFFED WITH PROSCIUTTO AND GORGONZOLA

Prep: 10 minutes   Cook: 20 minutes   Serves: 2

2 veal loin chops, cut
¾ inch thick, about
12 ounces each
1 thin slice prosciutto or ham,
cut in half
2 tablespoons crumbled
gorgonzola or other blue
cheese

2 tablespoons olive oil
1½ teaspoons chopped fresh
rosemary or ½ teaspoon
dried
⅛ teaspoon pepper
½ cup dry white wine

1. Trim excess fat from veal. With a small sharp knife, slit a pocket in meaty part of each chop, cutting toward bone. Stuff pockets with prosciutto and cheese; fasten closed with toothpicks.

2. In a large skillet, heat olive oil. Cook chops over medium-high heat, turning once, about 4 minutes, or until browned outside.

3. Sprinkle rosemary and pepper over veal and pour wine into pan. Bring to a boil, reduce heat to medium-low, cover, and cook, turning once, until veal is tender and cooked through but still juicy, 10 to 15 minutes longer.

216 VEAL CHOPS STUFFED WITH SPINACH

Prep: 15 minutes   Cook: 35 minutes   Serves: 4

4 veal loin chops, cut ¾ inch
thick, about 12 ounces each
3 tablespoons olive oil
3 tablespoons minced onion
7 garlic cloves, minced
¼ cup finely chopped
prosciutto or ham

1 10-ounce package frozen
spinach, defrosted and
squeezed dry
¼ cup soft bread crumbs
½ teaspoon salt
¼ teaspoon pepper

1. Preheat oven to 375°. Trim excess fat from veal. With a small sharp knife, slit a pocket in meatiest side of each chop, cutting toward bone.

2. In a medium skillet, heat 1 tablespoon olive oil over medium heat. Add onion, garlic, and prosciutto or ham and cook about 2 minutes, or until onion is softened but not browned. Add spinach and bread crumbs; mix well. Season with salt and pepper. Stuff each chop with spinach mixture. Fasten with toothpicks.

3. In a large skillet, heat 2 tablespoons olive oil over medium-high heat. Add chops and cook, turning once, 4 minutes, or until browned on both sides. Place in a 13 x 11-inch baking dish. Bake 30 minutes, or until meat is tender and cooked through but still juicy.

217   OSSO BUCCO
Prep: 15 minutes   Cook: 1½ to 1¾ hours   Serves: 6

4   10- to 12-ounce veal shanks, cut into 1½-inch lengths
1½ teaspoons salt
½   teaspoon pepper
½   cup flour
4   to 6 tablespoons olive oil
1   medium onion, chopped
2   medium carrots, peeled and chopped
2   celery ribs, chopped

2   cups dry white wine
1   cup beef stock or canned broth
1   14-ounce can Italian peeled tomatoes, drained and chopped
¼   cup plus 2 tablespoons chopped fresh parsley
2   garlic gloves, minced
Grated zest of 1 lemon

1. Trim excess fat from veal. Season with 1 teaspoon salt and ¼ teaspoon pepper. Dredge in flour; shake off excess. In a nonreactive Dutch oven, heat 2 tablespoons olive oil over medium heat. Add as many pieces of veal as will fit in Dutch oven without crowding and cook, turning, 8 to 10 minutes, until browned on all sides. Remove and repeat until all veal is cooked, adding 2 more tablespoons oil if pan becomes dry.

2. Heat 2 tablespoons olive oil in same pan over medium heat. Add onion, carrots, and celery. Cook, stirring occasionally, 3 to 4 minutes, or until onion is softened. Add wine, broth, tomatoes, 2 tablespoons parsley, and remaining ½ teaspoon salt and ¼ teaspoon pepper. Return veal to pan, bring to boil, reduce heat to low, cover, and simmer 1 hour, or until fork tender. Remove veal shanks to a serving platter and cover with foil to keep warm.

3. Skim off fat from surface of pan juices. Boil uncovered until liquid is reduced to 3 cups.

4. Meanwhile, in a small bowl, toss together remaining ¼ cup parsley, garlic, and grated lemon zest to make a *gremolata*. When sauce is reduced, return veal to pan and reheat. Serve with *gremolata* sprinkled over top.

218   CALVES' LIVER WITH BROWN BUTTER, LEMON, AND SAGE

Prep: 15 minutes   Cook: 10 minutes   Serves: 4

1½ pounds calves' liver,
   trimmed and sliced
   ¼ inch thick
½ teaspoon salt
¼ teaspoon pepper
½ cup flour
1 egg
2 tablespoons water

1½ cups dry bread crumbs
2 to 4 tablespoons olive oil
4 tablespoons butter
6 fresh sage leaves or
   ¼ teaspoon dried
2 tablespoons fresh lemon
   juice

1. Season liver with salt and pepper. Spread flour on a plate or sheet of wax paper. In a wide shallow bowl, beat egg with water. Place bread crumbs on another plate or sheet of wax paper. Dredge veal in flour; shake off excess. Dip in egg, then coat with bread crumbs. Pat crumbs gently to help them adhere.

2. In a large frying pan, heat 2 tablespoons olive oil over medium heat. Add as many pieces of liver as will fit in pan without crowding and cook, turning once, 4 to 6 minutes, or until golden brown outside and just rosy inside. Add more oil as needed. Remove liver and cover with foil to keep warm. Repeat process until all liver is cooked.

3. Wipe out pan with paper towels. Add butter to pan and melt over medium heat. Add sage leaves and cook until butter just begins to turn brown, about 2 minutes. Remove from heat and add lemon juice. Pour over liver and serve at once.

Chapter 9

Pork

Fresh pork is high on the Italian list of choices for meat. It is said that they know how to cook every inch of the pig—from the snout to the tail. Here I've concentrated just on the parts you know well.

Thinly pounded scaloppine of pork are sautéed in a quick vinegar and garlic reduction, a boneless pork loin is simmered slowly in milk, a traditional specialty that yields an amazingly tender and succulent roast with a rich, caramelized brown gravy, chops are stuffed with apricots and prosciutto and finished in a white wine sauce, chunks of pork and sausages are stewed with zucchini, peppers, and carrots.

Most of the chapters in the book use pork products made in the Italian style. The most recognized are probably sausages and salamis. Fresh sausages seasoned with red pepper flakes come from Calabria, fennel sausages from Sicily, and the mild, generic Italian sweet sausage can be found all over the country. Salamis include the hard, peppery Genoa salami; the larger, smoked sopressata; and mortadella, which, with its white cubes of fat, are the Italian equivalent of what we call bologna. It is used in many fillings for ravioli as well as on the antipasto plate and in little sandwiches, called *pannini*.

Italy boasts some of the best hams in the world. The most famous, prosciutto di Parma, a mild, fragrant ham usually served in very thin slices, often with melon and figs, is now available in this country. Prosciutto is air cured, not smoked; it should be pink, moist, and supple.

Many recipes also call for pancetta, Italian bacon rolled and cured with spices but not smoked. If you cannot find pancetta, substitute Canadian bacon or American bacon blanched in a large pot of boiling water before cooking to remove some of the salt and smoky flavor.

219   PORK SCALOPPINE WITH VINEGAR AND GARLIC

Prep: 20 minutes   Cook: 15 minutes   Serves: 4 to 6

12 whole garlic cloves, peeled
1½ teaspoons red wine vinegar
1 cup water
1½ pounds boneless pork loin,
    cut into ¼-inch-thick
    slices

½ teaspoon salt
¼ teaspoon pepper
2 tablespoons butter
3 tablespoons olive oil

1. In a nonreactive small saucepan, bring garlic cloves, red wine vinegar, and water to a boil over medium heat. Cook tightly covered 10 minutes, or until garlic is soft but still holds its shape.

2. Trim excess fat from pork. Season with salt and pepper. In a nonreactive large frying pan, melt butter with olive oil over medium-high heat. Add pork and cook, turning once, 6 minutes, or until browned on both sides and almost cooked through. Add garlic and its cooking liquid to pan. Cook uncovered until liquid is reduced to ½ cup, about 5 minutes. Season with additional salt and pepper.

220   PORK CUTLETS WITH LEMON-CAPER SAUCE

Prep: 20 minutes   Cook: 20 minutes   Serves: 4

8 thin slices boneless pork
    loin, 1½ to 2 pounds
½ teaspoon salt
½ teaspoon pepper
¼ cup flour
2 eggs
1 tablespoon water

1½ cups dry bread crumbs
2 to 4 tablespoons olive oil
6 tablespoons butter
2 lemons—1 halved, 1 sliced
3 tablespoons capers, rinsed
    and drained

1. Preheat oven to 350°. Pat pork dry. Season with salt and pepper. Dust with flour, dip in eggs beaten with water, then dredge in bread crumbs to coat; pat gently to help crumbs adhere.

2. In a large frying pan, heat 2 tablespoons olive oil over medium-high heat. Add as many pieces of breaded pork as will fit in pan without crowding and cook 1½ minutes on each side; transfer to a baking sheet. Repeat with remaining meat, adding more oil as needed. Bake pork 10 minutes, or until tender and white throughout but still moist.

3. In a medium frying pan, heat 6 tablespoons butter over medium heat 2 minutes, or until it just begins to turn brown. Immediately squeeze juice of halved lemon into pan and add capers. Arrange pork on a platter, pour sauce over, and garnish with lemon slices.

221   PORK AND FENNEL

Prep: 15 minutes   Cook: 1¾ to 2 hours   Serves: 6

1   boneless pork loin roast,
    2½ to 3½ pounds,
    trimmed of fat, rolled,
    and tied
¾   teaspoon salt
½   teaspoon pepper
4   tablespoons olive oil

1   large onion, thinly sliced
1   fennel bulb, trimmed and
    thinly sliced, or 2 cups
    sliced celery and 2
    tablespoons fennel seeds
1   cup water

1. Season pork with salt and pepper. In a Dutch oven, heat oil over medium heat. Add pork and cook, turning several times, 6 to 8 minutes, or until browned all over. Remove to platter. Wipe Dutch oven clean with paper towels.

2. Heat 2 tablespoons olive oil in Dutch oven over medium heat. Add onion and fennel (or celery and fennel seeds) and cook, stirring, 5 minutes, or until softened. Return pork to Dutch oven. Add water and bring to a boil. Reduce heat to low, cover, and cook 1½ hours, or until meat is tender when tested with a fork and juice runs clear. Slice pork and serve with fennel and onion.

222   ROAST PORK WITH MARSALA

Prep: 20 minutes   Cook: 1½ hours   Serves: 6 to 8

The *arrosti*, or roasts, of Italy are usually special-day or Sunday fare. The Italians are very fond of roast pork, and even cold pork sandwiches are a favorite.

1   boneless pork loin roast,
    about 3½ pounds,
    trimmed of fat, rolled,
    and tied
6   garlic cloves, cut in half
3   bay leaves, cut in half

¾   teaspoon salt
½   teaspoon pepper
2   tablespoons olive oil
1   cup dry Marsala or dry
    sherry
½   cup water

1. Preheat oven to 475°. With a sharp paring knife, make 12 slits in pork roast and stud with pieces of garlic. Slip bay leaves under string all around roast. Place pork in a nonreactive small roasting pan. Rub roast with salt, pepper, and olive oil.

2. Roast pork 15 minutes. Turn oven down to 350° and roast 1 hour longer, turning once. Remove meat to a carving board; cover with foil to keep warm.

3. Skim fat from pan juices. Set pan over low heat, add Marsala and water, and bring to a boil, scraping up brown bits from bottom of pan. Boil until liquid is reduced to ¾ cup, about 5 minutes.

4. Remove string and bay leaf from roast. Slice pork and drizzle pan juices over meat.

223   PORK BRAISED IN MILK

Prep: 5 minutes   Marinate: 2 to 8 hours
Cook: 1 hour to 1 hour 10 minutes   Serves: 6

Commonly found in Italy, this dish is sometimes cooked in sheep or goat's milk. The pork is tender and succulent from cooking in milk. This classic dish has its origins in Emilia-Romagna, where the cuisine is rich, and pork and dairy products are abundant.

1 boneless pork loin, 2½ to 3 pounds	¼ teaspoon pepper
2 tablespoons olive oil	3 garlic cloves, chopped
1 tablespoon chopped fresh rosemary or ½ teaspoon dried	2 tablespoons olive oil
	1½ cups milk
	2 tablespoons white wine vinegar

1. Trim excess fat from pork. Rub surface with olive oil, rosemary, pepper, and garlic. Marinate at least 2 hours at room temperature or 8 hours in refrigerator.

2. In a nonreactive Dutch oven, heat olive oil over medium-high heat. Add pork and cook, turning several times, 6 to 8 minutes, or until browned. Reduce heat to very low. Add milk and vinegar. Cover and cook, turning once or twice, 50 to 60 minutes, or until tender but not falling apart.

3. Remove meat to carving board; cover with foil to keep warm. If liquid in pan has not turned brown, cook over low heat until thickened and light brown. Season with salt and additional pepper. Carve pork into ½-inch slices and spoon sauce over.

224   SKEWERED PORK AND SAUSAGES

Prep: 15 minutes   Cook: 12 to 15 minutes   Serves: 4 to 6

While cooking, the bread becomes golden and well seasoned from the sausages. Serve with rigatoni with tomato sauce or my favorite, a dish of roasted peppers.

1 pound boneless pork loin, cut into 1½-inch pieces	3 sweet or hot Italian sausages, cut into 2-inch pieces
10 2-inch cubes Italian bread	

1. Trim excess fat from pork. Thread pork, bread, and sausages onto 8 to 10 long metal skewers, alternating ingredients until they are all used up.

2. Set skewers in a shallow baking pan and broil 3 inches from heat, turning frequently, 12 to 15 minutes, or until pork and sausages are browned and cooked through and bread is golden and crusty.

225 PORK CHOPS STUFFED WITH SMOKED CHEESE

Prep: 15 minutes   Cook: 25 to 35 minutes   Serves: 6

6 pork loin chops, cut 1 inch thick, about 10 ounces each
½ teaspoon salt
½ teaspoon pepper
1 cup soft bread crumbs

½ cup shredded smoked mozzarella or smoked Gouda cheese
¼ cup chopped prosciutto or ham
2 tablespoons olive oil
½ cup water

1. Trim excess fat from chops. With a sharp knife, slit a pocket in meaty part of each chop, cutting toward bone. Season chops with salt and ¼ teaspoon pepper.

2. In a small bowl, combine bread crumbs, cheese, prosciutto or ham, and remaining ¼ teaspoon pepper. Stuff filling into chops; fasten closed with toothpicks.

3. In a large frying pan, heat olive oil over medium-high heat. Add chops and cook, turning once, 3 to 5 minutes, or until browned on both sides. Add water and bring to a boil. Reduce heat to low, cover, and cook 20 to 30 minutes, or until tender and white throughout, turning once. Remove toothpicks and serve.

226 PORK CHOPS WITH APRICOTS AND PROSCIUTTO

Prep: 15 minutes   Cook: 25 to 35 minutes   Serves: 6

6 pork loin chops, cut 1 inch thick, about 10 ounces each
½ teaspoon salt
¼ teaspoon pepper

6 slices prosciutto or ham
6 dried apricots
1½ tablespoons olive oil
1 cup dry white wine
½ cup water

1. Trim excess fat from chops. With a sharp paring knife, slit a pocket in meaty part of each chop, cutting toward bone. Season chops with salt and pepper. Stuff each chop with a slice of prosciutto or ham and an apricot.

2. In a nonreactive large frying pan, heat olive oil over medium-high heat. Add pork chops and cook, turning once, 3 to 5 minutes, or until browned on both sides. Add wine and water and bring to a boil. Reduce heat to low, cover tightly, and cook 20 to 30 minutes, or until pork is tender and white throughout.

227   PORK AND SAUSAGES CONTADINA
Prep: 15 minutes   Cook: 30 to 35 minutes   Serves: 4 to 6

Here is a homey Italian meal in a pot. Serve this hearty dish over polenta, rice, or pasta. Leftovers make a great hero.

1½ pounds boneless pork loin, cut into 1½-inch pieces
½ teaspoon salt
¼ teaspoon pepper
2 tablespoons olive oil
6 links hot Italian sausage, about 1½ pounds
1 large onion, thickly sliced
3 medium zucchini, cut into 1½-inch chunks

2 green bell peppers, cut into 1½-inch squares
6 carrots, peeled and cut into 1-inch pieces
½ cup balsamic or red wine vinegar
4 cups hot cooked polenta, rice, or pasta

1. Preheat oven to 400°. Trim excess fat from pork. Season with salt and pepper. Heat olive oil in a nonreactive large, flameproof casserole over medium-high heat. Add pork and cook, turning, 5 minutes, or until browned on all sides. Remove with a slotted spoon and set aside.

2. Prick sausages all over with tines of a fork and add to casserole. Cook, turning, 5 minutes, or until lightly browned all over. Remove sausages and set aside. Pour off all but 2 tablespoons fat from casserole.

3. Add onion, zucchini, peppers, and carrots to pan. Stir to coat with oil. Return pork and sausages to pan. Transfer to oven and bake uncovered 20 to 25 minutes, turning several times, until pork and sausages are cooked through and vegetables are just tender. Remove from oven and pour vinegar over all. Stir to mix and serve over polenta, rice, or pasta.

228 SAUSAGES AND WHITE BEANS
Prep: 10 minutes   Cook: 35 to 40 minutes   Serves: 6

Luganega sausage is a common lightly spiced sausage often called sweet —meaning only that it is not hot. It is usually not a link sausage.

1½ **pounds lightly spiced sausage, such as luganega, cut into 2-inch pieces**
2 **tablespoons olive oil**
1 **cup chopped carrot**
1 **cup chopped celery**
2 **garlic cloves, chopped**

1 **14-ounce can Italian peeled tomatoes, drained and chopped**
1 **16-ounce can white beans, preferably cannellini, rinsed and drained**
Salt and pepper to taste

1. Prick sausage all over with tines of a fork. In a nonreactive Dutch oven, heat oil over medium heat. Add sausage and cook, turning, 5 minutes, or until lightly browned all over.

2. Add carrot, celery, and garlic to Dutch oven. Cook, stirring, 1 minute. Add tomatoes and bring to a boil. Reduce heat to low, cover, and cook 25 to 30 minutes, or until sausage is cooked through.

3. Add white beans and simmer 5 minutes. Season with salt and pepper.

229 SAUSAGES AND CABBAGE
Prep: 10 minutes   Cook: 40 minutes   Serves: 6

Cabbage is popular all over the world. The Italians prefer Savoy cabbage, with its milder flavor and more tender leaf. This is a great one-pot dish for hearty dining.

6 **links fennel or sweet Italian sausages**
2 **tablespoons olive oil**
1 **14-ounce can Italian peeled tomatoes, drained and chopped**

1 **cup water**
1 **large onion, sliced**
1 **small head of cabbage, preferably Savoy, about 1 pound, cored and shredded**

1. Prick sausages all over with tines of fork. In a nonreactive Dutch oven, heat olive oil over medium heat. Add sausages and cook, turning several times, 5 minutes, or until lightly browned all over. Spoon off fat.

2. Add tomatoes, water, onion, and cabbage to Dutch oven. Bring to a boil, reduce heat to low, cover, and cook 35 minutes, or until sausages are cooked through and vegetables are tender.

230 PORK STEW WITH TOMATOES AND PEPPERS

Prep: 20 minutes   Cook: 30 minutes   Serves: 6

Yellow and red peppers can be sweeter than summer fruit. If you are lucky enough to find yellow tomatoes, this dish will definitely take on "airs."

2 pounds boneless pork loin, cut into 1-inch pieces
¾ teaspoon salt
½ teaspoon pepper
2 tablespoons olive oil
1 medium onion, chopped
2 large bell peppers, red and yellow if possible, cut into 1½-inch squares

1 14-ounce can Italian peeled tomatoes, drained and chopped
2 tablespoons chopped fresh basil or 1 teaspoon dried
1 tablespoon chopped fresh parsley

1. Trim excess fat from pork. Season with salt and pepper. In a nonreactive Dutch oven, heat olive oil over medium-high heat. Add pork and cook, tossing, 3 to 5 minutes, or until lightly browned on all sides.

2. Add onion and bell peppers and cook 2 to 3 minutes, or until onion is softened. Add tomatoes and bring to a boil. Reduce heat to low, cover, and cook 20 minutes, or until pork is tender. Add basil and parsley. Season with additional salt and pepper, if needed.

Chapter 10

Beef

Beef has had a greater place on the Italian-American table than in Italy. The scarcity of grazing land and a natural choice to eat those things available in the area has not allowed beef to develop in Italian cuisine. What you will find most commonly are thin beefsteaks quickly seared and sauced with mushrooms or a little pan wine sauce, or the large Florentine rib chop, dressed with olive oil and herbs.

The large braised pieces of meat lend themselves well to Italian seasonings, and I have given you several recipes that can be used with less costly pieces of beef.

The Val di Chiana beef of northern Italy is from an enormous animal that produces a lean muscle not well marbled with fat, similar to beef now being marketed as "lite" in this country.

Probably the most familiar Italian beef dishes are meatballs and thin rolled beef called *braciolini*. Delicious and savory, they are served alone or cooked in sauces and used with pastas. There are those who say this form of spaghetti and meatballs is an Italian-American development, and you would never find this in Italy. More recent immigrants from northern Italy will tell you the very same thing, but that is a continuing argument about what is traditional and which regional specialties are valid.

231 BEEF STEW WITH SWEET AND HOT PEPPERS

Prep: 20 minutes   Cook: 1¾ hours   Serves: 6 to 8

Peperoncini are mildly hot pickled peppers.

2 pounds boneless beef chuck, cut into 2-inch pieces
1¼ teaspoon salt
½ teaspoon pepper
2 tablespoons olive oil
1 large onion, thinly sliced
¼ teaspoon dried rosemary

1 14-ounce can Italian peeled tomatoes, drained and chopped
2 cups water
2 medium green bell peppers, cut into 1-inch strips
12 peperoncini (Italian pickled peppers), seeded and halved lengthwise

1. Trim excess fat from beef. Season with ¾ teaspoon salt and ¼ teaspoon pepper. In a nonreactive large frying pan, heat oil over medium heat. Add meat and cook, turning, 5 minutes, or until browned on all sides. Remove meat to plate with slotted spoon.

2. Add onion to pan and cook, stirring, 2 to 3 minutes, or until softened. Return beef to pan along with rosemary, tomatoes, and water. Bring to a boil, reduce heat to low, cover, and cook 1¼ hours, or until meat is tender. Add peppers and peperoncini. Cook 10 minutes longer, or until peppers are tender. Season with remaining ½ teaspoon salt and ¼ teaspoon pepper.

232 BRAISED BEEF IN ESPRESSO

Prep: 10 minutes   Cook: 2¾ to 3¼ hours   Serves: 6 to 8

Use instant espresso coffee for a rich sauce and delicious flavor.

1 boneless beef rump roast, 3½ to 4 pounds
1¼ teaspoons salt
½ teaspoon pepper
2 tablespoons olive oil
2 cups chopped onion

1 garlic clove, minced
2 teaspoons fresh thyme leaves or ½ teaspoon dried
1 cup brewed espresso coffee
½ cup dry red wine

1. Trim excess fat from roast. Season with ¾ teaspoon salt and ¼ teaspoon pepper.

2. Heat oil in a nonreactive Dutch oven over medium-high heat. Add meat and cook, turning, about 10 minutes, or until evenly browned all over. Add onion, garlic, thyme, espresso, wine, and remaining ½ teaspoon salt and ½ teaspoon pepper. Bring to a boil, reduce heat to low, cover, and simmer 2½ to 3 hours, turning several times, until meat is fork tender.

3. Remove meat from Dutch oven. Skim fat off pan juices and strain into a warmed gravy boat. Carve meat into thin slices. Serve with pan juices.

233   ROLLED BEEFSTEAK WITH CURRANTS AND RAISINS

Prep: 25 minutes   Cook: 55 minutes   Stand: 10 minutes   Serves: 6

The flavors here are sweet from the currants and sour from the vinegar. This is good hot or cold with rice.

2 cups soft bread crumbs	3 tablespoons olive oil
½ cup plus 2 tablespoons currants or raisins	¾ teaspoon salt
½ cup pine nuts	½ teaspoon pepper
¼ cup grated Romano cheese	¼ pound paper-thin slices capocollo or salami
¼ cup chopped fresh parsley	¼ cup flour
2 tablespoons chopped fresh mint or ¾ teaspoon dried	1 large onion, sliced
2 slices beef top round steak, cut ½ inch thick, about 1 pound each	2 cups water
	¼ cup red wine vinegar

1. In a medium bowl, combine bread crumbs, ½ cup currants or raisins, pine nuts, Romano cheese, parsley, mint, and pepper.

2. Trim excess fat from steak. Pound steak between two pieces of wax paper or plastic wrap until flattened to ¼-inch thickness. Brush with 1 tablespoon olive oil. Season with ½ teaspoon salt and ¼ teaspoon pepper.

3. Cover surface of each steak with capocollo. Cover capocollo with bread crumb mixture. Roll up jelly-roll fashion. Tie with string or fasten with toothpicks. Season with remaining ¼ teaspoon salt and ¼ teaspoon pepper; dust with flour.

4. In a nonreactive large, flameproof casserole, heat remaining olive oil over medium-high heat. Add steak rolls and cook, turning, 5 minutes, or until evenly browned all over. Add onion and water to pan. Bring to boil, reduce heat to low, cover, and cook 30 minutes, turning several times, until meat is fork tender but still holds its shape.

5. Add 2 tablespoons currants and vinegar to casserole. Cook 15 minutes. Remove rolls to cutting board. Let stand 10 minutes before carving.

6. Skim fat off pan juices and strain into a warmed gravy boat. Carve each beef roll into thin slices and serve with pan sauce.

234   FLORENTINE STEAK WITH BRANDY AND MUSHROOMS

Prep: 10 minutes   Cook: 25 minutes   Serves: 4

There are a whole group of mushrooms being marketed as wild, when in fact they are cultivated mushrooms. Shiitake and oyster mushrooms are in this category. They have a delicious flavor. Those of you who live where cèpes or morels can be found are most fortunate.

4 boneless beef rib steaks, cut ½ inch thick, 6 to 8 ounces each
1¼ teaspoons salt
½ teaspoon pepper
5 tablespoons butter
2 tablespoons olive oil
2 garlic cloves, minced
½ cup finely chopped onion

1 pound fresh mushrooms such as shiitakes, oyster mushrooms,cèpes, or morels, sliced
¼ cup brandy, warmed
½ cup canned beef broth
2 tablespoons finely chopped fresh parsley

1. Trim excess fat from steaks. Season with ¾ teaspoon salt and ¼ teaspoon pepper.

2. In a nonreactive large frying pan, melt 3 tablespoons butter with 1 tablespoon olive oil over medium heat. Add garlic and onion and cook 2 to 3 minutes, or until onion is softened. Add mushrooms and cook 4 to 5 minutes, or until they begin to color. Pour brandy into pan and carefully ignite with a match. Shake pan until flames subside. Add stock, bring to boil over high heat, and cook until liquid is reduced to ½ cup, about 5 minutes. Season with remaining ½ teaspoon salt, ¼ teaspoon pepper, and parsley.

3. In another large frying pan over high heat, melt remaining 2 tablespoons butter with 1 tablespoon oil. Add steaks and cook 3 minutes on one side and 3 to 4 minutes on second side, or longer to desired degree of doneness. Remove steaks to a platter and pour mushrooms and sauce over.

235   BRAISED BEEF WITH SAUSAGES AND SWISS CHARD

Prep: 15 minutes   Cook: 1 hour 20 minutes   Serves: 6 to 8

6 hot Italian sausages, about 1½ pounds
2 pounds beef rump roast, cut into 2-inch pieces
½ teaspoon salt
¼ teaspoon pepper
½ cup flour
3 tablespoons olive oil
1 medium onion, chopped

½ cup dry red wine
1 cup water
1 14-ounce can Italian peeled tomatoes, drained and chopped
1 pound Swiss chard, cut into 3-inch pieces, stems included

1. Prick sausages all over with tines of a fork. Cook in a medium frying pan over medium heat 5 to 6 minutes, turning several times, until lightly browned all over. Remove sausages to paper towels to drain.

2. Trim excess fat from roast. Season with salt and pepper. Dust with flour; shake off excess. In a nonreactive large, flameproof casserole, heat olive oil over medium heat. Add meat and cook, turning, about 10 minutes, or until browned on all sides. Remove meat to platter with a slotted spoon. Drain oil from pan and wipe out with paper towel.

3. Heat 1 tablespoon olive oil in cleaned casserole over medium heat. Add onion and cook 2 to 3 minutes, or until softened. Return meat to casserole, along with sausages, wine, water, and tomatoes. Bring to a boil, reduce heat to low, cover, and simmer 45 minutes, or until beef is fork tender.

4. Add Swiss chard to pan. Cover and cook 15 minutes, or until chard is tender. Remove meat, sausages, and chard from pan to warmed platter. Skim fat from pan juices. Season Swiss chard and pan juices with salt and pepper if needed.

---

236 POT ROAST WITH TOMATOES, WINE, AND VEGETABLES
Prep: 20 minutes   Cook: 1½ to 1¾ hours   Serves: 6 to 8

The Italians don't often cook large pieces of meat, but when they do they are succulent, savory, and delicious.

1 beef rump roast, 2½ to 3 pounds	1 14-ounce can Italian peeled tomatoes, drained and chopped
½ teaspoon salt	
¼ teaspoon pepper	1 tablespoon fresh thyme leaves or 1 teaspoon dried
¼ cup flour	
3 tablespoons olive oil	4 medium carrots, peeled and halved
1 medium onion, chopped	
3 garlic cloves, chopped	4 medium zucchini, cut in 2-inch pieces
2 bay leaves	
2 cups dry red wine	2 medium red bell peppers, cut into 2x2-inch squares
2 cups water	

1. Trim excess fat from roast. Season with salt and pepper. Dust with flour. In a nonreactive large Dutch oven, heat olive oil over medium heat. Add rump roast and cook, turning, 10 minutes, or until evenly browned all over.

2. Add onion and cook 2 to 3 minutes, or until softened. Add garlic, bay leaves, wine, water, tomatoes, thyme, and remaining salt and pepper. Bring to a boil, reduce heat to low, cover, and simmer 45 to 60 minutes, or until meat is tender.

3. Add carrots, zucchini, and bell peppers. Cover and cook 15 minutes, or until vegetables are tender. Remove meat to a carving board, cut into ¼-inch slices, and place with vegetables on a warmed serving platter; cover with foil to keep warm.

4. Skim fat from pan juices. If necessary, boil over high heat to reduce to 2½ to 3 cups. Season with additional salt and pepper, if needed. Serve meat and vegetables with pan sauce.

237 BRAISED BEEF WITH CLOVES AND TURNIPS

Prep: 10 minutes   Cook: 2½ to 2¾ hours   Serves: 6 to 8

Sweet turnips and spicy cloves are a flavor combination from northern Italy.

1 boneless beef rump roast, 2½ to 3 pounds	10 whole cloves
1¼ teaspoon salt	2 cups canned beef broth
½ teaspoon pepper	1 cup water
¼ cup flour	12 small white turnips, peeled,
3 tablespoons olive oil	halved if larger than
1 large onion, chopped	2 inches in diameter

1. Trim excess fat from roast. Season with salt and pepper. Dust lightly with flour. In a Dutch oven, heat oil over medium heat. Add meat and cook, turning, 10 minutes, or until evenly browned all over. Add onion and cloves. Cook 2 to 3 minutes, or until onion is softened. Add stock and water and bring to boil. Reduce heat to low, cover, and cook 2 hours, or until meat is fork tender.

2. Add turnips to pot. Cook covered 15 minutes, or until tender. Remove meat and turnips.

3. Skim fat from pan juices. Strain juices, pushing as much onion through sieve as possible. If necessary, return juices to Dutch oven and boil over high heat until reduced to 2½ to 3 cups of sauce. Season with salt and pepper. Carve meat into thin slices and serve with sauce.

238 BEEF WITH CAPERS AND BLACK OLIVES (Fettina di Manzo)

Prep: 10 minutes   Cook: 15 minutes   Serves: 4 to 8

You don't have to pound the steak, but I find thin, quickly cooked pieces of meat delicious with the savory sauce, which is also good cold.

4 to 8 beef strip steaks, cut ¾ inch thick, 2 to 2¼ ounces each	1 14-ounce can Italian peeled tomatoes, drained and chopped
3 tablespoons olive oil	1 cup black olives, pitted and chopped
Salt and pepper to taste	2 tablespoons capers, rinsed
½ cup chopped onion	and drained
2 garlic cloves, chopped	½ cup water

1. Trim excess fat from steaks. Cut horizontally in half so they are very thin (or ask your butcher to do this). Pound steaks between two pieces of wax paper or plastic wrap until flattened to ½-inch thickness. Brush with 1 tablespoon olive oil. Season lightly with salt and pepper.

2. In a nonreactive medium frying pan, heat remaining 2 tablespoons olive oil over medium heat. Add onion and cook 2 to 3 minutes, or until softened. Add garlic and cook 1 minute longer. Add tomatoes, olives, capers, and water. Bring to a boil, reduce heat to medium-low, cover, and cook 5 minutes. Season with salt and pepper to taste.

3. Light a hot fire in a grill or preheat a broiler. Grill or broil beef 3 inches from heat 4 minutes. Turn and cook 3 minutes more. Pour sauce over steak.

---

239   SICILIAN BRACIOLA
Prep: 25 minutes   Cook: 1¾ hours   Serves: 4 to 6

Spoon the sauce over cooked fettuccine and serve the sliced meat in the center.

12 ounces ground chuck	4 ounces provolone, thinly
1 egg	sliced
¼ cup grated Romano cheese	2 hard-cooked eggs, quartered
1 tablespoon chopped fresh	¼ cup flour
parsley	3 tablespoons olive oil
Pinch of grated nutmeg	1 medium onion, chopped
1 teaspoon salt	1½ cups dry red wine
½ teaspoon pepper	1 14-ounce can Italian peeled
2 beef top round steaks, cut	tomatoes, drained and
½ inch thick, 1 to 1¼	chopped
pounds each	1 cup water
4 ounces capocollo, thinly	
sliced	

1. In a medium bowl, combine ground chuck, egg, cheese, parsley, nutmeg, ½ teaspoon salt, and ¼ teaspoon pepper. Mix with your hands or a wooden spoon to blend well.

2. Trim excess fat from steaks. Layer half each of capocollo and then provolone cheese on each round steak. Spread ground beef mixture evenly over cheese. Place 4 egg quarters down center of each steak. Roll up steaks around eggs, jelly-roll fashion. Tie with string or fasten with toothpicks. Rub with remaining ½ teaspoon salt and ¼ teaspoon pepper. Dust with flour to coat lightly.

3. In a nonreactive large Dutch oven, heat oil over medium-high heat. Add meat roll and cook, turning, 5 minutes, or until evenly browned all over. Add onion and cook 2 to 3 minutes, or until softened. Add wine, tomatoes, and water. Bring to a boil and reduce heat to low. Cover and simmer 1½ hours, turning several times.

4. Remove meat rolls to warmed platter; cover loosely with foil to keep warm. Quickly boil pan sauce over medium-high heat until reduced to 2½ cups. Remove string or picks from meat and cut each roll into three pieces. Serve with sauce.

240 MEAT LOAF WITH HARD-BOILED EGGS
Prep: 15 minutes   Cook: 30 minutes   Serves: 6 to 8

This meat loaf is very good hot or cold, served with green sauce. You might try a spicy tomato juice with this.

2 to 3 slices Italian bread cut into ½-inch cubes, to make 1 cup	2 teaspoons fresh thyme leaves or ½ teaspoon dried
1 6-ounce can tomato juice	2 tablespoons chopped fresh parsley
2 pounds ground beef chuck	
2 eggs	1½ teaspoons salt
¼ cup finely chopped onion	¼ teaspoon pepper
2 garlic cloves, chopped	4 hard-cooked eggs, peeled

1. Preheat oven to 350°. In a large bowl, combine bread and tomato juice. Let stand 10 minutes to soften bread. Add beef, eggs, onion, garlic, thyme, parsley, salt, and pepper. Mix with your hands or a wooden spoon to blend well.

2. On a piece of wax paper set on a baking sheet, flatten meat into a 12x8-inch rectangle. Arrange a line of hard-cooked eggs lengthwise down center of rectangle. Using paper to help lift meat, roll from long side into a sausage shape. Pinch edges to seal. Bake, seam side down, 30 minutes, until firm to touch.

241 STEAK WITH GORGONZOLA
Prep: 10 minutes   Cook: 7 to 10 minutes   Serves: 4

Steak and blue cheese is a good combination. Gorgonzola gives this dish an even bigger boost in flavor. Salt the meat only lightly, as the cheese is salty.

3 ounces gorgonzola or other blue cheese	1 tablespoon olive oil
3 tablespoons butter, softened	½ teaspoon salt
1 boneless top sirloin steak, cut ½ inch thick, 1½ to 2 pounds	½ teaspoon pepper
	2 garlic cloves, minced

1. In a small bowl, mash cheese and butter together with a fork. Set gorgonzola butter aside.

2. Preheat broiler. Trim excess fat from steak. Brush with olive oil. Season with salt, pepper, and garlic. Place steak on rack in broiler pan 3 to 4 inches from heat; broil 3 minutes on one side, 3 to 5 minutes on the other, depending on desired degree of doneness. Spread gorgonzola butter over one side of meat. Broil 30 seconds longer. Slice meat thin and serve.

242   CHUCK STEAK PIZZAIOLA
Prep: 10 minutes   Cook: 45 minutes to 1 hour   Serves: 4 to 6

Named after the pizza man, this is a favorite inexpensive family dish that I like to serve with roasted potatoes.

1 beef chuck steak, cut 1 inch
  thick, 1½ to 2 pounds
1 small onion, chopped
1 14-ounce can Italian peeled
  tomatoes, drained and
  chopped

1 tablespoon chopped fresh
  oregano or 1 teaspoon
  dried
2 garlic cloves, chopped
½ teaspoon salt
  Pinch of hot pepper flakes
2 tablespoons olive oil

1. Preheat oven to 350°. Trim excess fat from steak. Place in a shallow glass baking dish with plenty of space around meat. In a medium bowl, combine onion, tomatoes, oregano, garlic, salt, hot pepper flakes, and olive oil. Spread over top of steak.

2. Bake steak uncovered 45 minutes to 1 hour, or until tender. Slice steak and serve with tomato sauce from pan.

243   MEAT LOAF WITH MOZZARELLA
Prep: 20 minutes   Cook: 35 to 40 minutes   Serves: 6

This will make a good inside-out Italian hamburger if you want to serve it sliced on a bun.

½ cup tomato juice
2 to 3 slices Italian bread,
  trimmed of crust and cut
  into ½-inch cubes, to
  make 1 cup
2 pounds ground beef chuck
¼ cup finely chopped onion
¼ cup finely chopped celery
2 eggs

1 teaspoon dried oregano
1½ teaspoons salt
¼ teaspoon pepper
8 ounces mozzarella cheese,
  sliced
2 cups marinara sauce,
  homemade (page 131) or
  jarred, heated

1. Preheat oven to 350°. In a large bowl, combine tomato juice and bread. Let stand 10 minutes to soften bread. Add beef, onion, celery, eggs, oregano, salt, and pepper. Mix with your hands or a wooden spoon to blend well.

2. On a piece of wax paper set on a baking sheet, flatten meat into a 12x8-inch rectangle. Arrange mozzarella slices in a lengthwise line down center of rectangle. Using paper to help lift meat, roll up jelly-roll fashion from one long side. Pinch edges to seal. Bake for 35 to 40 minutes, or until firm. Serve with heated marinara sauce.

244   BEEF STEW WITH ARTICHOKES AND PEAS
Prep: 15 minutes   Cook: 1 hour 10 minutes   Serves: 6

When they're in season, Italians use artichokes whenever they can. In Italy, trimmed little baby artichokes are usually added to stews. In this country, frozen artichoke hearts are a tremendous time-saver.

2 pounds boneless beef
   chuck, cut in 1-inch pieces
½ teaspoon salt
¼ teaspoon pepper
2 tablespoons olive oil
1 medium onion, chopped
1 14-ounce can Italian peeled
   tomatoes, drained and
   chopped

2 cups water
1 10-ounce package frozen
   artichoke hearts,
   defrosted
1 10-ounce package frozen
   peas, defrosted
½ teaspoon dried sage leaves
2 tablespoons chopped fresh
   parsley

1. Trim excess fat from beef. Season with salt and pepper. In a nonreactive Dutch oven, heat olive oil over medium heat. Add beef and cook, turning, 5 minutes, or until browned on all sides. Add onion and cook 2 to 3 minutes, or until softened. Add tomatoes and water and bring to a boil. Reduce heat to low, cover, and cook 45 minutes, or until meat is tender.

2. Add artichoke hearts and cook uncovered 5 minutes. Add peas, sage, and parsley and cook 3 minutes longer.

245   STEAK PIZZAIOLA ALLA RICK
Prep: 10 minutes   Cook: 10 to 15 minutes   Serves: 2 to 4

This sauce is almost raw. You can combine everything several hours ahead of time and heat just before serving. This is best on the barbecue, served with grilled vegetables.

4 beef strip steaks, cut ½ inch
   thick, 6 to 8 ounces each
3 tablespoons olive oil
1 teaspoon salt
¼ teaspoon pepper
1 small onion, chopped
1 14-ounce can Italian peeled
   tomatoes, drained and
   chopped

2 teaspoons chopped fresh
   oregano leaves or
   ½ teaspoon dried
2 garlic cloves, chopped
   Pinch of hot pepper flakes

1. Trim excess fat from steaks. Pound steaks between two pieces of wax paper or plastic wrap until flattened to ¼-inch thickness. Brush with 1 tablespoon olive oil. Season with ½ teaspoon salt and pepper.

2. In a nonreactive medium saucepan, heat remaining 2 tablespoons olive oil over medium heat. Add onion and cook 2 to 3 minutes, or until softened. Add tomatoes, oregano, garlic, remaining ½ teaspoon salt, and hot pepper flakes. Bring to a boil, reduce heat to low, and cook 7 to 8 minutes to blend flavors. Cover and keep warm.

3. Light a hot fire in a grill or preheat broiler. Grill or broil steaks 3 inches from heat 2 minutes. Turn and cook 1 to 2 minutes more, being careful not to overcook. Spoon sauce over beef.

246   STEAK MARSALA WITH MUSHROOMS
Prep: 15 minutes   Cook: 20 minutes   Serves: 4

Marsala, which comes from Sicily, is used all over Italy in sauces and desserts. Grill the steaks on your barbecue if you can.

4 boneless beef rib steaks, cut ½ inch thick, 6 to 8 ounces each	1 pound fresh mushrooms, stems trimmed
3 tablespoons olive oil	2 tablespoons chopped fresh parsley
1 teaspoon salt	2 teaspoons fresh thyme leaves or ½ teaspoon dried
½ teaspoon pepper	
2 tablespoons butter	
½ cup finely chopped onion	½ cup dry Marsala or sherry

1. Trim excess fat from steaks. Brush with 1½ tablespoons olive oil. Season with ½ teaspoon salt and ¼ teaspoon pepper.

2. In a nonreactive large frying pan, melt butter with remaining 1½ tablespoons olive oil over medium heat. Add onion and cook 2 to 3 minutes, or until softened. Add mushrooms, parsley, and thyme. Cook, stirring, until mushrooms begin to color, 4 to 5 minutes. Add marsala and cook 3 to 5 minutes, or until liquid is reduced by half. Season with remaining ½ teaspoon salt and ¼ teaspoon pepper. Cover and keep warm over very low heat.

3. Light a hot fire in a grill or preheat broiler. If grilling, cook 3 minutes on one side, then turn and cook 2 to 3 minutes on second side, or longer to desired degree of doneness. If broiling, place steaks on rack in broiler pan about 3 inches from heat; broil 3 to 4 minutes on one side, 2 to 3 minutes on the other, depending on desired degree of doneness. Spoon mushrooms over top to serve.

247   MEATBALLS IN CAPER SAUCE

Prep: 15 minutes   Cook: 25 to 30 minutes   Serves: 6 to 8

These meatballs are from Sicily, where capers are grown and used abundantly.

1   cup soft bread crumbs
¼   cup milk
1½   pounds ground beef chuck
½   teaspoon salt
½   teaspoon pepper
4   tablespoons capers, rinsed
    and drained

1   egg
¼   cup flour
2   tablespoons olive oil
½   cup dry white wine
1   cup canned beef broth
1   tablespoon chopped fresh
    parsley

1. In a large bowl, combine bread crumbs and milk. Let stand 5 minutes to soften bread. Add ground chuck, salt, pepper, 2 tablespoons capers, and egg. Mix with your hands or a wooden spoon to blend well. Form into 1-inch meatballs. Dust lightly with flour.

2. In a nonreactive large frying pan, heat oil over medium heat. Add meatballs and cook, turning, 5 to 6 minutes, or until evenly browned all over. Add wine and stock to pan and bring to a boil. Reduce heat to low, cover, and simmer 15 minutes. Add remaining capers and parsley just before serving.

Chapter 11

Lamb

"On Sundays the roast was often lamb." I guess that statement covers a lot of ethnic and not-so-ethnic backgrounds. The statement varies, of course, in what follows. How it was seasoned, whether it was served well done or pink, or very rare, and what went along with it on the plate. The Italians stud lamb with garlic and rosemary and rub the surface with salt, black pepper, and olive oil. They roast it to just barely pink and serve it, depending upon which region you are from, with a few roasted potatoes, or beans, or firm slices of polenta. Roast Lamb with Pomegranate Juice is a unique dish I hope you'll try.

A whole roast lamb is not an easy thing to serve in a restaurant, so it is still in the realm of home cooking, which, for those who eat out frequently, makes it even more special.

Boned leg of lamb makes excellent stew, whether you choose sweet peppers, garlic, or fennel as the primary flavoring. And lamb steaks are excellent value. Cut from the leg, they are meaty and not as fat as some other cuts of meat.

Italians are particularly fond of meat on the bone, so included here are recipes for Braised Lamb Shanks and chops—Milanese, with Mint Pesto, in Red Wine.

---

248 ROSEMARY ROAST LAMB
Prep: 15 minutes   Cook: 1¾ hours   Serves: 6 to 8

This is the most traditional way to cook lamb throughout the Mediterranean.

1 leg of lamb, 4½ to 5 pounds	½ teaspoon pepper
1 tablespoon olive oil	8 garlic cloves, cut into slivers
1 teaspoon salt	2 tablespoons dried rosemary

1. Preheat oven to 425°. Trim excess fat from lamb. With point of a small paring knife, make tiny slits in surface of lamb. Slip a piece of garlic clove and a bit of rosemary into each slit. Rub lamb with olive oil; season with salt and pepper. Sprinkle any remaining rosemary over lamb.

2. Roast at 425° 15 minutes. Reduce oven temperature to 375° and roast 1½ hours longer, or until medium-rare.

249 ROAST LAMB WITH POMEGRANATE JUICE

*Prep: 10 minutes   Marinate: 3 hours   Cook: 1¼ to 1¾ hours
Serves: 6 to 8*

This roast and sauce are a rich, dark brown when finished. Unsweetened pomegranate juice is available in health food stores and Middle Eastern groceries.

1 leg of lamb, 4½ to 5 pounds	½ teaspoon pepper
4 cups unsweetened	2 tablespoons cold butter
pomegranate juice	Pomegranate seeds, for
2 tablespoons olive oil	garnish (optional)
1 teaspoon salt	

1. Preheat oven to 425°. Trim excess fat from lamb. Place in a large bowl. Pour 2½ cups pomegranate juice around lamb. Let marinate at room temperature 2 to 3 hours, turning several times.

2. Remove lamb from marinade. Pat meat dry; rub with olive oil, and season with salt and pepper.

3. Place leg of lamb in a roasting pan and roast 15 minutes. Reduce oven temperature to 325°. Cook, turning twice, 1 to 1½ hours, until medium-rare.

4. Remove lamb to a cutting board. Pour off fat from pan. Add remaining 1½ cups pomegranate juice to roasting pan and bring to a boil over medium-high heat, scraping up any brown bits from bottom of pan. Cook, stirring, until reduced by half, 3 to 5 minutes. Remove from heat and swirl in butter. Season with additional salt and pepper. Carve lamb, pour sauce over, and garnish with fresh pomegranate seeds, if available.

250 SWEET AND SOUR LAMB

Prep: 10 minutes   Cook: 40 to 45 minutes   Serves: 4

Agro dolce—sweet and sour—is a favorite way of cooking strong-flavored meat, such as lamb or venison. I like to serve this with wide noodles, like pappardelle.

3 pounds boneless leg of	3 tablespoons olive oil
lamb, cut into 1-inch	¼ cup tomato paste
pieces	1 cup water
1 teaspoon salt	½ cup red wine vinegar
½ teaspoon pepper	2 teaspoons sugar

1. Trim excess fat from lamb. Season with salt and pepper. In a nonreactive large frying pan or flameproof casserole, heat olive oil over medium-high heat. Add meat and cook, turning several times, 5 minutes, or until browned on all sides.

2. Add tomato paste, water, vinegar, and sugar. Bring to a boil, reduce heat to low, cover, and simmer 30 minutes, or until lamb is fork tender.

3. Uncover and boil 5 to 8 minutes, until sauce is thickened slightly.

251   ROLLED LAMB WITH CLOVES OF GARLIC
Prep: 15 minutes   Cook: 1½ hours   Serves: 6 to 8

16 garlic cloves, unpeeled
2   tablespoons chopped fresh
    parsley
2   teaspoons fresh oregano
    leaves or ¾ teaspoon
    dried

1   leg of lamb, boned, 3½ to
    4 pounds
1½ teaspoons salt
¾   teaspoon pepper
1½ tablespoons olive oil

1. Preheat oven to 350°. Bake unpeeled garlic cloves in a small baking pan covered with foil 15 minutes. Peel garlic. Increase oven temperature to 475°.

2. Set lamb on flat work surface, boned side up. Scatter whole garlic cloves, parsley, and oregano over lamb. Season with 1 teaspoon salt and ¼ teaspoon pepper. Roll up roast and tie at 2-inch intervals. Rub lamb with olive oil. Season with remaining salt and pepper. Place lamb in an open roasting pan.

3. Roast lamb at 475° 15 minutes. Reduce oven temperature to 350° and cook 1¼ hours longer, or until lamb is medium-rare. Serve with pan juices.

252   LAMB CHOPS MILANESE
Prep: 15 minutes   Cook: 10 to 15 minutes   Serves: 4

8   lamb rib chops, cut about
    1 inch thick, 5 to 6 ounces
    each
1   teaspoon salt
½   teaspoon pepper
½   cup flour
2   eggs

2   tablespoons water
1½ cups dry bread crumbs
3   tablespoons grated
    Parmesan cheese
2   to 3 tablespoons butter
2   to 3 tablespoons olive oil
    Lemon wedges

1. Trim excess fat from chops. Pound chops between two pieces of wax paper or plastic wrap, being careful not to separate meat from bone, until meat is flattened to about ¼-inch thickness. Season on both sides with salt and ¼ teaspoon pepper.

2. Spread flour on a plate or sheet of wax paper. In wide shallow bowl, beat eggs and water until well blended. On another plate or sheet of wax paper, combine bread crumbs, Parmesan cheese, and remaining ¼ teaspoon pepper. Dredge chops in flour. Dip in beaten eggs, then in seasoned bread crumbs; pat gently to help crumbs adhere.

3. In a large frying pan, melt 1 tablespoon butter with 1 tablespoon olive oil over medium heat. Add two or three of the chops and cook, turning once, 5 minutes, or until golden brown on both sides. Drain on paper towels. Repeat with remaining chops, adding more butter and oil, if needed. Serve with lemon wedges.

253   BRAISED LAMB SHANKS

Prep: 15 minutes   Cook: 1¾ hours   Serves: 6

Another one-dish meal. Serve with lots of garlic bread. Any leftover sauce and bits of meat will dress pasta beautifully.

6 lamb shanks, about 10 ounces each	1 tablespoon fresh thyme leaves or ½ teaspoon dried
1¼ teaspoons salt	12 garlic cloves, peeled
½ teaspoon pepper	1 14-ounce can Italian peeled tomatoes, drained and chopped
½ cup flour	
¼ cup olive oil	
1 large onion, chopped	1 cup dry red wine
2 cups chopped celery	1 cup water
1 cup chopped carrot	Garlic Bread (page 196)
2 tablespoons fresh rosemary or 1 teaspoon dried	

1. Trim excess fat from lamb. Season with ¾ teaspoon salt and ¼ teaspoon pepper. Dust with flour; shake off excess. In a nonreactive large, flameproof casserole, heat 2 tablespoons olive oil over medium-high heat. Add lamb shanks and cook, turning several times, 10 minutes, or until nicely browned all over. Remove shanks to platter. Pour off oil from casserole and wipe out with paper towels.

2. Heat remaining 2 tablespoons oil in casserole. Add onion, celery, carrots, rosemary, and thyme. Cook 3 to 4 minutes, or until vegetables are softened. Add garlic, tomatoes, wine, and water. Bring to a boil, reduce heat to low, and simmer 3 minutes.

3. Return lamb shanks to casserole. Cover and simmer over low heat 1½ hours, or until tender. Remove shanks from pan. Skim fat from pan juices. Season juices with additional salt and pepper, if needed. Serve with meat.

254   BONED ROLLED LAMB WITH PESTO

Prep: 20 minutes   Cook: 1½ hours   Serves: 6 to 8

Delicious hot or cold. Serve with Italian potato salad.

1 leg of lamb, boned, 3½ to 4 pounds	¾ cup pesto, homemade (page 77) or jarred
	1½ cups soft bread crumbs

1. Preheat oven to 450°. Trim excess fat from lamb. Open lamb with cut side up. Smear pesto over meat. Sprinkle bread crumbs over pesto. Roll up lamb and tie securely with kitchen string at 2-inch intervals. Place in open roasting pan.

2. Roast lamb at 450° 15 minutes. Reduce oven temperature to 350° and roast 1¼ hours, or until medium-rare. Remove to cutting board and cut into thin slices to serve.

255   LAMB STEW WITH GREEN BEANS AND BASIL

Prep: 15 minutes   Cook: 40 minutes   Serves: 6

This was the usual lamb dish prepared in my mother's kitchen. The tomatoes, beans, and basil were from my father's garden.

3 pounds lean lamb stew meat, cut into 1½-inch cubes	1 14-ounce can Italian peeled tomatoes, drained and chopped
1¼ teaspoons salt	1 pound green beans
½ teaspoon pepper	2 tablespoons chopped basil leaves or ¾ teaspoon dried
2 tablespoons olive oil	
3 garlic cloves, chopped	1 tablespoon chopped fresh parsley
1 small onion, chopped	
1 cup water	

1. Trim excess fat from lamb. Season with ¾ teaspoon salt and ¼ teaspoon pepper. In a large flameproof casserole, heat oil over medium heat. Add lamb and cook, turning several times, until lightly browned, about 5 minutes.

2. Add garlic and onion to pan. Cook, stirring, 2 minutes. Add water and tomatoes, bring to a boil, reduce heat to low, cover, and simmer 20 minutes.

3. Add green beans, basil, and remaining salt and pepper. Cook until lamb and beans are tender, about 15 minutes longer. Garnish with chopped parsley.

256   LAMB CHOPS IN RED WINE

Prep: 5 minutes   Cook: 6 to 10 minutes   Serves: 4

8 lamb rib chops, cut about 1 inch thick, about 7 ounces each	2 tablespoons olive oil
	½ cup dry red wine
1 teaspoon salt	1 teaspoon dried thyme
½ teaspoon pepper	2 tablespoons chopped fresh parsley
2 tablespoons butter	

1. Trim excess fat from chops. Pound chops between two pieces of wax paper or plastic wrap, being careful not to separate meat from bone, until meat is flattened to about ¼-inch thickness. Season on both sides with salt and pepper.

2. In a nonreactive large frying pan, melt 1 tablespoon butter with 1 tablespoon olive oil over medium heat. Add chops and cook, turning once, 4 to 6 minutes, or until barely pink in center. Remove chops to plate and cover with foil to keep warm. Repeat with remaining chops, adding more butter as needed.

3. Add wine and thyme to pan. Boil over high heat, scraping up browned bits from bottom of pan, until reduced to about 2 tablespoons, 2 to 3 minutes. Add parsley. Pour sauce over chops.

257   LAMB STEAKS WITH ARTICHOKES

Prep: 10 minutes   Cook: 35 minutes   Serves: 4

Baby lamb or kid is often prepared this same way.

4   lamb steaks, about ¾ inch
    thick, cut from leg, about
    8 ounces each
½   teaspoon salt
¼   teaspoon pepper
2   tablespoons olive oil
½   cup chopped prosciutto or
    ham

1   medium onion, chopped
1   cup dry white wine
1   tablespoon tomato paste
1   teaspoon dried thyme
1   8½-ounce can small
    artichoke hearts

1. Trim excess fat from steaks. Season with salt and pepper.

2. In a nonreactive large skillet or flameproof casserole, heat olive oil over medium-high heat. Add lamb steaks and cook, turning once, 3 to 4 minutes, until lightly browned on both sides. Add prosciutto or ham, onion, wine, tomato paste, and thyme. Bring to a boil, reduce heat to low, cover, and cook for 25 minutes, or until lamb is tender. Add artichoke hearts and simmer 3 minutes longer. Season with additional salt and pepper.

258   LAMB ROTOLO WITH HAM, SAGE, AND GARLIC

Prep: 20 minutes   Cook: 1¾ hours   Serves: 6

1   leg of lamb, boned, 3½ to
    4 pounds
6   garlic cloves, chopped
12 fresh sage leaves, chopped,
    or 1½ teaspoons dried
1½ cups soft bread crumbs

3½ tablespoons olive oil
4   very thin slices prosciutto or
    ham
1   teaspoon salt
½   teaspoon pepper
1   cup dry red wine

1. Preheat oven to 450°. Trim excess fat from lamb. Open lamb cut side up.

2. In a small bowl, combine garlic, sage, bread crumbs, and 2 tablespoons olive oil. Arrange prosciutto or ham slices on lamb, overlapping if necessary. Spread bread mixture evenly over ham. Roll up lamb and tie securely with kitchen string at 2-inch intervals. Rub with remaining 1½ tablespoons olive oil. Season with salt and pepper. Place in open roasting pan.

3. Roast lamb at 450° 15 minutes. Reduce heat to 350° and roast 1¼ hours, or until medium-rare. Remove meat to cutting board; skim fat off pan juices. Set roasting pan over medium heat and stir in wine. Bring to a boil, scraping up any browned bits from bottom of pan. Cook until reduced by half, about 3 minutes. Season with salt and pepper. Slice meat and serve with pan juices.

259   LAMB BRAISED WITH FENNEL
Prep: 15 minutes   Cook: 1 hour to 1 hour 5 minutes   Serves: 6

This dish can be beautiful with fresh fennel. If not available, 1 tablespoon fennel seed will impart some of the flavor, and 4 celery ribs, coarsely chopped, can simulate the texture.

3 pounds boneless leg of lamb
1 teaspoon salt
½ teaspoon pepper
3 tablespoons olive oil
1 large onion, thinly sliced

1 fennel bulb, trimmed and coarsely chopped
¼ cup chopped fresh parsley
2½ cups milk

1. Cut lamb into 6 equal pieces. Season with salt and pepper. In a large flameproof casserole, heat oil over medium heat. Add lamb and cook, turning several times, 5 to 7 minutes, or until browned on all sides. Remove lamb with a slotted spoon and set aside.

2. Add onion and fennel to casserole. Cook covered over medium-low heat, stirring occasionally, 3 to 5 minutes, or until softened.

3. Add parsley and milk. Return lamb to pan. Bring just to a simmer, reduce heat to very low, cover, and cook, turning several times, 35 to 40 minutes, or until lamb is tender. While lamb is cooking, stir bottom of pan well with wooden spoon occasionally to prevent milk from burning.

260   LAMB CHOPS WITH MINT PESTO
Prep: 15 minutes   Cook: 7 to 8 minutes   Serves: 4

1 cup packed fresh mint leaves
½ cup fresh parsley leaves
¼ cup walnuts
3 garlic cloves, chopped
1 cup plus 2 tablespoons extra-virgin olive oil

2 tablespoons white wine vinegar
1¾ teaspoons salt
½ teaspoon pepper
8 lamb shoulder chops, about 7 ounces each

1. Place mint, parsley, walnuts, and garlic in a food processor. Process until chopped. With machine on, pour 1 cup olive oil through feed tube in a slow stream. Continue to process until pesto is finely chopped but not pureed. Season with vinegar, ¾ teaspoon salt, and ¼ teaspoon pepper. Set mint pesto aside.

2. Light a hot fire in a grill or preheat a broiler. Trim excess fat from chops. Season with remaining 1 teaspoon salt, ¼ teaspoon pepper, and 2 tablespoons olive oil. Grill or broil 3 inches from heat 4 minutes on one side. Turn and cook 2 minutes more, or until cooked to desired doneness. Serve with mint pesto.

261 ROASTED LAMB SHANKS
Prep: 20 minutes   Cook: 1¾ hours   Serves: 6

These little roasts of lamb provide generous servings. The roast potatoes and garlic make it a one-dish meal.

6 **lamb shanks, about 12 ounces each**	9 **large red potatoes, peeled and halved**
3 **tablespoons olive oil**	12 **whole garlic cloves, peeled**
¾ **teaspoon salt**	2 **tablespoons fresh rosemary or 1 teaspoon dried**
¼ **teaspoon pepper**	

1. Preheat oven to 450°. Trim all fat from lamb. Rub with 1 tablespoon olive oil. Season with salt and pepper.

2. In a large baking pan, toss potatoes with remaining 2 tablespoons olive oil. Put lamb and garlic in pan. Scatter rosemary over top.

3. Cook at 450° 15 minutes. Reduce heat to 350° and cook, turning several times, 1½ hours, or until shanks are fork tender.

262 LAMB WITH SWEET RED PEPPERS
Prep: 15 minutes   Cook: 50 minutes   Serves: 4 to 6

3 **pounds boneless leg of lamb, cut into 1½-inch pieces**	2 **garlic cloves, chopped**
1 **teaspoon salt**	2 **cups hot water**
½ **teaspoon pepper**	3 **tablespoons chopped fresh parsley**
3 **tablespoons olive oil**	2 **large red bell peppers, cut into 1½- to 2-inch pieces**

1. Trim excess fat from lamb. Season with ½ teaspoon salt and ¼ teaspoon pepper. In a large frying pan or flameproof casserole, heat oil over high heat. Add lamb and cook, turning frequently, 3 to 5 minutes, or until browned on all sides.

2. Add garlic, water, and remaining ½ teaspoon salt and ¼ teaspoon pepper. Bring to a boil, reduce heat to medium, and cook partially covered 30 minutes. Uncover and cook 10 minutes longer, or until lamb is fork tender.

3. Add parsley and red peppers to pan. Cook 10 minutes, or until peppers are just tender.

263 NORTHERN ITALIAN LAMB STEW WITH TURNIPS AND MUSHROOMS

Prep: 15 minutes   Cook: 1¼ hours   Serves: 6

Turnips, cabbage, and buckwheat flour find their way to Italian dishes from the northern areas of Austria, Switzerland, and Yugoslavia.

4 pounds boneless leg of lamb, cut into 2-inch pieces
1½ teaspoons salt
½ teaspoon pepper
½ cup flour
3 tablespoons olive oil
1 large onion, chopped
2 garlic cloves, chopped
1 cup Chianti or other dry red wine

2 cups water
2 bay leaves
6 small carrots, peeled
12 medium white turnips, peeled and cut in half
1 pound fresh whole mushrooms
1 teaspoon dried thyme

1. Trim excess fat from lamb. Season with 1 teaspoon salt and ¼ teaspoon pepper. Dust lightly with flour; shake off excess.

2. In a nonreactive Dutch oven, heat 1½ tablespoons olive oil over medium-high heat. Add lamb and cook, turning frequently, 6 minutes, or until browned on all sides. Add onion and garlic and cook 2 to 3 minutes, or until onion is softened. Add Chianti, water, and bay leaves. Bring to a boil, reduce heat to medium-low, cover, and cook 35 minutes. Add carrots and turnips and cook covered 15 minutes, or until vegetables are tender.

3. Meanwhile, in a large frying pan, heat remaining 1½ tablespoons olive oil over medium heat. Add mushrooms and cook, stirring, 5 minutes, or until lightly browned. Season with thyme and remaining ½ teaspoon salt and ¼ teaspoon pepper. Add to stew and simmer 5 minutes.

Chapter 12

Vegetables, Frittatas, and Tortas

Vegetables play an important role in any Italian meal, from the simplest method of preparing them—blanching, then quickly tossing them in hot olive oil and garlic—to the vegetable stews and pasta sauces with vegetables that are especially prevalent in the south.

Everyone has a very definite idea of the perfectly cooked vegetable. A little crunch is good, but you should be able to put your fork into it without having it pop off your plate. Al dente, or underdone, potatoes, are wrong in anyone's book. Too, vegetables that are not cooked beyond the rock stage have not been allowed to develop their full flavor, and any sauce will probably slip off the surface. Vegetables that are overdone, on the other hand, are sad to behold.

Unless you live where there is a long growing season, you are limited in variety for most of the year, except for frozen and canned vegetables and whatever fresh vegetables are trucked in, sometimes not of the best quality. Use fresh whenever possible, although there are good-quality frozen vegetables; peas and spinach come to mind. Tomatoes are very important to Italian cooking, especially the southern dishes, so feast when they are in full season. There are some fairly good canned tomatoes that can be used and are, in fact, often used in Italian homes. Recommended are peeled whole tomatoes (drain and chop them) and tomatoes crushed with puree, which are a very good product for thick tomato sauces.

Vegetables in Italy are often served as a separate course in a meal, not part of a plate with meat and potatoes. A dish of roasted peppers at a table has as much importance as a dish of pasta or a serving of meat or fish. Vegetables also show up in antipasti, in egg dishes, soups, pasta sauces, and rice, and very often as a single dish, or *contorno*, to round out a meal. Dishes are made colorful with red and green peppers, zucchini, and a variety of beans—such as green, yellow wax, romanos, favas, and fresh cranberry beans, all of which enrich the Italian table.

Summer gardeners can really "cook Italian" when all these delicious vegetables are available. Italians are also fond of leafy vegetables and lettuces such as arugula, spinach, broccoli rabe, escarole, Swiss chard, and dandelion, and they use them generously. And vegetables like peppers and artichokes shine when they are stuffed with a savory filling.

A final word: A *frittata* is an Italian omelet, cooked slowly until just set in the center. Combined with any variety of vegetables and cheeses, they provide a great way to use leftovers and are just as good warm, cold, or at room temperature.

264　BRAISED ARTICHOKES

Prep: 10 minutes　Cook: 50 minutes to 1 hour　Serves: 4

4　medium artichokes
1　lemon, cut in half
1　tablespoon olive oil
4　slices pancetta or bacon, cut in 1-inch pieces, about 4 ounces
1　large onion, chopped
1　14-ounce can Italian peeled tomatoes, drained and chopped

1　cup water
1　tablespoon chopped fresh oregano or 1 teaspoon dried
2　tablespoons chopped fresh parsley
1　teaspoon salt
½　teaspoon pepper

1. Using a sharp stainless steel knife, cut 1 inch from top of each artichoke. Rub with cut side of lemon.

2. In a nonreactive large, flameproof casserole with a tight-fitting cover, heat olive oil over medium heat. Add pancetta and onion and cook 3 to 4 minutes, or until onion is softened. Add tomatoes, water, oregano, parsley, salt, and pepper. Bring to a boil, reduce heat to low, and cook 3 to 4 minutes to blend flavors.

3. Add artichokes to casserole and cover. Simmer 35 to 45 minutes, or until leaf pulls easily away from artichoke and is tender. Drain. When cool enough to handle, pull center leaves apart and, with a melon baller, gently scrape hairy "choke" from center of artichoke. Serve artichokes in shallow soup bowls with tomato sauce from casserole.

265　STUFFED ARTICHOKES SICILIAN

Prep: 20 minutes　Cook: 45 minutes　Serves: 4

4　medium artichokes
3　cups soft bread crumbs
2　tablespoons chopped fresh parsley
3　garlic cloves, chopped

3　flat anchovy fillets, chopped
¼　cup grated Parmesan cheese
4　tablespoons olive oil
4　slices lemon

1. With a sharp stainless-steel knife, cut 1 inch from top of each artichoke. Pull center leaves apart, and with a melon baller gently scrape hairy "choke" from center. Set aside.

2. In a small bowl, combine bread crumbs, parsley, garlic, anchovies, and Parmesan cheese. Stuff center of artichokes with most of bread stuffing. Force remainder down between some of larger leaves.

3. Place artichokes in single layer in a Dutch oven. Pour in 1 inch of water. Drizzle 1 tablespoon olive oil over each artichoke and place a slice of lemon on top. Bring to a simmer over medium heat, reduce heat to medium-low, cover, and cook 40 minutes, or until leaves pull out easily, adding a little water from time to time if needed. Serve hot or at room temperature.

266   ARTICHOKES AND PEAS WITH MINT
Prep: 2 minutes   Cook: 10 minutes   Serves: 4 to 6

Mint is a favorite herb in Italy, even though it is less commonly associated with Italian food in this country. It is especially a favorite of the Romans.

1 10-ounce package frozen
   artichoke hearts
1 10-ounce package frozen
   peas
¼ cup heavy cream
2 tablespoons finely chopped
   onion

1 tablespoon chopped fresh
   mint or 1 teaspoon dried
¼ teaspoon salt
½ teaspoon pepper

1. In a medium saucepan, cook frozen artichokes in 1 cup boiling water for 4 minutes, breaking up gently with fork. Drain and return to pan.

2. Add peas to artichokes and cover. Cook covered over very low heat for 3 minutes to heat through. Add cream and onion to pan and simmer 2 minutes, or until cream is bubbly and hot. Stir in mint and season with salt and pepper.

267   ASPARAGUS BUNDLES WITH PROSCIUTTO
Prep: 10 minutes   Cook: 9 to 12 minutes   Serves: 4

Here's a great first course that can be prepared hours ahead and finished off just before serving.

1 pound medium asparagus
4 thin slices prosciutto or
   ham, about 1 ounce

3 tablespoons butter, melted
¼ cup grated Parmesan cheese

1. Preheat oven to 375°. Cut 2 inches from stem ends of asparagus. Use a swivel-bladed vegetable peeler to scrap bottom half of asparagus stalks. Cook asparagus in a large saucepan of boiling salted water until crisp-tender, 3 to 4 minutes, depending on thickness. Drain in a colander and rinse under cold running water. Drain well.

2. Divide cooled asparagus into four bunches. Wrap each portion of asparagus with a piece of ham to make four bundles. Place in a 17 x 11-inch baking dish. Drizzle butter over top and sprinkle with Parmesan cheese.

3. Bake 6 to 8 minutes, or until Parmesan begins to turn a golden brown.

268   WHITE ASPARAGUS BUNDLES PARMESAN
Prep: 5 minutes   Cook: 5 minutes   Serves: 2 to 4

Fresh white asparagus are very difficult to find. Canned white asparagus can be very delicious when cooked this way.

1 1-pound can white asparagus, drained	1 teaspoon paprika
4 tablespoons butter	¼ cup grated Parmesan cheese

Preheat broiler. Arrange asparagus in a 9-inch glass pie plate and dot with butter. Sprinkle with paprika and Parmesan cheese. Broil 3 inches from heat 4 to 5 minutes, or until asparagus is heated through and cheese begins to turn a golden brown.

269   THE BEST BEETS
Prep: 10 minutes   Cook: none   Serves: 4 to 6

2 garlic cloves, minced	½ teaspoon freshly ground
2 flat anchovy fillets, chopped	pepper
3 tablespoons red wine vinegar	⅛ teaspoon salt

3 tablespoons extra-virgin
     olive oil
	1 15-ounce can sliced beets,
	    drained

	2 tablespoons chopped fresh parsley

In a medium bowl, combine garlic, anchovies, vinegar, olive oil, pepper, and salt. Beat with a fork to blend. Add beets and toss. Taste for salt, remembering that anchovies are salty, and correct seasoning if needed. Garnish with chopped parsley.

270   BROCCOLI WITH GOLDEN GARLIC AND LEMON
Prep: 10 minutes   Cook: 10 minutes   Serves: 2 to 4

This is not a difficult recipe, but its success depends upon not burning the garlic.

1 bunch broccoli, about 1 pound	½ teaspoon salt
¼ cup extra-virgin olive oil	⅛ teaspoon pepper

3 garlic cloves, cut into thin
     slivers
	3 tablespoons fresh lemon
	    juice

1. Cook broccoli in a large saucepan of boiling salted water 5 to 6 minutes, or until crisp tender. Drain in a colander. Arrange in a serving dish and cover with foil to keep warm.

2. In a small frying pan, warm olive oil over low heat. Stir in garlic and cook slowly until golden brown, being careful not to burn, 1 to 2 minutes. Add salt, pepper, and lemon juice. Pour over broccoli.

271 BROCCOLI RABE
Prep: 5 minutes   Cook: 10 to 12 minutes   Serves: 4

This delicious vegetable should be well cooked. It has a slightly bitter but pleasant taste and can be enjoyed hot or at room temperature.

2 bunches broccoli rabe, 1½ to 2 pounds	2 tablespoons red wine vinegar
2 tablespoons olive oil	½ teaspoon salt
1 garlic clove, finely chopped	¼ teaspoon pepper
Pinch of hot pepper flakes	

1. Cook broccoli rabe in a large saucepan of boiling salted water 8 to 10 minutes, or until tender. Drain in a colander.

2. In a nonreactive large frying pan, heat olive oil over medium heat. Add garlic and hot pepper flakes and cook 30 seconds, or until garlic is fragrant, being careful not to burn it. Add broccoli rabe to pan and cook, tossing, 1 minute, or until heated through. Remove from heat. Sprinkle vinegar, salt, and pepper over broccoli rabe and toss again.

272 CARROTS WITH MARSALA
Prep: 5 minutes   Cook: 15 minutes   Serves: 4 to 6

Carrots are often a very neglected vegetable. Be sure to follow the instructions carefully; do not be tempted to add all the stock at once, for the result will not be as rich and delicious.

1½ pounds carrots, peeled	¼ teaspoon salt
1½ cups Chicken Stock (page 48) or reduced-sodium canned broth	⅛ teaspoon pepper
	1½ tablespoons sugar
	¼ cup dry Marsala or sherry

1. Cut carrots into ½-inch slices. In a nonreactive medium frying pan, combine carrots with ¾ cup stock, salt, and pepper. Cover tightly and cook, shaking pan several times, over medium heat 3 minutes, or until stock is almost evaporated.

2. Add another ¾ cup stock, cover, and cook as above. Repeat process until all the stock has evaporated. Sprinkle sugar over carrots and cook, stirring, 2 minutes, or until carrots begin to brown. Add Marsala or sherry and cook, stirring occasionally, until wine evaporates to a glaze, 2 to 3 minutes.

273   EGGPLANT PARMIGIANA

Prep: 1 hour   Stand: 35 to 40 minutes   Cook: Serves: 6

A very rich version. This can be prepared a day ahead and cooked just before serving.

2 eggplants, 1¼ to 1½ pounds each	½ to ¾ cup olive oil
2 tablespoons coarse (kosher) salt	3½ cups marinara sauce, homemade (page 131) or jarred
½ cup flour	2 cups Besciamella Sauce (recipe follows)
3 eggs	
2 tablespoons water	2 cups shredded mozzarella cheese, about 8 ounces
2½ cups dry bread crumbs	
1 teaspoon salt	½ cup grated Parmesan cheese
½ teaspoon pepper	

1. Trim ends and peel skin from eggplant. Slice eggplant into ¼-inch rounds. Sprinkle with coarse salt and layer in a colander. Place a plate with a weight on top (such as two 1-pound cans) and let drain 35 to 40 minutes. Pat slices dry with paper towels.

2. Spread flour on a flat plate or sheet of wax paper. In a wide shallow bowl, beat eggs and water until well blended. On another plate or piece of wax paper, combine bread crumbs with salt and pepper. Dredge eggplant slices in flour. Dip in beaten egg, then dredge in seasoned bread crumbs; pat gently to help crumbs adhere.

3. In a large frying pan, heat ½ cup olive oil over medium heat. Add 3 to 4 slices of eggplant at a time, being careful not to crowd pan, and cook 3 to 4 minutes, or until golden brown on both sides. Remove eggplant to drain on paper towels while cooking remaining pieces, adding remaining ¼ cup olive oil to pan if needed.

4. Spread ½ cup marinara sauce over bottom of 13 x 9-inch baking dish. Place a single layer of eggplant on sauce. Spread ½ cup besciamella sauce over eggplant; top with 1 cup marinara sauce, ¼ cup of the mozzarella, and 2 tablespoons Parmesan cheese. Make 3 more layers, ending with the Parmesan cheese.

5. Bake 30 minutes, or until bubbly and brown on top. Let stand 5 minutes before serving.

BESCIAMELLA SAUCE
Makes about 2 cups

1 cup milk	3 tablespoons flour
1 cup Chicken Stock (page 48) or reduced-sodium canned broth	½ teaspoon salt
	⅛ teaspoon pepper
	¼ teaspoon grated nutmeg
4 tablespoons butter	⅛ teaspoon dried thyme

1. In a small saucepan, combine milk and chicken stock. Bring just to a simmer over medium-low heat. Keep warm.

2. In a heavy medium saucepan, melt butter over low heat. Add flour and cook, stirring, 2 to 3 minutes without allowing flour to brown.

3. Remove pan from heat and whisk in hot milk and stock. Return to low heat and cook, whisking occasionally, 4 to 5 minutes, until sauce is medium thick. Season with salt, pepper, nutmeg, and thyme.

274 EGGPLANT WITH SUN-DRIED TOMATOES
Prep: 1 hour   Stand: 35 to 40 minutes   Cook: 20 minutes   Serves: 6

This is eggplant parmigiana with a face lift. Something old with a fresher look.

2 **eggplants, 1¼ to 1½ pounds each**	6 **sun-dried tomatoes in oil, drained and cut into thin slivers**
2 **tablespoons coarse (kosher) salt**	½ **cup chopped fresh basil or 2 tablespoons dried**
½ **cup flour**	⅔ **cup grated Parmesan cheese**
3 **eggs**	2 **cups marinara sauce, homemade (page 131) or jarred, heated**
2 **tablespoons water**	**Whole basil leaves, for garnish**
2½ **cups dry bread crumbs**	
1 **teaspoon salt**	
½ **teaspoon pepper**	
½ **to ¾ cup olive oil**	
1 **pound mozzarella cheese, thinly sliced**	

1. Trim ends from eggplant. Slice unpeeled eggplant into ¼-inch rounds. Sprinkle with coarse salt and layer in a colander. Place a plate with a weight on top (such as two 1-pound cans) and let drain 35 to 40 minutes. Pat slices dry with paper towels.

2. Spread flour on a flat plate or sheet of wax paper. In a wide shallow bowl, beat eggs and water until well blended. On another plate or piece of wax paper, combine bread crumbs with salt and pepper. Dredge eggplant pieces in flour. Dip in beaten egg, then in seasoned bread crumbs; pat gently to help crumbs adhere.

3. In a large frying pan, heat ½ cup olive oil over medium heat. Add 3 to 4 slices of eggplant at a time, being careful not to crowd pan, and cook 3 to 4 minutes, or until golden brown on both sides. Remove eggplant to drain on paper towels while cooking remaining pieces, adding remaining ¼ cup olive oil to pan if needed.

4. Set eggplant slices on an oiled 15 x 12-inch baking sheet in a single layer. Lay slices of mozzarella on eggplant rounds, overlapping as necessary. Top with pieces of sun-dried tomato and chopped basil. Sprinkle with Parmesan cheese.

5. Bake 15 minutes, until eggplant is heated through and cheese is melted and bubbly. To serve, spoon heated marinara sauce down center of each row of eggplant. Garnish with basil leaves.

275   GREEN BEANS WITH TOMATOES AND BASIL

Prep: 10 minutes   Cook: 15 to 18 minutes   Serves: 6

1 pound green beans	1 tablespoon chopped fresh
1½ tablespoons olive oil	basil or ½ teaspoon dried
1 small onion, finely chopped	1 tablespoon chopped fresh
1 14-ounce can Italian peeled	parsley
tomatoes, drained and	½ teaspoon salt
chopped	¼ teaspoon pepper

1. Cook beans in a large saucepan of boiling salted water 5 minutes; beans will still be crisp. Drain in a colander and rinse under cold running water. Drain well.

2. Meanwhile, in a large frying pan, heat olive oil over medium heat. Add onion and cook 2 to 3 minutes, or until softened. Add tomatoes, basil, and parsley. Cook 3 minutes to heat and combine flavors. Stir beans into pan and cook 5 to 6 minutes, or until crisp tender. Season with salt and pepper.

276   GREEN BEANS WITH PROVOLONE CHEESE

Prep: 10 minutes   Cook: 10 minutes   Serves: 4

Provolone is a good sharp cheese easily found in most grocery stores. The provolone will melt slightly and season the beans deliciously.

1 pound green beans,	½ cup water
preferably romano pole	½ teaspoon salt
beans	⅛ teaspoon pepper
2 garlic cloves, minced	8 ounces provolone cheese,
1½ tablespoons olive oil	cut into ¼-inch dice

1. Cook beans in a large saucepan of boiling salted water 5 minutes; beans will still be crisp. Drain in a colander and rinse under cold running water. Drain well.

2. In a large frying pan, cook garlic in olive oil over medium heat until fragrant, about 30 seconds, being careful not to burn. Add beans to pan and stir to coat with oil. Add water to pan and cook, stirring occasionally, 3 to 4 minutes, or until crisp tender. Season with salt and pepper.

3. Remove pan from heat. Add provolone to hot beans and toss. Serve immediately.

277   LEEKS AND BEL PAESE CHEESE
Prep: 15 minutes   Cook: 45 to 50 minutes   Serves: 6

Leeks are not commonly used in modern-day Italy, but when they are, they are often cooked with cheese.

**4 medium leeks, about
    5 ounces each**
	**1 tablespoon minced fresh
	    parsley**

3½ tablespoons butter	**¼ teaspoon pepper**
2 cups milk	**4 ounces Bel Paese cheese, thinly sliced**

1. Trim all but 1 inch of the green ends from leeks. Trim root ends and remove any coarse outer leaves. Place leeks on a cutting board and cut in half lengthwise, using a sharp knife. Wash cut leeks twice in cold water, or until all sand and grit is removed. Drain and pat dry. Cut leeks crosswise into 1-inch pieces.

2. In a large saucepan, melt 3 tablespoons butter over medium heat. Stir leeks into butter and cook 2 to 3 minutes, or until slightly translucent. Pour milk into pan and cook, stirring, over medium-high heat 2 to 3 minutes, or until milk is heated through. Reduce heat to low and cover pan. Cook 20 to 25 minutes, or until leeks are tender. Drain in a colander, discarding milk.

3. Preheat oven to 350°. Grease a 1-quart casserole with remaining ½ tablespoon butter. Add leeks to casserole and sprinkle with parsley and pepper. Cover with Bel Paese. Bake 15 to 18 minutes, or until cheese is melted and leeks are heated through.

278   GRILLED MUSHROOMS
Prep: 10 minutes   Cook: 6 to 8 minutes   Serves: 4

12 large fresh mushrooms	**1 teaspoon salt**
2 tablespoons olive oil	**¼ teaspoon pepper**
2 garlic cloves, minced	**Lemon wedges**

**1 tablespoon minced fresh
     oregano or 1 teaspoon
     dried**	

1. Prepare a hot fire in a grill or preheat a broiler.

2. Wipe mushrooms clean with a damp towel. Cut stem ends level with caps. In a small bowl, combine olive oil, garlic, and oregano. Brush mushrooms with oil mixture. Season mushrooms with salt and pepper.

3. Place mushroom caps, stem side down, on an oiled grill rack or in a broiler pan set 4 to 6 inches from heat. Grill or broil 3 to 5 minutes until well marked from grill. Turn over and cook 3 minutes longer, or until mushrooms are tender but still hold their shape. Serve with lemon wedges.

279   MUSHROOMS TRIFOLATA

Prep: 10 minutes   Cook: 7 to 10 minutes   Serves: 4 to 6

This recipe is especially good if you mix in some wild mushrooms; you need to purchase just a few ounces. *Trifolata* means thinly sliced.

2 tablespoons butter	2 teaspoons fresh thyme
2 tablespoons olive oil	leaves or ½ teaspoon
¼ cup chopped onion	dried
2 garlic cloves, minced	1 teaspoon salt
2 pounds mushrooms, thinly	¼ teaspoon pepper
sliced	¼ teaspoon grated nutmeg
2 tablespoons chopped	
parsley	

1. In a large frying pan, melt butter with olive oil over medium heat. Add onion and garlic and cook 2 to 3 minutes, or until onion is softened.

2. Add mushrooms to pan, increase heat to medium-high, and cook, stirring, 5 to 6 minutes, or until lightly browned around edges. Stir in parsley, thyme, salt, pepper, and nutmeg.

280   POTATO PIZZAIOLA

Prep: 10 minutes   Cook: 50 minutes   Serves: 6

This is how the pizza man would make potatoes.

3½ to 4 pounds large red	1 14-ounce can Italian peeled
potatoes	tomatoes, drained and
3 tablespoons olive oil	chopped
4 garlic cloves, minced	¾ cup grated Parmesan cheese
1 tablespoon chopped fresh	1½ teaspoons salt
oregano or 1 teaspoon	½ teaspoon freshly ground
dried	pepper

1. Preheat oven to 350°. Cook potatoes in a large saucepan of boiling salted water, for 10 minutes only. Drain potatoes and remove skins. Cut potatoes into ½-inch slices.

2. Brush an 11 x 7-inch baking dish with 1 teaspoon olive oil. Place one third layer of potatoes in baking dish, overlapping slightly. Season with one third each of the garlic, oregano, tomatoes, remaining olive oil, Parmesan, salt, and pepper. Repeat layers twice, using remaining ingredients. Bake 40 minutes, or until potatoes are tender when tested with a knife and lightly browned and bubbly.

281 PEAS WITH PANCETTA AND BITTER GREENS

Prep: 5 minutes   Cook: 6 to 8 minutes   Serves: 4

1 tablespoon butter
2 tablespoons chopped onion
¼ cup chopped pancetta or bacon (2 ounces)
1 10-ounce package frozen peas
¾ cup water

1 cup packed arugula or watercress leaves
1 tablespoon extra-virgin olive oil
½ teaspoon salt
⅛ teaspoon pepper

1. In a medium frying pan, melt butter over medium heat. Add onion and pancetta or bacon and cook 2 to 3 minutes, or until onion is softened.

2. Add peas, water, and arugula. Increase heat to medium-high and cook, stirring frequently, 3 to 4 minutes, until peas are tender and greens wilted. Stir in olive oil, salt, and pepper.

282 STUFFED PEPPERS

Prep: 15 minutes   Cook: 1 hour   Serves: 6

In the summer we had stuffed peppers for supper at least once a week. We liked them best late in the season when the peppers would begin to turn red.

6 small to medium red or green bell peppers, 1¾ to 2 pounds
2 tablespoons olive oil
1 medium onion, chopped
1 pound sweet or hot Italian sausage, casings removed
2 cups cooked rice

1 tablespoon chopped fresh parsley
¼ cup grated Parmesan cheese
1 egg
½ teaspoon salt
½ teaspoon pepper
2 cups tomato sauce
½ cup water

1. Preheat oven to 350°. Cut tops from peppers and remove seeds and ribs, keeping peppers whole. Brush outside of peppers with 2 teaspoons olive oil.

2. In a medium frying pan, heat remaining olive oil over medium heat. Add onion and cook 2 to 4 minutes, or until softened. Crumble sausage meat into pan and cook, stirring to break up lumps, until it begins to lose its pinkness, 5 to 7 minutes.

3. Using a slotted spoon, remove sausage and onion to a medium bowl. Add rice, parsley, Parmesan cheese, and egg. Toss to mix. Season with salt and pepper.

4. Stuff peppers, with rice and sausage filling, mounding top slightly. Place peppers in a 13 x 9-inch baking dish. Mix tomato sauce with water and pour into dish around peppers. Bake 45 minutes.

283   ROASTED POTATOES
Prep: 10 minutes   Cook: 45 minutes   Serves: 6

Simple, and always best with roasted meats or grilled chicken.

4 large baking potatoes	1 teaspoon salt
3 tablespoons olive oil	¼ teaspoon pepper

1. Preheat oven to 375°. Cook potatoes in a large saucepan of boiling salted water for 10 minutes only. Drain and peel off skins. Cut potatoes into thick chunks about 2 x 1 inch.

2. Pour olive oil into a 13 x 9-inch baking dish. Add potatoes and toss to coat with oil. Season with salt and pepper. Roast, turning once, 35 minutes, or until tender inside and crispy brown outside.

284   RED CABBAGE WITH VINEGAR AND BLACK OLIVES
Prep: 10 minutes   Cook: 12 to 15 minutes   Serves: 6 to 8

⅓ cup extra-virgin olive oil	16 black olives, preferably
1 medium onion, thinly sliced	Niçoise
4 cups shredded red cabbage	Salt and pepper to taste
3 tablespoons balsamic or red wine vinegar	

In a nonreactive large frying pan, heat olive oil over medium heat. Add onion and cook 3 to 5 minutes, until soft. Add red cabbage to pan and cook, tossing, for 2 to 3 minutes in oil, until color turns bright and cabbage is well coated with oil. Cover and cook 6 to 8 minutes, until cabbage is crisp-tender. Stir in balsamic vinegar and olives. Season with salt and pepper.

285   PEAS WITH MINT AND TOMATOES
Prep: 5 minutes   Cook: 10 to 13 minutes   Serves: 4

When available, use fresh red or yellow tomatoes, peeled and chopped.

3 tablespoons butter	1 tablespoon chopped fresh
2 tablespoons chopped onion	mint or 1 teaspoon dried

1 14-ounce can Italian peeled
      tomatoes, drained and
      chopped
	½ teaspoon salt

	⅛ teaspoon pepper
1 10-ounce package frozen peas	

1. In a medium frying pan, melt butter. Add onion and cook over medium heat 2 to 3 minutes, or until softened. Add tomatoes and cook 5 minutes to heat and blend flavors.

2. Add peas and mint and cook uncovered until liquid is reduced and peas are tender, 3 to 5 minutes. Season with salt and pepper.

---

286   DIRTY PEAS
Prep: 5 minutes   Cook: 10 to 12 minutes   Serves: 2 to 4

"Dirty peas" is a rather unattractive dish with great flavor. Only those you love will understand.

3 tablespoons butter	½ cup Chicken Stock (page 48)
1 tablespoon olive oil	or reduced-sodium
¼ cup chopped onion	canned broth
¼ cup chopped prosciutto or ham	3 tablespoons cream
	½ teaspoon salt
1 10-ounce package frozen peas	¼ teaspoon pepper

1. In a medium frying pan, melt butter with olive oil over medium heat. Add onion and prosciutto or ham and cook 2 to 3 minutes, or until onion is softened. Add peas and stock, increase heat to medium-high, and cook uncovered 3 minutes.

2. Add cream and cook 3 to 5 minutes, until liquid is reduced and peas begin to collapse and turn brown. Season with salt and pepper.

---

287   MASHED POTATOES CASALINGA
Prep: 15 minutes   Cook: 35 minutes   Serves: 4 to 6

6 baking potatoes, 3½ to 4 pounds	¼ teaspoon pepper
	½ cup finely chopped salami
4 tablespoons butter, cut up	4 ounces Italian fontina or
1½ cups hot milk	Gruyère cheese, diced
1 teaspoon salt	3 scallions, minced
	1 garlic clove, minced

1. In a large saucepan of boiling salted water, cook potatoes 30 minutes, or until tender. Drain and remove skins.

2. Return potatoes to saucepan and mash with a potato masher over very low heat until no lumps remain and potatoes are dry. Add butter and continue to mash until butter is melted.

3. Gradually stir in hot milk and beat with a wooden spoon until well blended. Season mashed potatoes with salt and pepper. Stir in salami, cheese, scallions, and garlic.

288   SPINACH ALLA ROMANA
Prep: 10 minutes   Cook: 6 minutes   Serves: 2

This is such a great dish, I like to serve it as a single course all by itself.

2 pounds fresh spinach, washed and stems removed	2 ounces thinly sliced prosciutto, shredded
1 tablespoon olive oil	3 tablespoons golden raisins
2 tablespoons pine nuts	1 tablespoon butter
1 garlic clove, minced	¼ teaspoon salt
	⅛ teaspoon pepper

1. In a nonreactive large frying pan over medium-high heat, cook spinach, covered, in water that clings to leaves 2 to 3 minutes, or until spinach is wilted but still bright green and all the water is evaporated. Drain and squeeze to remove excess liquid. Set aside.

2. In a medium frying pan, heat olive oil over medium heat. Add pine nuts and garlic and cook, stirring, until garlic is fragrant and pine nuts are golden, about 30 seconds. Add spinach, prosciutto, and raisins and cook about 2 minutes, until heated through. Stir in butter until melted. Season with salt and pepper.

289   RICE AND ONION TORTA
Prep: 10 minutes   Cook: 1 to 1¼ hours   Serves: 8 to 10

Cooked in a large baking pan and cut into small squares, this is good cocktail food.

2 cups water	3 tablespoons chopped fresh basil or 2 teaspoons dried
1 cup long-grain rice	
2 tablespoons butter	1 teaspoon chopped fresh oregano or ¼ teaspoon dried
2 tablespoons olive oil	
2 large onions, chopped	2 tablespoons minced fresh parsley
5 eggs	
1¼ cups grated Parmesan cheese	

1. Preheat oven to 350°. In a medium saucepan, bring water to a boil over high heat. Stir in rice, cover tightly, reduce heat to low, and simmer until rice is tender, about 20 minutes. Set aside.

2. In a large frying pan, melt butter in 1 tablespoon olive oil over medium heat. Cook onions, stirring, 4 to 6 minutes, or until soft but not brown.

3. In a large bowl, beat eggs lightly. Add cooked rice, onions, 1 cup Parmesan cheese, basil, oregano, and parsley. Stir to combine. Brush an 11 x 8-inch baking pan with remaining 1 tablespoon olive oil. Pour egg-onion mixture into pan and smooth evenly with a spatula. Sprinkle remaining ¼ cup Parmesan cheese over top. Bake 40 to 45 minutes, or until mixture is cooked through and set and lightly browned on top.

290 TOMATOES BEL PAESE

Prep: 15 minutes   Cook: 20 to 25 minutes   Serves: 6 to 8

4 large ripe tomatoes, 1½ to
  2 pounds
2 ounces Bel Paese cheese, cut
  into ¼-inch dice
2 tablespoons capers, rinsed
  and drained

1 tablespoon minced fresh
  parsley
¼ teaspoon pepper
1½ tablespoons extra-virgin
  olive oil

1. Preheat oven to 350°. Cut tomatoes in half crosswise and squeeze gently to extract seeds and juice. Using a teaspoon, scoop out remaining pulp from center of tomatoes to form cups. Chop pulp and place in a medium bowl. Add cheese, capers, parsley, and pepper and toss together to combine.

2. Brush a 12 x 8-inch baking dish with ½ tablespoon olive oil. Spoon tomato-cheese mixture into tomato cups and arrange them in baking dish. Drizzle remaining olive oil over tomatoes. Bake 20 to 25 minutes, or until cheese has melted and tomatoes are heated through but still hold their shape.

291 STUFFED TOMATOES

Prep: 10 minutes   Cook: 50 minutes   Serves: 6

1 10-ounce package frozen
  spinach
2 tablespoons butter
1 small onion, chopped
2 cups soft bread crumbs
¼ cup grated Parmesan cheese

½ teaspoon salt
¼ teaspoon grated nutmeg
1 egg, beaten
6 medium tomatoes (2 to
  2½ pounds)
1 teaspoon olive oil

1. Preheat oven to 350°. Cook spinach according to directions on package. Drain in colander and press out water with back of a wooden spoon. In a small frying pan, heat 1 tablespoon butter over medium heat. Add onion and cook for 2 to 3 minutes, or until softened. Remove from heat.

2. In a medium bowl, combine onion, spinach, bread crumbs, Parmesan cheese, salt, and nutmeg. Stir in egg and mix to blend well.

3. With a sharp knife, slice 1 inch from top of each tomato. Turn tomatoes over and squeeze gently to extract seeds and juice. Using a teaspoon, scoop out remaining pulp from center of tomatoes to form cups. Chop pulp and stir into spinach mixture. Spoon spinach filling into tomatoes and arrange in a 9-inch buttered baking dish. Drizzle olive oil over tomatoes. Bake 35 minutes. Serve hot or cold.

292 ZUCCHINI STUFFED WITH ZUCCHINI
Prep: 20 minutes   Cook: 30 minutes   Serves: 6 or 12

Prepare these ahead of time and cook just before serving.

6 medium zucchini, about 6 ounces each	½ cup soft bread crumbs
3 tablespoons olive oil	1 tablespoon chopped fresh parsley
½ cup chopped onion	½ cup grated Parmesan cheese
1 cup finely chopped prosciutto or ham, about 3 ounces	1 egg
	½ teaspoon salt
	¼ teaspoon grated nutmeg

1. Preheat oven to 350°. Trim ends from zucchini, but leave whole. Cook zucchini in a large saucepan of boiling salted water 3 minutes; drain and rinse under cold running water. Cut zucchini in half lengthwise. Scoop out centers to form a trench down middle of each zucchini half. Chop zucchini centers and place in a medium bowl.

2. In a medium frying pan, heat 2 tablespoons olive oil over medium heat. Add onion and cook 2 to 3 minutes, or until softened. Stir in prosciutto or ham, chopped zucchini, bread crumbs, and parsley. Cook, stirring once or twice, 2 minutes. Remove from heat and stir in ¼ cup Parmesan cheese, egg, salt, and nutmeg.

3. Stuff zucchini with bread crumb mixture. Place zucchini in a flameproof baking dish just large enough to hold them. Drizzle remaining 1 tablespoon olive oil over zucchini and sprinkle with remaining ¼ cup Parmesan cheese.

4. Bake 20 minutes, or until heated through. Transfer to the broiler and broil 3 inches from heat until golden brown on top, 1 to 2 minutes.

293 ZUCCHINI, PEPPER, AND TOMATO STEW
Prep: 20 minutes   Cook: 10 to 15 minutes   Serves: 4 to 6

Stir in a few beaten eggs to this finished stew. Pile into a cut loaf of Italian bread for a hero sandwich.

1½ pounds medium zucchini	1 tablespoon chopped fresh oregano or 1 teaspoon dried
2 red and/or green bell peppers (1 to 1¼ pounds)	
3 tablespoons olive oil	½ teaspoon dried rosemary
1 large onion, chopped	1 cup water
2 garlic cloves, chopped	¾ teaspoon salt
1 14-ounce can Italian peeled tomatoes, drained and chopped	½ teaspoon pepper
	¼ cup red wine vinegar (optional)
2 tablespoons chopped fresh parsley	

1. Trim ends from zucchini. Cut zucchini into 2-inch rounds. Core and seed peppers, then cut into 1-inch squares.

2. In a nonreactive large frying pan, heat olive oil over medium heat. Add onion and garlic and cook 2 to 3 minutes, or until onion is softened. Add zucchini and peppers and cook, stirring, 2 to 3 minutes, or until vegetables are crisp tender.

3. Add tomatoes, parsley, oregano, rosemary, and water. Bring to a boil, reduce heat to low, cover, and cook 5 to 6 minutes, or until vegetables are tender. Uncover, increase heat to medium-high, and cook 2 to 3 minutes to reduce any excess liquid. Season with salt and pepper.

4. Serve hot. Or, to serve chilled or at room temperature, let cool, then stir in vinegar.

---

294 SALAMI AND ROASTED PEPPER FRITTATA
Prep: 5 minutes   Cook: 10 minutes   Serves: 2

4 **eggs**	Half a 7.25-ounce jar roasted
½ **teaspoon salt**	red peppers, drained and
⅛ **teaspoon pepper**	cut into 1-inch strips,
1 **tablespoon water**	about ½ cup
2 **tablespoons olive oil**	2 **tablespoons chopped fresh**
6 **thin slices salami**	basil or 1 teaspoon dried
	2 **tablespoons grated**
	Parmesan cheese

1. Preheat oven to 375°. In a medium bowl, beat eggs, salt, pepper, and water until well blended.

2. In a 9-inch frying pan with a heatproof handle, heat olive oil over medium heat. Pour eggs into pan, cook, shaking pan and stirring at same time with a wooden spoon. As eggs begin to set around edges, stir them into center. When eggs are half cooked, 2 to 3 minutes, scatter salami and peppers on top. Sprinkle with basil and Parmesan cheese.

3. Place pan on middle rack of oven. Bake 2 to 3 minutes, or until set. Remove pan from oven with a heatproof mitt. Slip a spatula around edge of pan to loosen. Cut into wedges to serve.

295   SWISS CHARD AND CHICK-PEAS
Prep: 10 minutes   Cook: 20 minutes   Serves: 4 to 6

This is good as a vegetable, but equally good tossed with cooked shell or bow-tie pasta.

2 bunches of Swiss chard, about 1½ pounds
¼ cup olive oil
1 medium onion, chopped
3 garlic cloves, chopped
1 16-ounce can chick-peas, rinsed and drained

1 14-ounce can Italian peeled tomatoes, drained and chopped
1 cup water
¾ teaspoon salt
¼ teaspoon pepper

1. Separate stems from leaves of chard. Slice stems into 2-inch pieces; set leaves aside. In a large saucepan, cook chard stems in boiling salted water 2 minutes. Add chard leaves and cook 3 minutes longer. Drain well.

2. In a large frying pan, heat oil over medium heat. Add onion and cook 2 to 3 minutes, or until softened. Add garlic and cook 1 minute longer. Add Swiss chard, chick-peas, tomatoes, and 1 cup water. Partially cover and simmer 12 minutes, or until flavors blend and excess liquid evaporates. Season with salt and pepper.

296   FRITTATA WITH MARINATED ARTICHOKES AND HAM
Prep: 5 minutes   Cook: 10 minutes   Serves: 2

4 eggs
½ teaspoon salt
⅛ teaspoon pepper
1 tablespoon water
1½ tablespoons olive oil
1 6-ounce jar marinated artichokes, drained

2 ounces thinly sliced and quartered prosciutto or ham, cut into 2 x 1-inch strips
2 tablespoons grated Parmesan cheese

1. Preheat oven to 375°. In a medium bowl, beat eggs, salt, pepper, and water until well blended.

2. In a 9-inch frying pan with a heatproof handle, heat olive oil over medium heat. Pour eggs into pan. Cook, shaking pan and stirring at same time with a wooden spoon. As eggs begin to set around edges, stir them into center. When eggs are half cooked, 2 to 3 minutes, scatter artichokes and ham on top. Sprinkle with Parmesan cheese.

3. Place pan on middle rack of oven. Bake 2 to 3 minutes, or until set. Remove pan from oven with a heatproof mitt. Slip a spatula around edge of pan to loosen. Cut into wedges to serve.

297   ARTICHOKE TORTA

Prep: 25 minutes   Chill: 30 minutes   Cook: 50 to 55 minutes
Serves: 10 to 12

SIMPLE PASTRY

2¼ cups sifted all-purpose flour	1 egg
½ teaspoon salt	¼ cup cold water
1 stick (8 tablespoons) butter	

FILLING

2 6-ounce jars marinated artichokes, drained	1 teaspoon salt
	¼ teaspoon pepper
2 tablespoons olive oil	4 ounces ham, cut into ¼-inch dice
½ pound fresh mushrooms, quartered	
	8 ounces Italian fontina or Gruyère cheese, grated
6 eggs	
¼ cup heavy cream	

1. In a large bowl, combine 2 cups flour and salt. Rub butter into flour with fingers until it resembles fine cornmeal. Make a well in center.

2. In a small bowl, beat egg and water together with a fork to blend. Pour mixture into well and incorporate flour into liquid ingredients until a soft dough is formed.

3. Flour a work surface and turn dough onto it. Knead dough until it holds its form. Divide dough in half. Place each piece of dough between 2 sheets of plastic wrap. Flatten each into a 6-inch disk, wrap tightly, and refrigerate at least 30 minutes.

4. Preheat oven to 350°. Cut artichokes into quarters; set aside. Heat oil in a medium frying pan over medium-high heat. Add mushrooms and cook, stirring, 4 to 5 minutes, or until browned. Stir in artichokes. Remove from heat and set aside.

5. In a large bowl, beat eggs and cream with salt and pepper. Stir in ham, cheese, mushrooms, and artichokes.

6. Remove 1 disk of pastry from refrigerator. Roll out between 2 sheets of plastic wrap into an 11-inch round. Fit pastry into a 10-inch tart pan with removable bottom. Press pastry against sides and trim off any excess. Roll out remaining pastry to an 11-inch round. Remove top plastic wrap and cut pastry into 1-inch strips.

7. Pour filling into prepared tart shell. Arrange pastry strips in a lattice pattern on top; trim off any excess. Bake torta 45 to 50 minutes, or until pastry is lightly browned and egg mixture is cooked through and firm to touch.

298 ASPARAGUS FRITTATA
Prep: 5 minutes   Cook: 10 to 12 minutes   Serves: 2

¼ pound asparagus tips
4 eggs
½ teaspoon salt
1 tablespoon water
2 tablespoons olive oil

2 ounces mozzarella cheese,
  thinly sliced
1 tablespoon grated Parmesan
  cheese

1. Preheat oven to 375°. In a medium saucepan, cook asparagus in boiling salted water about 3 minutes, or until crisp tender. Drain into a colander and rinse under cold running water to stop the cooking. Drain and pat dry. If tips are long, cut in half.

2. In a medium bowl, beat eggs, salt, and water until well blended.

3. In a 9-inch frying pan with a heatproof handle, heat olive oil. Pour eggs into pan. Cook, shaking pan and stirring at same time with a wooden spoon. As eggs begin to set around edges, stir them into center. When eggs are half cooked, 2 to 3 minutes, scatter asparagus, mozzarella cheese, and Parmesan cheese on top.

4. Transfer pan to middle rack of oven. Bake 2 to 3 minutes, or until set and cheese begins to melt. Remove pan from oven with a heatproof mitt. Slip a spatula around edge of pan to loosen. Cut into wedges to serve.

Chapter 13

The Italian Way with a Loaf of Bread

It's amazing what the Italians do with bread dough. Pizza features dough flattened into a relatively thin round and covered with as many toppings as your imagination can come up with. A calzone is basically a pizza made into a turnover, with the topping becoming a filling. Focaccia is the classic Italian flat bread, usually baked up with distinctive seasonings. Bread sticks, crisp and irresistible, lend themselves to a variety of flavors. Zeppoli fries the bread dough for an intriguing effect, and heroes are super-sandwiches run riot.

While I've included a recipe for Traditional Pizza Dough, you may be delighted to learn that you can achieve excellent results from frozen bread dough, which comes in one-pound loaves in the freezer section of your local supermarket. Try classic pies, like Pizza Margherita, with marinara sauce, basil, and cheese, and Peperoncini and Pepperoni Pizza, for those who like it spicy. Trendier recipes include Pizza with Artichokes and Sun-Dried Tomatoes, Smoked Salmon Pizza, and Pizza Bianco (White Pizza), which features garlic and cheese.

The same pizza or bread dough is used to encase sausage and cheese or salami, cheese and Swiss chard for hefty calzones, turnovers that are ideal for picnics and eating out of hand.

Focaccia, using the same dough, is a flat bread that requires only one rising and can be prepared start to finish in little more than an hour. Rosemary and garlic, blue cheese and walnuts are a couple of the flavor duos that make this bread so appealing with other foods or by itself as a snack.

In this chapter, I've taken plain store-bought bread sticks and turned them into sweet and spicy treats you can whip up in minutes. Savory and sweet are the recipes for zeppoli, too, which sandwich a hint of flavor inside the pizza or bread dough and fry it in sticks until crisp and golden brown.

Take a fully baked loaf of bread, and Italian cooking turns it into divinity. How much Garlic Bread can you eat? This chapter features a variety of flavored breads, as well as the overstuffed heros, called submarines or grinders in different parts of the country. While most are Italian-American conventions, no one will quibble about how good they are. They can be stuffed with meat, cheese, pickled vegetables . . . They are delicious and can be enormously creative. I like to pull out some of the center of the bread to create a little holding place for the fillings. It's fun to make very long versions of these sandwiches for parties and cut them to order, depending on how much your family or friends think they can eat. They are best if made and allowed to sit for about half an hour to allow the flavors to blend.

299 GARLIC BREAD
Prep: 10 minutes   Cook: 15 minutes   Serves: 8 to 10

Here's an Italian classic that will never go out of style.

1½ sticks (6 ounces) butter, softened
6 garlic cloves, minced

1 1-pound loaf of Italian or French bread

1. Preheat oven to 375°. Cut butter into small pieces. Use a fork or electric mixer to mix garlic and butter until well blended.

2. Cut bread in half lengthwise. Spread cut sides with garlic butter. Wrap each piece in foil. Bake 15 minutes, or until butter has melted and bread is heated through. Remove foil and cut crosswise into serving pieces.

300 TOMATO GARLIC BREAD
Prep: 10 minutes   Cook: 3 to 5 minutes   Serves: 8 to 10

Soooo good!

1½ sticks (6 ounces) butter
5 garlic cloves, minced
5 tablespoons tomato paste

1 1-pound loaf of Italian or French bread
⅓ cup grated Parmesan cheese

1. Preheat broiler. Use a fork or electric mixer to mix butter, garlic, and tomato paste until well blended.

2. Cut bread in half lengthwise. Spread cut sides with butter mixture. Sprinkle with Parmesan cheese. Place bread pieces on a baking sheet. Broil 4 to 5 inches from heat 3 to 5 minutes, or until lightly browned.

301 ANCHOVY BREAD
Prep: 10 minutes   Cook: 2 to 3 minutes   Serves: 6 to 12

Delicious served with a simple tomato salad. Leftover anchovy-garlic oil can be stored in the refrigerator and used for salad dressings.

2 garlic cloves, minced
5 flat anchovy fillets, drained
¾ cup olive oil

½ teaspoon pepper
12 slices of Italian or French bread, cut ½ inch thick

1. Preheat broiler. Use a fork to mash garlic and anchovies in small bowl. Beat in olive oil and pepper.

2. Generously brush tops of bread slices with anchovy-oil mixture. Place on a baking sheet. Broil 3 to 4 inches from heat 2 to 3 minutes, or until lightly browned.

302   GRILLED BREAD WITH ITALIAN HERBS
Prep: 5 minutes   Cook: 5 to 7 minutes   Serves: 6 to 8

This simple preparation is perfect for barbecue days. Serve along with grilled zucchini, eggplant, and peppers brushed with the same herb oil.

1 cup olive oil
2 tablespoons chopped fresh oregano or 1½ teaspoons dried
1 tablespoon chopped fresh rosemary or ½ teaspoon dried

12 slices of Italian or French bread, cut 1½ inches thick

1. In a small bowl, combine olive oil with oregano and rosemary. Beat with a fork to blend.

2. Prepare a medium fire in a grill, or use an existing fire. When coals are ashen, brush both sides of bread with herb oil and place along outer edges of cooking grid. Grill, turning once, 5 to 7 minutes, or until bread is lightly toasted and marked from the grill.

303   PIZZA WITH ARTICHOKES AND SUN-DRIED TOMATOES
Prep: 15 minutes   Bake: 12 to 15 minutes
Makes: 2 12-inch pizzas   Serves: 4

This is a good party pizza, cut into small pieces and passed.

1 recipe Traditional Pizza Dough or 1 pound frozen bread dough, defrosted
2 tablespoons cornmeal
1 28-ounce can Italian peeled tomatoes, drained and chopped
2 teaspoons salt
1 teaspoon pepper
6 garlic cloves, chopped
1 tablespoon chopped fresh oregano or 1 teaspoon dried

16 slices mozzarella cheese, about 8 ounces
2 6-ounce jars marinated artichokes, drained
8 sun-dried tomatoes, packed in oil, drained and cut into thin strips
½ cup grated Parmesan cheese
3 tablespoons olive oil

1. Preheat oven to 500°. Divide pizza dough in half and roll into two 12-inch circles. Sprinkle each of two baking sheets with 1 tablespoon cornmeal. Place dough circles on cornmeal.

2. Spread tomatoes evenly over dough; sprinkle with salt, pepper, garlic, and oregano. Top with mozzarella cheese, artichokes, and sun-dried tomatoes. Sprinkle with Parmesan cheese, then drizzle each with 1½ tablespoons olive oil.

3. Bake until crusty and brown around the edges, 12 to 15 minutes.

304 TRADITIONAL PIZZA DOUGH

Prep: 10 minutes   Stand: 10 to 12 minutes   Rise: 1 to 2 hours
Makes: 2 12-inch pizzas or 1 10 x 8-inch focaccia   Serves: 4

1 cup warm water (about 100°)	3 cups unbleached
¼ teaspoon sugar	all-purpose flour
1 envelope (¼ ounce) active	1 teaspoon salt
dry yeast	1 tablespoon olive oil

1. In small bowl, combine ¼ cup water with sugar and yeast. Let stand in a warm place for 10 to 12 minutes. The yeast will become bubbly and give off a yeasty odor.

2. In another bowl, combine flour and salt. Make a well in flour, add proofed yeast, remaining ¾ cup warm water, and olive oil. Begin mixing flour and liquid together with your hand; mix until you form a dough that cleans sides of bowl.

3. Clean off your hands. Lightly flour a work surface. Place dough on surface and begin to knead with heel of your hand, turning and folding dough as you knead it. Knead 5 to 8 minutes, or until dough becomes smooth and elastic. Put dough into a clean bowl and let rise, covered with a kitchen towel, in a warm place (75° to 80°) 1 to 2 hours, until doubled in bulk.

4. At this point, punch dough down with fist. Knead 1 minute. You are now ready to shape dough according to recipe. If only making one pizza, divide dough in half and wrap remaining piece of dough to freeze for future use.

305 PIZZA MARGHERITA

Prep: 10 minutes   Bake: 12 to 15 minutes
Makes: 2 12-inch pizzas   Serves: 4

This is the most traditional Neapolitan pizza.

1 recipe Traditional Pizza	16 thin slices mozzarella
Dough or 1 pound frozen	cheese, about 8 ounces
bread dough, defrosted	½ cup grated Parmesan cheese
2 tablespoons cornmeal	3 tablespoons shredded fresh
3 cups marinara sauce,	basil or 2 teaspoons dried
homemade (page 131) or	4 tablespoons olive oil
jarred	

1. Preheat oven to 500°. Divide pizza dough in half and roll into two 12-inch circles. Sprinkle each of two baking sheets with 1 tablespoon cornmeal. Place dough circles on cornmeal. Spread sauce evenly over dough; top with mozzarella, Parmesan cheese, and basil. Drizzle each with 2 tablespoons olive oil.

2. Bake until crusty and brown around edges, 12 to 15 minutes.

306 PEPERONCINI AND PEPPERONI PIZZA

Prep: 15 minutes   Bake: 12 to 15 minutes
Makes: 2 12-inch pizzas   Serves: 4

Peperoncini are pickled little green peppers easily found in a grocery store or deli. Serve the pizza with more peperoncini on the side.

1 recipe Traditional Pizza Dough or 1 pound frozen bread dough, defrosted	2 garlic cloves, minced
	½ teaspoon pepper
2 tablespoons cornmeal	16 slices mozzarella, about 8 ounces
2 cups marinara sauce, homemade (page 131) or jarred	12 ounces thinly sliced pepperoni
	16 peperoncini in vinegar, drained and halved
	½ cup grated Parmesan cheese

1. Preheat oven to 500°. Divide pizza dough in half and roll into two 12-inch circles. Sprinkle each of two baking sheets with 1 tablespoon cornmeal. Place dough circles on cornmeal.

2. Spread sauce evenly over dough; sprinkle with garlic and black pepper. Top with mozzarella cheese, pepperoni, and peperoncini. Sprinkle with Parmesan cheese.

3. Bake until cheese is bubbly and crust is brown around edges, 12 to 15 minutes.

307 PIZZA BIANCO (WHITE PIZZA)

Prep: 10 minutes   Bake: 12 to 15 minutes
Makes: 2 pizzas   Serves: 2 to 4

Called white because there is no tomato.

1 recipe Traditional Pizza Dough or 1 pound frozen bread dough, defrosted	6 large garlic cloves, chopped
	½ teaspoon pepper
	¼ cup olive oil
2 tablespoons cornmeal	2 cups shredded mozzarella cheese, about 8 ounces
2 tablespoons chopped basil leaves or 1 tablespoon dried	16 thin slices fontina cheese, about 8 ounces
	½ cup grated Parmesan cheese

1. Preheat oven to 500°. Divide pizza dough in half and roll into two 12-inch circles. Sprinkle each of two baking sheets with 1 tablespoon cornmeal. Place dough circles on cornmeal.

2. In small bowl, combine basil, garlic, pepper, and olive oil. Spread mixture evenly over dough. Top with mozzarella, then fontina cheese. Sprinkle with Parmesan.

3. Bake until cheese is bubbly and crust is brown around edges, 12 to 15 minutes.

308   SMOKED SALMON PIZZA

Prep: 15 minutes   Cook: 20 to 25 minutes
Makes: 2 12-inch pizzas   Serves: 4

This untraditional pizza is wonderful for brunch.

1 recipe Traditional Pizza Dough or 1 pound frozen bread dough, defrosted	½ teaspoon pepper
2 tablespoons cornmeal	16 thin slices smoked salmon, about 12 ounces
½ cup olive oil	1 cup sour cream
6 cups sliced onions, about 5 medium	½ cup capers, rinsed and drained
2 teaspoons salt	2 tablespoons chopped fresh dill or 2 teaspoons dried

1. Preheat oven to 500°. Divide pizza dough in half and roll into two 12-inch circles. Sprinkle each of two baking sheets with 1 tablespoon cornmeal. Place dough rounds on cornmeal.

2. In a large frying pan, heat olive oil over medium heat. Add onions and cook, stirring occasionally, 10 to 12 minutes, or until softened but not browned. Season with salt and pepper. Let cool to room temperature.

3. Spread onions and olive oil evenly over pizza dough. Bake 10 to 12 minutes, or until crusty and brown around the edges. Cover each pizza with smoked salmon slices. Top with sour cream and sprinkle with capers and dill.

309   TOMATO ANCHOVY PIZZA

Prep: 10 minutes   Cook: 10 to 12 minutes
Makes: 2 12-inch pizzas   Serves: 4

1 recipe Traditional Pizza Dough or 1 pound frozen bread dough, defrosted	2 tablespoons chopped fresh oregano or 2 teaspoons dried
2 tablespoons cornmeal	¼ cup olive oil
1 2-ounce can flat anchovy fillets, drained	12 thin slices mozzarella, about 10 ounces
4 garlic cloves, chopped	
3 cups marinara sauce, homemade (page 131) or jarred	

1. Preheat oven to 500°. Divide pizza dough in half and roll into two 12-inch circles. Sprinkle each of two baking sheets with 1 tablespoon cornmeal. Place dough circles on cornmeal.

2. Pat anchovies dry. In a small bowl, combine garlic, sauce, oregano, and olive oil. Spread mixture evenly over pizza dough. Top with cheese, then anchovies.

3. Bake 10 to 12 minutes, or until cheese is bubbly and crust is brown around edges.

310   BLUEBERRY FOCACCIA
Prep: 30 minutes   Rise: 45 minutes   Bake: 30 minutes
Serves: 8 to 10

This combination is not as untraditional as it may seem. It is inspired by Italian flat breads baked with wine grapes and rosemary, called *schiacciate con l'uva*. Serve with a dab of sour cream or mascarpone cheese.

4 tablespoons butter, melted	1 cup blueberries
1 recipe Traditional Pizza	¾ cup sugar
Dough or 1 pound frozen	
bread dough, defrosted	

1. Preheat oven to 350°. Brush a 10 x 8-inch pan with 1 tablespoon butter. Pat or roll dough to fit pan. Brush surface with remaining 3 tablespoons butter. Indent surface of dough by pressing all over with your fingertips. Top with blueberries and sugar, pressing gently into dough.

2. Let dough rise, covered with a kitchen towel, in a warm place (75° to 80°) 45 minutes, or until doubled in bulk.

3. Bake focaccia 30 minutes, or until puffy and lightly golden.

311   FOCACCIA WITH BLUE CHEESE AND WALNUTS
Prep: 10 minutes   Rise: 45 minutes   Bake: 30 minutes
Serves: 6 to 8

Red wine and a simple salad turn this into a delightful meal.

3 tablespoons olive oil	8 ounces blue cheese,
1 recipe Traditional Pizza	preferably gorgonzola,
Dough or 1 pound frozen	crumbled
bread dough, defrosted	
1½ cups coarsely chopped	
walnuts	

1. Preheat oven to 350°. Brush a 10 x 8-inch baking pan with 1 tablespoon olive oil. Pat or roll dough to fit pan. Brush surface with remaining 2 tablespoons oil. Indent surface of dough by pressing all over with your fingertips. Scatter walnuts and cheese over dough. Let rise, covered with a kitchen towel, in a warm place (75° to 80°) 45 minutes, or until doubled in bulk.

2. Bake focaccia 30 minutes, or until puffy and lightly golden.

312   FOCACCIA WITH ROSEMARY AND GARLIC
Prep: 10 minutes   Rise: 45 minutes   Bake: 30 minutes
Serves: 6 to 8

This traditional focaccia is as delicious as it is fragrant.

1 recipe Traditional Pizza
  Dough or 1 pound frozen
  bread dough, defrosted
3 tablespoons olive oil
2 large garlic cloves, minced

2 tablespoons chopped fresh
  rosemary or 1 teaspoon
  dried
1 tablespoon coarse (kosher)
  salt

1. Preheat oven to 350°. Brush a 10 x 8-inch baking pan with 1 tablespoon olive oil. Pat or roll dough to fit pan. Brush surface with remaining 2 tablespoons oil. Sprinkle garlic, rosemary, and coarse salt over dough. Indent surface of dough by pressing all over with your fingertips. Let dough rise, covered with a kitchen towel, in a warm place (75° to 80°) 45 minutes, or until doubled in bulk.

2. Bake focaccia 30 minutes, or until puffy and lightly golden on top.

313   CHEESE AND SWISS CHARD CALZONE
Prep: 15 minutes   Cook: 22 to 25 minutes
Makes: 2 8-inch calzones   Serves: 2 to 4

1 recipe Traditional Pizza
  Dough or 1 pound frozen
  bread dough, thawed
  Cornmeal
2 tablespoons olive oil
1 10-ounce package frozen
  Swiss chard or spinach,
  defrosted
1 garlic clove, minced

1 teaspoon salt
1 teaspoon pepper
2 eggs
2 cups ricotta cheese, about
  1 pound
¼ cup grated Parmesan cheese
8 ounces sliced salami, cut
  into thin strips

1. Preheat oven to 425°. Divide pizza dough in half and roll into two 8-inch circles. Sprinkle cornmeal over a large baking sheet.

2. In a medium frying pan, heat olive oil over medium heat. Add chard and garlic and cook 2 to 3 minutes, or until chard is wilted and garlic is fragrant. Season with ½ teaspoon salt and ½ teaspoon pepper. Let cool to room temperature.

3. In a medium bowl, combine eggs with ricotta cheese, Parmesan cheese, salami, and remaining ½ teaspoon each salt and pepper. Stir in chard or spinach.

4. Cover half of each dough circle with half of filling, leaving a ½-inch border around edge. Fold dough over filling to form a turnover. Press edges with tines of a fork to seal.

5. Bake 18 to 20 minutes, or until calzone are puffed and deep golden brown.

314   SAUSAGE AND CHEESE CALZONE
Prep: 20 minutes   Bake: 33 to 35 minutes
Makes: 2 8-inch calzones   Serves: 2 to 4

In Naples, calzone are eaten as "street food." In other parts of Italy they are knife-and-fork food.

1 recipe Traditional Pizza
    Dough or 1 pound frozen
    bread dough, defrosted
2 tablespoons cornmeal
4 links sweet or hot Italian
    sausage, about 1 pound
1 cup marinara sauce,
    homemade (page 131) or
    jarred, plus more, if
    desired

¼ teaspoon hot pepper flakes
½ teaspoon crushed fennel
    seeds
1½ cups grated mozzarella,
    about 6 ounces
¼ cup grated Parmesan cheese

1. Preheat oven to 425°. Divide pizza dough in half and roll into two 8-inch circles. Sprinkle cornmeal over large baking sheet.

2. Remove sausages from casings. Crumble uncooked sausage meat into a medium saucepan and cook, stirring, over medium heat until no longer pink, about 10 minutes. Stir in 1 cup sauce, hot pepper flakes, and fennel seeds. Cook 5 minutes more. Cool and skim fat from top.

3. Cover half of each dough circle with mozzarella cheese, leaving a ½-inch border around edge. Top with sausage filling. Sprinkle with Parmesan cheese. Fold dough over filling to form a turnover. Press edges with tines of a fork to seal.

4. Bake 18 to 20 minutes, or until calzone are puffed and deep golden brown. Serve with additional sauce, if desired.

315   SWEET ZEPPOLI
Prep: 25 minutes   Cook: 12 minutes   Serves: 10

On bread-baking days in southern Italy, all the scraps of dough went into making these delicious bits of fried bread.

1 recipe Traditional Pizza
    Dough or 1 pound frozen
    bread dough, defrosted
    Flour

Vegetable oil, for deep
    frying
Confectioners' sugar

1. Knead dough a few times on a lightly floured board. Roll into a rectangle about ½ inch thick. Cut dough into 2 x 3-inch rectangles.

2. In a large saucepan or deep-fat fryer, heat oil to 350° on a deep-fat thermometer. Fry dough a few pieces at a time without crowding, turning once, until golden brown, 2 to 3 minutes. Drain on paper towels and dust with confectioners' sugar. Serve hot.

316 ZEPPOLI WITH SUN-DRIED TOMATOES AND BASIL

Prep: 15 minutes   Stand: 20 minutes   Cook: 10 to 12 minutes
Serves: 10

1 recipe Traditional Pizza
Dough or 1 pound frozen
bread dough, defrosted

8 sun-dried tomato halves,
packed in oil, drained
and coarsely chopped
2 tablespoons chopped fresh
basil or 2 teaspoons dried

1. On a lightly floured board, flatten dough to a small disk about diameter of your hand. Lay chopped tomatoes and basil on disk and fold dough over, kneading with your right hand and folding over with left. Knead and fold 10 to 12 times. Let dough rest about 20 minutes, covered with a kitchen towel.

2. On a work surface dusted with flour, roll dough into a rectangle about ½ inch thick. Cut dough into 3 x 2-inch rectangles.

3. In a large saucepan or deep-fat fryer, heat vegetable oil to 350° on a deep-fat thermometer. Fry dough, a few pieces at a time without crowding, turning once, until golden brown, 2 to 3 minutes. Drain on paper towels. Serve hot.

317 ZEPPOLI WITH ANCHOVIES

Prep: 20 minutes   Stand: 20 minutes   Cook: 10 to 12 minutes
Serves: 10

From Calabria, these are especially popular at Christmas and on St. Joseph's Day in March. Serve as an appetizer or along with salad or soup.

1 recipe Traditional Pizza
Dough or 1 pound frozen
bread dough, defrosted
1 2-ounce can flat anchovy
fillets, drained and
coarsely chopped

2½ quarts vegetable oil, for
deep frying

1. On a lightly floured board, flatten dough to a small disk about diameter of your hand. Lay anchovies on disk and fold dough over, kneading with your right hand and folding over with left. Knead and fold 10 to 12 times. Let dough rest about 20 minutes, covered with a kitchen towel.

2. On a work surface dusted with flour, roll dough into a rectangle about ½ inch thick. Cut dough into 3 x 2-inch rectangles.

3. In a large saucepan or deep-fat fryer, heat vegetable oil to 350° on a deep-fat thermometer. Fry dough, a few pieces at a time without crowding, turning once, until golden brown, 2 to 3 minutes. Drain on paper towels. Serve hot.

318   MEATBALL HERO
Prep: 10 minutes   Cook: 25 minutes   Serves: 2 to 3

Cooking time here is based on your having meatballs and sauce left over.

1 recipe meatballs in tomato
  sauce (from Spaghetti and
  Meatballs, page 52)
1 1-pound loaf of Italian or
  French bread

⅔ cup grated Romano cheese
8 slices mozzarella cheese,
  about 4 ounces

1. Preheat oven to 375°. Remove meatballs from tomato sauce and slice into ½-inch pieces. In a small saucepan, warm tomato sauce over low heat 5 to 7 minutes, or until heated through.

2. Cut bread in half lengthwise and remove some of soft center from bottom half. Arrange meatball pieces in hollowed-out portion of bread. Spoon 1 cup warm tomato sauce over meatballs. Sprinkle with Romano cheese. Arrange mozzarella slices over all, then replace top half of bread.

3. Wrap in foil and bake until cheese has melted and meatballs are heated through, about 20 minutes. Remove foil and slice crosswise into individual portions.

319   TUNA HERO
Prep: 20 minutes   Press: 1 hour   Cook: none   Serves: 2 to 3

This piquant sandwich is ideal picnic fare.

⅓ cup red wine vinegar
2 garlic cloves, minced
1 teaspoon salt
½ teaspoon pepper
1 tablespoon chopped fresh
  basil or 1 teaspoon dried
1 cup olive oil
1 1-pound loaf of Italian or
  French bread

1½ cups diced ripe tomato
½ cup diced onion
12 cooked fresh green beans
  (optional)
2 hard-cooked eggs, quartered
1 6½-ounce can oil-packed
  tuna, drained

1. In a small bowl combine vinegar, garlic, salt, pepper, basil, and oil. Beat with fork to blend.

2. Cut bread in half lengthwise and remove some of soft center from bottom half. Brush both cut sides of bread with half the dressing.

3. In a medium bowl, toss tomato and onion with remaining dressing. Arrange green beans over bottom half of bread. Top with tomato-onion mixture, then eggs and tuna. Replace top half of bread, pressing down lightly, and wrap loosely in foil. Weight with a book or other 1-pound weight and let rest for about 1 hour for flavors to blend. Remove foil and cut into diagonal slices to serve.

320   SATURDAY HERO
Prep: 15 minutes   Cook: 25 to 30 minutes   Serves: 2 to 3

This was a favorite of the men in my family, so we often served it for Saturday lunch when they were likely to be around.

4 Italian sausages, about
   1¼ pounds
1 medium onion, chopped
1 garlic clove, minced
3 tablespoons olive oil
3 green bell peppers, cut into
   1-inch squares
1 cup chopped tomatoes,
   fresh or canned

1 teaspoon dried oregano
1 tablespoon chopped fresh
   parsley
1 cup water
1 1-pound loaf of Italian or
   French bread
3 eggs

1. Preheat oven to 375°. Prick sausages all over with a fork. Place in a small pan and roast in oven, turning once, 15 to 18 minutes, or until no longer pink.

2. Meanwhile, in a large frying pan, over medium heat, cook onion and garlic in olive oil until softened, about 2 minutes. Stir in peppers. Add tomatoes, oregano, parsley, and water. Bring to a boil, reduce heat to low, and cook, stirring occasionally, 5 minutes, or until most of excess liquid has evaporated.

3. Cut bread in half lengthwise and remove some of soft center from bottom half.

4. In a small bowl, whisk eggs until well blended and stir into pepper mixture. Turn off heat and cover for 1 minute to allow eggs to set. Cut sausages in half lengthwise and place in hollowed-out bread. Spoon egg and pepper mixture over sausage. Replace top half of bread. To serve, cut into diagonal slices.

321   EGGPLANT RELISH HERO
Prep: 10 minutes   Serves: 2 to 3

1 1-pound loaf of Italian or
   French bread
1 recipe Caponata with Red
   and Green Peppers
   (page 9)

16 thin slices of capocollo or
   other salami, about
   2 ounces
9 thin slices Italian fontina
   cheese, 4 to 5 ounces

1. Cut bread in half lengthwise and remove some of soft center from bottom half of bread.

2. Spoon caponata into hollowed-out portion of bread. Top with capocollo, folding in half, if necessary. Arrange cheese slices over capocollo and replace top half of bread. To serve, cut into 3- to 4-inch diagonal slices.

322 EGGPLANT HOT HERO
Prep: 10 minutes   Cook: 25 minutes   Serves: 4 to 6

Prepared deli food can be a boon for today's busy cooks. Unless you have leftover eggplant parmigiana on hand, simply purchase it already made from a reliable delicatessen.

1 1-pound loaf of Italian or French bread
½ recipe Eggplant Parmigiana (page 180), or 1 pound store-bought eggplant parmigiana
8 ounces thinly sliced salami

⅓ cup grated Romano cheese
6 slices mozzarella, about 3 ounces
2 cups marinara sauce, homemade (page 131) or jarred (optional)

1. Preheat oven to 350°. Cut loaf of bread in half lengthwise and remove some of soft center from bottom half.

2. Separate slices of eggplant from casserole into layers no more than 1 inch thick. Arrange salami on bottom half of bread, then top with eggplant. Sprinkle with Romano cheese; top with mozzarella. Replace top half of bread.

3. Wrap in foil and place on baking sheet. Bake until heated through, about 25 minutes. To serve, cut into diagonal slices. Pass hot marinara sauce, if desired.

323 VENETIAN HERO
Prep: 15 minutes   Cook: none   Serves: 2 to 3

Part of a Venetian antipasto is often a zesty combination of red pepper, sardines, and eggs with a sage-tomato-butter sauce. I like to wrap it all in a loaf of bread and serve as a sandwich.

1 1-pound loaf of Italian or French bread
1½ sticks butter (6 ounces)
3 tablespoons tomato paste
3 garlic cloves, minced
1 teaspoon dried sage leaves
1 7.25-ounce jar roasted bell peppers, drained and coarsely chopped

2 4¼-ounce cans boneless, skinless sardines, drained
4 hard-cooked eggs, cut into ½-inch slices
1 teaspoon pepper

1. Cut bread in half lengthwise and remove some of soft center from bottom half.

2. Use a fork or electric mixer to mix butter, tomato paste, garlic, and sage until well blended.

3. Spread butter mixture over cut sides of bread. Top with roasted peppers, sardines, and then eggs. Season generously with pepper. Replace top half of bread and press gently. To serve, cut into 3- to 4-inch diagonal slices.

324   SAUSAGE AND PEPPER HERO
Prep: 10 minutes   Cook: 30 minutes   Serves: 6

6 fennel sausage links, 2 to
  2½ pounds
1 tablespoon olive oil
1 medium onion, chopped
2 green bell peppers, cut into
  1½-inch squares
1 14-ounce can Italian peeled
  tomatoes, drained and
  chopped

½ cup water
½ teaspoon salt
¼ teaspoon pepper
2 tablespoons chopped fresh
  parsley
6 long Italian rolls

1. Cut fennel sausages into 3 pieces each. In a nonreactive large frying pan, heat oil over medium heat. Add sausages and cook, turning, 10 minutes, or until browned and cooked through.

2. Spoon off fat from pan. Add onion and peppers. Cook, stirring, 5 minutes. Add tomatoes, water, salt, and pepper. Bring to a boil, reduce heat to low, cover, and cook 15 minutes. Stir in parsley. Spoon sausages with peppers and sauce onto split rolls.

325   CINNAMON BREAD STICKS
Prep: 10 minutes   Cook: 8 to 10 minutes   Serves: 6

Commercially purchased bread sticks work very well for this recipe. Serve warm with coffee or hot chocolate.

¾ cup sugar
1 tablespoon cinnamon
1 5-ounce package plain bread
  sticks

1 stick (8 tablespoons) butter,
  melted

1. Preheat oven to 325°. Combine sugar and cinnamon in a shallow bowl. Brush bread sticks all over with butter, then roll lightly in sugar and cinnamon mixture.

2. Place bread sticks on a wire rack fitted in a rimmed baking sheet and bake 8 to 10 minutes, or until lightly browned.

326   CINNAMON ALMOND BREAD STICKS

Prep: 10 minutes   Bake: 8 to 10 minutes   Serves: 6 to 8

These are good for a brunch or for dessert.

¾ cup blanched almonds
½ cup sugar
½ teaspoon cinnamon

1 5-ounce package plain bread sticks
1 egg white, beaten with 2 tablespoons water

1. Preheat oven to 325°. Pulverize almonds coarsely in a blender or food processor. Add sugar and cinnamon just to combine. Transfer to a shallow bowl.

2. Brush bread sticks all over with egg white and roll lightly in almond-sugar mixture. Place on a wire rack fitted in a rimmed baking sheet and bake 8 to 10 minutes, or until lightly browned.

327   SPICY SEEDED BREAD STICKS

Prep: 10 minutes   Bake: 12 to 15 minutes   Serves: 6 to 8

Spicy and hot, these will perk up any soup or salad.

½ cup sesame seeds
3 tablespoons poppy seeds
2 tablespoons hot pepper flakes
2 tablespoons coarse salt

1 5-ounce package plain bread sticks
1 egg white, beaten with 2 tablespoons water

1. Preheat oven to 350°. In a wide shallow bowl, combine sesame and poppy seeds with pepper flakes and salt.

2. Brush bread sticks all over with egg white and roll lightly in seed mixture. Place on a wire rack fitted in a rimmed baking sheet and bake 12 to 15 minutes, or until lightly browned.

328   HAM AND CHEESE PANINI

Prep: 5 minutes   Cook: 5 to 7 minutes   Serves: 4

These are thin sandwiches of Italian prosciutto or deli ham and cheese. Don't try to overload them with filling, for they just won't be as good.

4 tablespoons butter, softened	4 slices Italian fontina cheese,
8 slices of firm white	about 2 ounces
sandwich bread	
8 slices deli ham or 24 thin	
slices prosciutto, about	
4 ounces	

1. Butter one side of each piece of bread. Place one fourth each of ham and cheese between 2 *unbuttered* sides. Trim away any excess ham and cheese. Form 4 sandwiches.

2. Preheat a griddle or large cast-iron frying pan over medium-low heat. Grill sandwiches, turning once, 5 to 7 minutes, or until cheese has melted and bread is golden brown. To serve, cut each sandwich into halves or quarters.

Chapter 14

Salads

A simple salad to an Italian is a few greens tossed with a little salt and olive oil. A little squeeze of lemon juice is arbitrary and left up to you and a wedge of lemon. The Italians love their greens. All kinds of lettuces, cultivated and wild, are cherished. A salad of tomatoes, basil, and olive oil—the best example of simplicity—is a joy.

Keep in mind that a basic dressing for all salads is oil and vinegar. The variations on that theme are enormous. There are strong, pungent vinegars, some with deep color and others pale. The range of olive oil is also enormous. There are very strict laws on what can be called "extra-virgin," "virgin," or just "olive oil." They are related to the choice and grading of olives, how the olive is pressed—whether by the natural weight of the olives or mechanical means—and how much acid is in the resulting oil. A rich, green oil may or may not mean the olive oil is full in flavor or delicate, so you will have to do some experimenting. Olive oil does not get better with age. Buy only small amounts if you are not going to use it frequently. Store olive oil away from heat and light. This is a good rule of thumb for oils, herbs, and spices as well. The top shelves in your kitchen are considerably warmer, especially in the summer, so store them on your lower shelves away from your stove. Experiment with the flavors of oils and vinegars, and remember a recipe cannot direct you as far as the exact flavor in this case. Each time you use a different oil and vinegar, the flavor will change. Find your favorite combination.

Fresh ingredients and specialty greens are not always available, but there are some very good substitutes. Radicchio, a red lettuce grown originally in the Veneto and now in California, can be found in some markets, but it is still very expensive. Red cabbage can be substituted for color, though the flavor is not the same. Arugula, or rocket, is a favorite of home gardeners. If you can't find it in the store, watercress is a very good substitute. In the case of rice salads, long-grain white rice should be used, cooked according to package directions. Many of these salads do well as part of an antipasto or as a whole meal.

329   ARUGULA, TOMATO, AND OLIVE SALAD
Prep: 10 minutes   Cook: none   Serves: 4

If you are lucky enough to find arugula, you will enjoy the slightly bitter flavor as a contrast to the richness of the olive oil.

1 garlic clove, minced
½ teaspoon salt
¼ teaspoon pepper
2 teaspoons chopped fresh
  oregano or ½ teaspoon
  dried
3 tablespoons red wine
  vinegar

⅓ cup extra-virgin olive oil
2 large ripe tomatoes, about
  1 pound
8 ounces arugula or 1 small
  head of curly endive
½ cup oil-cured black olives
1 small red onion, thinly
  sliced

1. In a large bowl, combine garlic, salt, pepper, oregano, vinegar, and olive oil. Beat with fork to blend.

2. Cut each tomato into 8 wedges. Toss tomatoes, arugula, olives, and onion together in bowl with dressing.

330   ARUGULA SALAD WITH PARMESAN CHEESE
Prep: 12 minutes   Cook: none   Serves: 6

⅓ cup olive oil
3 tablespoons red wine
  vinegar
1 teaspoon salt

½ teaspoon pepper
4 cups arugula or watercress
4 ounces Parmesan cheese, in
  one piece

1. In a serving bowl, combine olive oil, vinegar, salt, and pepper. Beat with a fork to blend. Add arugula to bowl with dressing and toss to coat.

2. With a swivel-bladed vegetable peeler or cheese slicer, shave off very thin slices of Parmesan cheese and scatter over top of salad.

331 ORANGES, RICOTTA, AND BASIL WITH BALSAMIC VINEGAR

Prep: 10 minutes   Cook: none   Serves: 4

The simplicity of this is beautiful, especially if on glass plates.

4 navel oranges
2 tablespoons balsamic
    vinegar
8 ounces ricotta cheese

3 tablespoons shredded fresh
    basil
Freshly ground pepper

1. With a very sharp knife, remove skins and all white pith from oranges. Slice oranges across to make ½-inch-thick rounds. Arrange slices on four chilled plates.

2. Sprinkle balsamic vinegar over oranges. Dot with ricotta cheese and scatter basil over all. Pass a pepper mill on the side.

332 ORANGES, ONIONS, AND BLACK OLIVES

Prep: 15 minutes   Cook: none   Serves: 4

4 navel oranges
1 medium red onion
12 oil-cured black olives, such
    as Niçoise or Calamata,
    pitted
3 tablespoons olive oil,
    preferably extra-virgin

1½ tablespoons fresh lemon
    juice
½ teaspoon salt
¼ teaspoon pepper

1. With a very sharp knife, remove skin and all white pith from oranges. Slice oranges across to make ½-inch-thick rounds. Arrange slices on a flat plate.

2. Cut red onion lengthwise in half; cut each half into thin slices. Scatter red onion and olives over oranges.

3. In a small bowl, combine olive oil, lemon juice, salt, and pepper. Beat with a fork to blend. Drizzle dressing over oranges. Serve at room temperature.

333   FENNEL, CURLY ENDIVE, AND DRY FIG SALAD

Prep: 10 minutes   Soak: 15 minutes   Cook: none   Serves: 4 to 6

This is a refreshing winter salad, with the licorice-y crunch of fresh fennel and the bite of curly endive. If you can't find fennel (finocchio) in your market, substitute celery.

6 ounces dried figs
1 cup hot water
2 small fennel bulbs, trimmed and cut into matchstick pieces
2 cups curly endive (chicory)

¼ cup olive oil
2 tablespoons balsamic vinegar
1 teaspoon salt
¼ teaspoon pepper

1. In a small bowl, soak figs in hot water for 15 minutes to soften slightly; drain. Cut each fig into quarters.

2. In a salad bowl, combine fennel, endive, and figs. Toss to mix.

3. In a small bowl, combine olive oil, vinegar, salt, and pepper. Beat with a fork to blend. Pour dressing over salad and toss.

334   ITALIAN BREAD AND TOMATO SALAD

Prep: 15 minutes   Stand: 15 minutes   Cook: none   Serves: 4

This classic Tuscan recipe, called *panzanella*, combines salad and bread basket all in one. It's a delicious starter, worth making when red ripe tomatoes and garden-crisp cucumbers are in season.

2 cups cubed (1-inch) Italian bread
2 large ripe tomatoes, about 1 pound, cut into 1-inch cubes
1 small cucumber, peeled, seeded, and cut into ¾-inch cubes
½ cup finely diced red onion

1 garlic clove, minced
½ cup extra-virgin olive oil
¼ cup red wine vinegar
1 tablespoon chopped fresh oregano or 1 teaspoon dried
1 teaspoon salt
½ teaspoon pepper

1. In a large bowl, combine bread, tomatoes, cucumbers, and onion.

2. In a small bowl, combine garlic, olive oil, vinegar, oregano, salt, and pepper. Beat with a fork to blend. Pour half the dressing over tomato combination and toss together. Gradually add remaining dressing, tossing to season bread. Use only as much as needed. Allow to stand for about 15 minutes and toss again.

335 WINTER BREAD SALAD
Prep: 15 minutes   Cook: none   Serves: 6 to 8

1 small head of radicchio
   (about 6 ounces)
16 peperoncini in vinegar,
    drained
2 cups cubed (1-inch) Italian
   bread
1 medium red onion, chopped
16 oil-cured black olives,
    preferably Niçoise, pitted
    if desired

2 garlic cloves, minced
1 tablespoon oregano leaves
   or ½ teaspoon dried
½ cup extra-virgin olive oil
¼ cup red wine vinegar
1 teaspoon salt
½ teaspoon pepper

1. Shred radicchio into thin slices, as for a slaw. Remove stems and seeds from peperoncini and cut into 1-inch pieces. In a salad bowl, combine radicchio, peperoncini, bread, onion, and olives.

2. In a small bowl, combine garlic, oregano, olive oil, vinegar, salt, and pepper. Beat with a fork to blend. Pour dressing over salad and toss.

336 RICE SALAD WITH CURRANTS, PINE NUTS, AND MINT
Prep: 5 minutes   Cook: 20 minutes   Serves: 8

This salad is excellent as a side dish with lamb.

2 cups long-grain rice
⅓ cup pine nuts
4 scallions
6 tablespoons olive oil
3 tablespoons white wine
   vinegar

1½ teaspoons salt
¼ teaspoon pepper
⅓ cup currants or raisins
½ cup shredded fresh mint

1. Preheat oven to 350°. Cook rice according to package directions. Transfer to a large bowl and let cool, tossing occasionally.

2. Meanwhile, in a dry medium frying pan, toast pine nuts over medium heat 2 to 3 minutes, or until fragrant and lightly browned, shaking pan frequently. Set aside to cool.

3. Trim scallion greens down to 3 inches. Cut remaining white and green of scallion into ½-inch pieces.

4. In a small bowl, combine olive oil, vinegar, salt, and pepper. Beat with a fork to blend.

5. Add scallions, currants or raisins, and mint to rice. Toss gently to mix. Pour dressing over salad and toss again.

337   RICE SALAD WITH PEAS AND TOMATOES
Prep: 15 minutes   Cook: 20 minutes   Serves: 8

Rice salads are very common in Italy in the summer. Serve on sliced tomatoes, or use to stuff tomatoes.

2 cups long-grain rice
2 large ripe tomatoes
2 celery ribs, cut into ½-inch dice
2 tablespoons chopped fresh basil or parsley
½ cup olive oil, preferably extra-virgin

3 tablespoons white wine vinegar
1½ teaspoons salt
¼ teaspoon pepper
1 cup frozen peas, defrosted

1. Cook rice according to package directions. As soon as rice is cooked, transfer to a large bowl and let cool, tossing occasionally.

2. Remove stem ends from tomatoes. Cut tomatoes crosswise in half and squeeze gently to extract seeds and juice. Cut tomatoes into ½-inch dice. Add tomatoes, celery, and basil to rice. Toss gently to mix.

3. In a small bowl, combine olive oil, vinegar, salt, and pepper. Beat with a fork to blend. Pour dressing over rice, add peas, and toss again.

338   RICE AND ARTICHOKE SALAD
Prep: 15 minutes   Cook: 20 minutes   Serves: 6

1½ cups long-grain rice
3 scallions
⅓ cup olive oil
3 tablespoons white wine vinegar
1 teaspoon salt
2 tablespoons chopped parsley

1 6-ounce jar artichoke bottoms, drained and quartered
1 4-ounce jar pimientos, drained and cut into thin strips
Freshly ground pepper

1. Cook rice according to package directions. Transfer to a large bowl and let cool, tossing occasionally.

2. Trim scallion greens down to 3 inches. Cut remaining white and green of scallion into ½-inch pieces.

3. In a small bowl, combine olive oil, vinegar, and salt. Beat with a fork to blend.

4. Add scallions and artichokes to rice. Toss to mix. Pour dressing over salad and toss again. Season with additional salt, if needed. Transfer to a salad bowl and garnish with a circle of pimiento strips. Grind pepper over top.

339 POTATO SALAD WITH SWEET PEPPERS AND BLACK OLIVES

Prep: 20 minutes   Cook: 25 to 35 minutes   Serves: 8

Use waxy potatoes, such as White Rose all-purpose potatoes or red boiling potatoes. Baking, or Russet, potatoes are mealy and will fall apart in a potato salad. If tiny new potatoes are in season, use them and leave the stems on.

3½ to 4 pounds all-purpose or boiling potatoes, scrubbed
6 scallions, cut into ½-inch pieces
1 14-ounce can black olives, pitted and cut in half
1 8-ounce jar pimientos, drained and cut into ½-inch dice

¼ cup shredded fresh basil leaves
¼ cup chopped fresh parsley
¾ cup olive oil
½ cup white wine vinegar
1½ teaspoons salt
½ teaspoon pepper

1. Bring potatoes to a boil in a large pot of salted water. Cover, reduce heat to medium-low, and cook 25 to 35 minutes, or until tender; drain. Peel and cut potatoes into 1- to 1½-inch pieces. Place in a large bowl along with scallions, olives, pimientos, basil, and parsley. Do not mix at this point.

2. In a small bowl, combine olive oil, vinegar, salt, and pepper. Beat with a fork to blend. Toss potatoes gently with dressing. Season with additional salt, if needed.

340 POTATO SALAD WITH PEPERONCINI AND RED ONIONS

Prep: 20 minutes   Cook: 20 to 30 minutes   Serves: 6 to 8

Spicy and easy. Leave the skins on. Good hot or cold.

3 pounds small red potatoes, scrubbed
1 cup diced red onion
12 peperoncini, stemmed, seeded, and chopped coarsely
2 tablespoons chopped fresh parsley

¾ cup olive oil
¼ cup white wine vinegar
2 teaspoons salt
½ teaspoon freshly ground pepper

1. Bring potatoes to a boil in a large pot of boiling water. Cover, reduce heat to medium, and cook 20 to 30 minutes, or until tender; drain. Cut into 1-inch pieces, if needed. Place in large bowl along with onions, peperoncini, and parsley. Do not mix at this point.

2. In a small bowl, combine olive oil, vinegar, salt, and pepper. Beat with a fork to blend. Toss potatoes gently with dressing. Season with additional salt, if needed. Chill.

341   CHICKEN SALAD WITH BLUE CHEESE
Prep: 15 minutes   Cook: 2 to 3 minutes   Serves: 4 to 6

This is another quick main-course salad. Great served with Garlic Bread (page 196).

½ cup pine nuts or walnuts
2 spit-roasted or barbecued chickens, about 2 pounds each, or Roasted Chicken (page 105)
3 celery ribs with leaves, sliced
1 medium red onion, thinly sliced
⅓ cup olive oil

¼ cup red wine vinegar
1 teaspoon chopped fresh oregano or ¼ teaspoon dried
1 teaspoon salt
½ teaspoon pepper
1 head of romaine lettuce
4 ounces gorgonzola or other blue cheese

1. In a dry medium skillet, toast nuts over medium heat, 2 to 3 minutes, or until nuts are fragrant and lightly browned, shaking pan frequently.

2. Remove chicken meat from bones. Tear into long strips about ½ inch wide; discard skin. In a large bowl, combine chicken with celery and red onion.

3. In a small bowl, combine olive oil, vinegar, oregano, salt, and pepper. Beat with a fork to blend. Pour half of dressing over chicken mixture and toss to coat.

4. Divide lettuce leaves among 4 to 6 large plates. Drizzle remaining dressing over leaves. Mound chicken salad on lettuce. Crumble cheese over chicken and sprinkle toasted pine nuts on top.

342   CHICKEN SALAD FROM LOMBARDY
Prep: 15 minutes   Cook: none   Serves: 4 to 6

2 spit-roasted or barbecued chickens, about 2 pounds each, or Roasted Chicken (page 105)
¾ cup walnut pieces
2 celery ribs, cut into ½-inch pieces
4 scallions, sliced

¼ cup golden raisins
½ cup extra-virgin olive oil
¼ cup red wine vinegar
1 teaspoon salt
½ teaspoon freshly ground pepper
1 head of romaine lettuce, torn into large bite-size pieces

1. Remove chicken meat from bones. Tear into long strips about ½ inch wide; discard skin. In a large bowl, combine chicken with walnuts, celery, scallions, and golden raisins.

2. In a small bowl, combine olive oil, vinegar, salt, and pepper. Beat with a fork to blend. Pour dressing over chicken salad and toss to coat.

3. Add lettuce to salad bowl and toss again to dress leaves.

343 RADICCHIO, WATERCRESS, AND RED ONION SALAD

Prep: 15 minutes   Marinate: 30 minutes   Cook: none   Serves: 6

This is my favorite salad. Its pleasing bite is especially good with roasted meats.

⅓ cup finely chopped red onion
⅓ cup red wine vinegar
¾ teaspoon salt

¼ teaspoon pepper
8 ounces radicchio
2 large bunches of watercress
⅓ cup extra-virgin olive oil

1. In a small bowl, marinate red onion in vinegar with salt and pepper for 30 minutes.

2. Shred radicchio into thin slices, as for a slaw. Remove thick stems from watercress. In a large bowl, combine radicchio and watercress. Toss lightly to mix.

3. Add olive oil to marinated red onion and beat with a fork to blend. Pour onion and dressing over salad and toss to coat.

344 ROMAINE SALAD WITH GARLIC-ANCHOVY DRESSING AND CROUTONS

Prep: 10 minutes   Cook: 15 to 20 minutes   Serves: 4 to 5

2 cups cubed (½-inch) Italian bread
⅓ cup plus 2 tablespoons extra-virgin olive oil
4 flat anchovy fillets
4 garlic cloves, minced
3 tablespoons red wine vinegar

½ teaspoon dry mustard
¼ teaspoon salt
½ teaspoon pepper
1 large head of romaine lettuce, torn into bite-size pieces
½ cup grated Parmesan cheese

1. Preheat oven to 325°. Toss bread with 2 tablespoons olive oil until lightly coated. Spread out bread cubes on a baking sheet and bake 10 minutes. Shake pan to turn cubes over and bake 5 to 10 minutes longer, or until golden brown.

2. In a small bowl, mash anchovies and garlic together with a fork. Add ⅓ cup olive oil, vinegar, mustard, salt, and pepper. Beat with a fork to blend.

3. Place lettuce in a salad bowl. Pour garlic-anchovy dressing over lettuce and toss to coat. Add croutons and toss again. Sprinkle Parmesan cheese over salad.

345 AVOCADOS WITH GORGONZOLA AND BALSAMIC VINEGAR

Prep: 10 minutes   Cook: none   Serves: 4

Serve this with thinly sliced prosciutto or ham and bread sticks for an easy lunch.

2 ripe avocados
2 tablespoons balsamic
    vinegar
½ teaspoon salt
¼ teaspoon pepper
3 tablespoons extra-virgin
    olive oil

2 tablespoons finely chopped
    red onion
¼ cup crumbled blue cheese,
    preferably gorgonzola

Cut each avocado in half and remove pit. In a small bowl, combine vinegar, salt, pepper, and olive oil. Beat with a fork to blend. Add red onion and blue cheese and stir just to mix. Spoon dressing into each avocado hollow. Eat with a spoon, right out of avocado shell.

346 SQUID SALAD

Prep: 30 minutes   Cook: 5 to 8 minutes   Serves: 4 to 6

Make this easy by using cleaned squid. Serve on a bed of lettuce with lemon wedges. The lightness of the squid and tartness of the dressing taste best if the salad is served slightly chilled.

1 pound squid, cleaned
3 tablespoons olive oil
3 garlic cloves, finely chopped
    Pinch of hot pepper flakes
½ cup dry white wine
1¼ teaspoons salt
¼ teaspoon dried oregano
2 celery ribs, thinly sliced
1 small red onion, thinly
    sliced
1 red bell pepper, cored,
    seeded, and thinly sliced

2 tablespoons chopped fresh
    parsley
2 tablespoons chopped fresh
    basil or 1 teaspoon dried
2 tablespoons red wine
    vinegar
1 tablespoon fresh lemon
    juice
½ teaspoon pepper
    Lemon wedges

1. Cut squid into thin ¼- to ½-inch circles. In a nonreactive large frying pan, heat 2 tablespoons olive oil over medium heat. Add garlic and hot pepper flakes and cook 30 seconds, or until garlic is fragrant but not brown. Immediately add squid to pan and cook, stirring frequently, 1 to 2 minutes, or until squid just turns pink. Add wine, ½ teaspoon salt, and oregano. Cook 1 minute and remove from heat. Set aside and let cool.

2. In a large bowl, combine celery, red onion, bell pepper, parsley, basil, vinegar, lemon juice, pepper, and remaining 1 tablespoon olive oil. Toss to mix. Add squid with its liquid and remaining ¾ teaspoon salt. Toss again. Serve with lemon wedges.

Chapter 15

Dolce—Dessert in Italian

Dolce, the "sweet," does not really translate as dessert. In Italy, the sweet is served at any time, as a snack, but seldom as dessert or at the end of a meal. The end of a meal is often just a piece of fruit or a little black coffee. To end a meal with a rich dessert is considered gilding the lily.

Italian-Americans, however, adopted the custom of dessert readily. The richness of an American diet was like heaven to so many of the Italians who came with the first waves of immigrants, many of them from areas where butter and cream were scarce; the land gave olives and vegetables, but no grazing land for meat or its products to become a major part of their diet. It became not unusual to have dinner in the Italian style with the succession of the antipasto, pasta, a meat course, salad, and then finish it off with lemon meringue pie or chocolate pudding icebox cake that someone made from a recipe from a box of graham crackers.

As a compromise, I've included some of the most popular recipes from Italian-American restaurants, like Italian Cheesecake and Biscuit Tortoni, and those holiday spectaculars, such as Cassata alla Siciliana and Zuppa Inglese. A very popular concoction, both here and in Italy, is Tiramisù. Rich with mascarpone cheese and ladyfingers—soaked in brandy and coffee and dusted with cocoa—this is usually enjoyed in the afternoon with black coffee. Last but not least, Italian Biscotti are cookies—but cookies very different from what we know as cookies. They're not very sweet but are very dry, and absolutely delicious when dipped in coffee and wine.

347   ITALIAN CHEESECAKE

Prep: 10 minutes   Chill: 15 to 30 minutes   Marinate: 30 minutes
Cook: 1 hour   Cool: 30 minutes   Serves: 8 to 10

Lemon-Marsala Pastry
   (recipe follows)
⅓ cup golden raisins
¼ cup dry Marsala or sherry
1 pound ricotta cheese
½ cup sugar
1 tablespoon flour

4 eggs, separated
¼ cup sour cream
¼ cup heavy cream
1 teaspoon vanilla extract
2 tablespoons pine nuts

1. Line bottom and 1 inch of side of a 9-inch springform pan with pastry, patting to even thickness. Refrigerate 30 minutes or freeze 15 minutes, until set.

2. Preheat oven to 350°. In a small bowl, combine raisins and Marsala. Let stand 30 minutes.

3. In a large bowl, combine ricotta, sugar, and flour. Beat with a wooden spoon until well blended. Add egg yolks, sour cream, heavy cream, and vanilla; beat to blend well.

4. In another large bowl, beat egg whites with electric mixer until stiff but not dry. Using a rubber spatula, gradually fold beaten egg whites into cheese mixture, one third at a time, just until combined. Drain raisins, discarding Marsala, and fold into batter along with pine nuts. Pour into prepared pan.

5. Bake cheesecake 50 to 60 minutes, until center is firm. Let cool 30 minutes. Slip a knife around edges of pan and release springform. Serve chilled or at room temperature.

LEMON-MARSALA PASTRY
Makes enough for a 9-inch single crust

1 stick (8 tablespoons)
   unsalted butter
1½ cups sifted flour
2 egg yolks

3 tablespoons sugar
1 teaspoon grated lemon zest
1 tablespoon dry Marsala or
   dry sherry

1. In a medium bowl, cut butter into flour until mixture resembles cornmeal. Make a well in center.

2. In a small bowl, combine egg yolks, sugar, lemon zest, and Marsala. Beat with a fork to blend. Pour mixture into well in flour and stir with a fork, gradually pulling flour into center until mixture blends to form a dough. Knead in bowl a few times to finish pulling dough together.

348   BAKED PEACHES
Prep: 15 minutes   Cook: 15 to 20 minutes   Serves: 4 to 8

When served, the filling resembles the pit of a peach. Serve with soft whipped cream and a glass of chilled Amaretto.

4 ripe freestone peaches	1 tablespoon almond liqueur,
1 tablespoon butter	such as Amaretto
¼ cup packed brown sugar	1 egg yolk
¼ cup finely chopped almonds	
6 Italian almond macaroons,	
such as Amaretti, crushed	

1. Preheat oven to 350°. Cut peaches in half from stem to root end. Give a little twist to free one side from pit. Gently twist pit from peach half and discard. Place peach halves, cut side up, in a 10-inch baking dish greased with the butter.

2. In a medium bowl, combine brown sugar, almonds, macaroons, almond liqueur, and egg yolk. Beat with a fork to blend well. Stuff each peach hollow with almond mixture. Bake 15 to 20 minutes, or until peaches are soft but still hold their shape. Serve warm.

349   GRILLED FRUIT
Prep: 20 minutes   Cook: 5 minutes   Serves: 4

These are delicious with zabaglione as a dessert, or as a side dish to grilled meats. This is a perfect dessert for outdoor barbecues.

8 dried pears	8 dried figs
8 dried peaches	

1. Prepare a medium fire in a grill, or use an existing fire.

2. If the fruit is plump and pliable, rinse with hot water. Drain and pat dry. If fruit is hard and dry, pour hot water over to cover and let steep 15 to 20 minutes. Drain and pat dry.

3. When coals are ashen, place fruit along edges of a lightly oiled grill rack and cook, turning once, 3 to 4 minutes, or until fruits are lightly browned.

350   BISCUIT TORTONI
Prep: 10 minutes   Cook: none   Freeze: 2 hours   Serves: 6 to 8

An Italian-American creation found often in old-time Italian restaurants.

½ cup finely chopped almonds	¼ cup confectioners' sugar
½ cup crushed Italian almond	2 cups heavy cream
macaroons, such as	3 tablespoons dark rum
Amaretti	

1. In a dry medium frying pan, toast almonds over medium heat 2 to 3 minutes, or until lightly browned, shaking pan frequently. Coarsely grind nuts in a food processor; set aside to cool.

2. In a medium bowl, mix macaroons and almonds with sugar and 1 cup cream.

3. In another medium bowl, whip remaining 1 cup cream until soft peaks form. Fold into almond mixture along with rum.

4. Spoon mixture into 6 to 8 individual paper muffin cups set in a muffin tin or foil baking cups placed on a baking sheet. Freeze until firm, at least 2 hours.

351   BISCOTTI
Prep: 30 minutes   Rest: 15 minutes   Cook: 1½ hours
Makes: 3½ to 4 dozen

These cookies were especially made at Easter time, the sugar glaze being tinted pale yellow, green, and pink.

5 cups all-purpose flour	2 teaspoons vanilla extract
1½ cups granulated sugar	2 cups sifted confectioners'
3 teaspoons baking powder	sugar
4 eggs	¼ cup cream
¾ cup milk	1 teaspoon lemon juice

1. Preheat oven to 350°. In a large bowl, combine flour, granulated sugar, and baking powder. Stir with a wooden spoon to mix. Make a well in center.

2. In a small bowl, beat eggs just enough to combine. Stir in milk and vanilla. Pour milk mixture into well in center of flour. Beat with wooden spoon until a soft dough forms. Cover with a kitchen towel and let rest 15 minutes.

3. Divide dough into five pieces. On a floured work surface, roll each piece into ½-inch-thick rope. Cut into 3-inch lengths and tie each into a loose knot. Place on a baking sheet and bake 12 to 15 minutes, until dry and still pale in color. Partially cool cookies.

4. While biscotti are cooling, in a medium bowl combine confectioners' sugar, cream, and lemon juice, beating with a fork until sugar dissolves and mixture is thoroughly blended. Dip tops of warm cookies into sugar glaze and set on a cookie sheet to dry.

---

352   ALMOND CHOCOLATE BISCOTTI
Prep: 30 minutes   Cook: 50 minutes   Makes: About 2 dozen

These dry twice-baked cookies store well and are best if dipped in a cup of coffee or a glass of wine.

1 cup whole blanched almonds, about 4 ounces
2¼ cups all-purpose flour
1 teaspoon baking powder
⅛ teaspoon salt
¾ cup sugar

2 whole eggs, lightly beaten
2 tablespoons water
3 ounces semisweet chocolate, coarsely chopped
1 egg white

1. Preheat oven to 375°. Spread almonds on a cookie sheet and toast in oven 5 to 7 minutes, or until almonds are light brown, shaking pan several times. Grind one third of nuts in a food processor; set aside in a large bowl. Chop remaining nuts coarsely and set aside in a small bowl.

2. Add flour, baking powder, and salt to large bowl containing ground almonds. Stir until well mixed. Make a well in center. Add sugar, whole eggs, and water to well. Using a fork, gradually stir flour and egg mixture together to form a dough. Using hands, knead dough 2 to 3 minutes while still in bowl. Add chocolate to bowl and gently knead in.

3. Divide dough into two pieces. On a floured work surface, roll each piece into ½-inch-thick rope. Place on a baking sheet. In a small bowl, beat egg white with a fork until foamy. Using a pastry brush, lightly brush each rope with egg white. Bake 20 minutes, or until pale brown.

4. Reset oven to 275°. Using a wide spatula, remove each rope to a cutting board. Using a sharp knife, cut into 1½-inch slices at a 45° angle. Return cookies to baking sheet and bake 30 minutes, until dry and firm. Let cookies cool before serving. Store in an airtight container for up to several weeks.

353   CASSATA ALLA SICILIANA
Prep: 30 minutes   Cook: none   Serves: 10 to 12

A cassata is a cake layered with ricotta and "encased" in whipped cream or chocolate. This is a version made simple with store-bought cake. You can use any liqueurs you wish, though the following are particularly aromatic.

1 14- to 16-ounce frozen pound cake, partially thawed
5 tablespoons maraschino liqueur
3 tablespoons orange liqueur, such as Grand Marnier
3 tablespoons anise liqueur, such as anisette
1 pound ricotta cheese
½ cup sugar

1 cup chocolate chips
½ cup chopped candied orange peel
1 cup chopped walnuts
1 teaspoon vanilla extract
   Chocolate Buttercream (recipe follows)
   Optional: silver candies, candied cherries or violets

1. Using a thin sharp knife, stand partially frozen cake on its side. Mark side evenly before cutting lengthwise into 3 equal layers. If top layer is rounded, shave top to make an even layer. Sprinkle one layer with 3 tablespoons of maraschino liqueur. Sprinkle orange liqueur over second layer and anise liqueur over third.

2. In a medium bowl, combine ricotta cheese, sugar, chocolate chips, candied orange peel, walnuts, vanilla, and remaining 2 tablespoons maraschino liqueur. Mix to blend.

3. Using a flexible spatula, evenly spread half of ricotta mixture over bottom layer of cake. Level ricotta and top with second slice of pound cake, pressing gently. Repeat with remaining ricotta and cake. Using a spatula, gently smooth exterior, removing any filling that has oozed out.

4. Using a flexible metal spatula, frost cake with chocolate buttercream. Decorate as desired.

CHOCOLATE BUTTERCREAM
Makes about 2 cups

1 cup sugar
3 tablespoons flour
⅛ teaspoon salt
1 cup milk
2 ounces (2 squares) unsweetened chocolate, broken into small pieces

2 sticks (½ pound) unsalted butter, softened
1 tablespoon orange liqueur, such as Grand Marnier
1 teaspoon vanilla extract

1. In a medium saucepan, mix sugar, flour, and salt. Whisk in milk until combined. Add chocolate and cook over medium-low heat, whisking frequently until smooth and thick and chocolate is melted, 8 to 10 minutes. Remove from heat and let cool.

2. In a large bowl, with an electric mixer, beat butter until light and fluffy. Gradually beat in chocolate mixture. When all the chocolate is combined with butter, stir in orange liqueur and vanilla. Cover and refrigerate until spreadable, about 15 minutes.

354   ZUPPA INGLESE
Prep: 10 minutes   Cook: 13 to 17 minutes   Chill: 2 to 3 hours
Serves: 6 to 8

This is very similar to English trifle, which the Italians adopted from the British. They thoroughly enjoyed it, and called it "English soup." Some versions are very elaborate, including different liquors and flavored custard. Serve with whipped cream.

¾ **cup slivered almonds, about**
    3 ounces
2 **cups milk**
3 **egg yolks, lightly beaten**
¼ **cup sugar**
¼ **cup flour**
⅛ **teaspoon salt**

    Grated zest of 1 lemon
6 **tablespoons sweet vermouth**
6 **tablespoons dark rum**
1 **4.4-ounce package dry**
    ladyfingers or
    Champagne biscuits
⅓ **cup apricot preserves**

1. Preheat oven to 350°. Spread almonds on a cookie sheet and toast in oven 5 to 7 minutes, until evenly browned, shaking pan several times.

2. In a medium saucepan, whisk together milk, egg yolks, sugar, flour, salt, and lemon zest until blended. Cook over medium-low heat, stirring, 8 to 10 minutes, or until medium thick. Do not allow to boil at any time. Remove from heat and cool.

3. In a small bowl, combine vermouth and rum. Place one third of the ladyfingers in a glass bowl and sprinkle them with ¼ cup of the liquors. Dot with one third of the apricot jam and pour one third of the custard over top. Repeat layers, finishing with custard. Top with toasted almonds. Cover with plastic wrap and refrigerate 2 to 3 hours. Serve spooned into wine glasses.

355   TIRAMISU

Prep: 20 minutes   Cook: none   Chill: 2 hours   Serves: 10 to 12

Tiramisù means "pick me up." A midafternoon dessert like this, with strong black coffee, certainly will help you on to the rest of the day. It has become an extremely popular Italian dessert anytime of day or evening. To really dress it up, purchase commercially made chocolate cups and spoon the dessert high into the cups. Dust with more cocoa.

1   4.4-ounce package dry
    ladyfingers or
    Champagne biscuits
½   cup brewed espresso coffee,
    cooled
2   tablespoons brandy
6   eggs, separated
6   tablespoons sugar

2   pounds mascarpone cheese,
    or 1½ pounds cream
    cheese mixed with ½ cup
    heavy cream and ¼ cup
    sour cream
4   tablespoons unsweetened
    cocoa powder

1. Spread ladyfingers on a large baking sheet. In a small bowl combine coffee and brandy. Sprinkle ladyfingers with mixture and set aside.

2. In a medium bowl, beat egg yolks and sugar with an electric mixer until thick and lemon colored, 4 to 5 minutes. Add mascarpone and blend on low speed until combined.

3. In a large bowl, beat egg whites with electric mixer until soft peaks form, 2 to 3 minutes. Using a rubber spatula, fold egg whites into mascarpone mixture. Line the bottom of an 8-cup soufflé dish with half the ladyfingers. Spread half the mascarpone mixture on the ladyfingers and sift 2 tablespoons of cocoa over the surface. Repeat layers, ending with cocoa. Cover with plastic wrap and refrigerate at least 2 hours. To serve, spoon out into a serving plate.

356   ZABAGLIONE

Prep: 5 minutes   Cook: 10 minutes   Serves: 4 to 6

The heady aroma of Marsala makes this dessert irresistible.

6   egg yolks
3   tablespoons sugar

½   cup sweet Marsala wine or
    sweet sherry

Whisk egg yolks and sugar together in top of a double boiler set over simmering water. Continue to whisk gently until mixture is tepid; then add Marsala and begin whisking vigorously until mixture is thick and foamy, 5 to 6 minutes total. Serve immediately in wine glasses.

357   COLD ZABAGLIONE

Prep: 10 minutes   Cook: 10 minutes   Chill: 2 hours   Serves: 4 to 6

Tart berries make an excellent counterpoint to this rich dessert.

6 egg yolks	1 cup cold heavy cream
3 tablespoons sugar	1 pint fresh raspberries or
½ cup sweet Marsala wine or	blueberries (optional)
sweet sherry	

1. Whisk egg yolks and sugar together in top of a double boiler set over simmering water. Continue to whisk gently until mixture is tepid; then add Marsala and begin whisking vigorously until mixture is thick and foamy, 5 to 6 minutes total.

2. Whip cream until soft peaks form. Gently fold whipped cream into warm zabaglione until blended. Cover and refrigerate until chilled, about 2 hours. Serve with fresh berries, if desired.

358   SWEET RISOTTO

Prep: 10 minutes   Cook: 25 to 30 minutes   Serves: 6 to 8

One of the best stove-top rice puddings. Italian Arborio rice lends itself well to a creamy rich result. Try it for brunch or as dessert.

2 tablespoons butter	½ teaspoon cinnamon
2 cups Arborio rice	½ cup golden raisins
3 cups boiling water	2 cups sliced strawberries
¼ teaspoon salt	1 cup blueberries
3 cups hot milk	1½ cups warm cream
¾ cup sugar	

1. In a large saucepan, melt butter over medium heat. Add rice to butter and stir until well coated. Add boiling water and salt. Cook, stirring, until water is absorbed, 5 to 6 minutes. Add 1 cup hot milk and reduce heat to low. Cook, stirring, until milk is absorbed, about 2 minutes. Repeat twice until all milk is used and rice is creamy and tender but still firm in center. Stir in sugar, cinnamon, and golden raisins.

2. In a small serving bowl combine strawberries and blueberries. Pass berries and a pitcher of warm cream along with warm rice pudding.

359   APRICOT PIE

Prep: 20 minutes   Chill: 30 minutes   Cook: 35 minutes   Serves: 8

This is easy because the pastry is not temperamental, and the filling can come out of a jar.

2 cups plus 2 tablespoons
   sifted flour
Pinch of salt
2 tablespoons granulated
   sugar
1 stick (8 tablespoons) butter
3 egg yolks

¼ cup milk
2 cups apricot jam
2 tablespoons orange liqueur,
   such as Grand Marnier
2 tablespoons heavy cream
Confectioners' sugar

1. In a large bowl, combine 2 cups flour with salt and sugar. Cut in butter until mixture resembles cornmeal. Make a well in center. In a small bowl, beat 2 egg yolks and milk to blend. Pour into well. Using a fork, gradually stir flour and egg mixture together to form a dough. Using hands, knead dough several times while still in bowl.

2. Divide dough in half and flatten each piece into a 6-inch disk. Sprinkle each with 1 tablespoon flour, wrap in plastic wrap, and refrigerate 30 minutes.

3. Preheat oven to 350°. Lightly flour a work surface. Remove one disk of dough from refrigerator. Roll out on floured surface to fit a 9-inch tart pan with a removable bottom. Press against sides of pan and trim off any excess. Do not be alarmed if dough falls apart. Simply press it back together; the result will still be excellent. Place tart shell in freezer. Roll second disk into a 9-inch circle and cut into 1-inch strips.

4. In a small bowl, combine jam and liqueur until well mixed. Remove prepared tart shell from freezer and fill with jam mixture. Arrange pastry strips in a lattice pattern on top; trim off any excess. Beat together remaining egg yolk and cream. Brush over top of pastry. Bake 35 minutes, or until pastry is golden brown. Serve at room temperature, first removing sides of pan and dusting top with confectioners' sugar.

360   CHOCOLATE AMARETTO BUDINO
Prep: 15 minutes   Cook: 30 minutes   Serves: 8

This is a cake and a sauce at the same time. It is very simple to prepare and almost foolproof. Serve with whipped cream.

2 cups all-purpose flour	1 teaspoon vanilla extract
1 tablespoon plus 1 teaspoon baking powder	2 tablespoons melted butter
½ teaspoon salt	1 cup packed dark brown sugar
2 cups granulated sugar	6 tablespoons brewed espresso coffee (instant is fine)
1¾ cups unsweetened cocoa powder	Whipped cream
1½ cups milk	
3 tablespoons Amaretto liqueur	

1. Preheat oven to 350°. In a large bowl, sift together flour, baking powder, salt, 1⅓ cups granulated sugar, and ¼ cup cocoa. Make a well in center. In a medium bowl, beat milk, 1 tablespoon amaretto, vanilla, and melted butter with a fork to blend well. Pour liquid ingredients into well in dry ingredients and stir with fork until well blended. Pour batter into a buttered 8-inch square baking pan. Using a rubber spatula, smooth top; set aside.

2. In a medium saucepan, combine remaining ⅔ cup granulated sugar, 1½ cups cocoa, 2 tablespoons Amaretto, brown sugar, and coffee. Stir with a wooden spoon over low heat until sugar and cocoa are melted, 2 to 3 minutes. Remove from heat and pour over ingredients in pan. Bake 30 minutes. Serve warm or at room temperature, spooned into dessert dishes and topped with whipped cream.

361   GRANITA DI CAFFE
Prep: 10 minutes   Cook: none   Freeze: 4 hours   Serves: 6

Remember, caffeine doesn't disappear when you cook or freeze it. If serving this at night, you may want to make it with decaffeinated coffee.

½ cup plus 1 tablespoon sugar	¾ cup heavy cream
6 cups brewed, very strong hot coffee (instant espresso is excellent for this)	1 tablespoon apricot or other fruit brandy

1. Stir ½ cup sugar into hot coffee to dissolve. Pour into freezer trays and freeze until icy, about 1½ hours. Stir and break up ice crystals with a fork. Freeze until firm, about 2½ hours longer.

2. In a medium bowl, whip cream with 1 tablespoon sugar until soft peaks form. Stir in brandy.

3. Serve *granita* immediately in chilled wine glasses. Top with cream.

362   CANNOLI WITH HAZELNUT CREAM
Prep: 15 minutes   Cook: 15 to 18 minutes   Serves: 6

Cannoli shells are available in Italian markets and specialty food shops. They come in packages of twelve; store unused shells in an airtight container for use at another time.

1 cup shelled hazelnuts	¼ cup shelled natural pistachio
2 cups heavy cream	nuts, coarsely chopped
½ cup granulated sugar	6 cannoli shells
½ teaspoon vanilla	Confectioners' sugar

1. Preheat oven to 350°. Scatter hazelnuts on a baking sheet and toast 15 to 18 minutes, or until nuts are lightly browned and skins are cracked. Remove as much of brown skins as possible by rubbing nuts in a kitchen towel. Crack nuts into coarse pieces by enclosing in a clean kitchen towel and hitting gently with a rolling pin.

2. In a medium bowl, whip cream with an electric mixer 2 to 3 minutes, or until thick. Briefly beat in granulated sugar and vanilla. Fold in hazelnuts and pistachios. Stuff cannoli shells with nut cream. Serve topped with a light sifting of confectioners' sugar.

363   BAKED APPLES
Prep: 20 minutes   Cook: 30 to 40 minutes   Serves: 6

6 green apples, such as	1 teaspoon cinnamon
Granny Smith or Pippin,	2 tablespoons butter, softened
about 3 pounds	1½ cups Chianti or other dry red
6 tablespoons sugar	wine
3 tablespoons currants or	½ cup water
raisins	
3 tablespoons chopped	
walnuts	

1. Preheat oven to 350°. Using an apple corer or melon baller, remove center of apples to within ½ inch of bottom of fruit.

2. In a small bowl, mix sugar, currants or raisins, walnuts, cinnamon, and 1 tablespoon butter. Divide mixture equally among apples to fill cavities. Use remaining 1 tablespoon butter to grease an 11 x 8½-inch baking dish. Arrange apples in dish, filling side up.

3. Pour wine and water around apples, then cover dish with foil. Bake 30 to 40 minutes, or until apples are tender. Serve in soup bowls or deep dessert dishes with wine sauce spooned around each apple.

364   APPLES IN CORNMEAL PASTRY

Prep: 30 minutes   Chill: 30 minutes
Cook: 35 to 45 minutes   Serves: 6 to 8

If this pastry falls apart, just patch it together.

APPLES

4 large cooking apples, such
as Granny Smith or
Pippin, about 2 pounds
¾ cup sugar
⅓ cup chopped walnuts

8 dried apricots, cut into
½-inch pieces
3 tablespoons golden raisins
3 tablespoons pine nuts
3 tablespoons unsalted butter,
softened
Cornmeal Pastry (recipe
follows)

1. Peel apples and cut crosswise in half. Remove cores. In a small bowl, mix sugar, walnuts, apricots, golden raisins, pine nuts, and butter. Stuff centers of apples with mixture. Set aside, covered.

2. Preheat oven to 350° F. Remove one disk of dough from refrigerator. Roll out to 11-inch circle between two sheets of plastic wrap. Fit into a 9- or 10-inch tart pan with a removable bottom. Press against sides.

3. Place apples, cut side down and in a single layer, in crust. Sprinkle any remaining sugar mixture over apples. Roll out remaining pastry and place over apples. Pinch edges and crimp to seal.

4. Bake 35 to 45 minutes, or until pastry is golden brown and apples are tender when pricked with a knife. Remove sides of pan to serve.

CORNMEAL PASTRY
Makes enough for a 10-inch double-crust tart

2½ cups plus 2 tablespoons
sifted flour
¾ cup cornmeal
1¼ cups sugar
¼ teaspoon salt

2⅔ sticks (13 ounces) unsalted
butter
4 egg yolks
2 tablespoons water

1. In a large bowl, combine 2½ cups flour, cornmeal, sugar, and salt. Using fingers, work butter into flour mixture until it resembles cornmeal. Make a well in center. In a small bowl, beat egg yolks and water to blend. Pour into well. Using a fork, gradually stir flour and egg mixture together to form a dough. Using hands, knead a few times while still in bowl.

2. Divide dough in half and flatten each piece into a 6-inch disk. Sprinkle each with 1 tablespoon flour, wrap in plastic wrap, and refrigerate 30 minutes.

365   LEMON ICE

Prep: 10 minutes   Cook: 8 to 10 minutes   Freeze: 4 hours
Serves: 6 to 8

I can't think of anything as refreshing as this lemon ice. We used to buy it in Italian bakeries, where it was proudly served in small white paper cups.

5 cups water	**6 tablespoons orange liqueur,**
⅔ cup sugar	**such as Grand Marnier**
1 teaspoon grated lemon zest	**(optional)**
½ cup fresh lemon juice	

1. In a medium saucepan, bring water, sugar, and lemon zest to boil; boil over high heat 5 minutes. Let cool 5 minutes; then stir lemon juice into sugar water.

2. Pour into a freezer tray and freeze 1½ hours, or until icy. Stir and break up ice crystals with a fork. Freeze again until firm, about 2½ hours longer. Serve in chilled wine glasses. To dress up this dessert, pour a little Grand Marnier over top of each serving.

Index

About the Author

Rick Marzullo O'Connell is a San Francisco-based chef, cooking teacher, and restaurant consultant.